'Ross Heaven's *The Journey To You* is a splendid contribution to this ancient body of knowledge and brings home its relevance to life today' Leo Rutherford, author of *Principles of Shamanism*

'Ross weaves together science and spirituality, the left brain and the right brain, in a highly imaginative, intelligent way. He is a visionary' Nick Williams, author of *The Work We Were Born To Do*

'A fascinating account of how psychology and spirit can come together in our explorations of the inner world and of other dimensions. And a great invitation to some wonderful inner journeys' Dr Dina Glouberman, author of *Life Choices, Life Changes*

'In each time of change for any society, the tools, resources, and guides that we need to navigate through such changes manifest "as if by magic" so we can shift, grow and change ourselves to meet the demands of the time. This book is such a guide and, with it in hand, we can navigate through the challenges that face us now, both individually and collectively' Alan Tickhill, Director of The Raven Lodge of Shamanic and Personal Development

'Intriguing . . . A fresh and accessible approach to an ancient practice. *The Journey To You* will make the concept of Shamanism relevant to modern-day spiritual seekers' Paula Croxon, Editorial Manager, Waterstone's *Online*

'*The Journey To You* opens new doors for learning about this marvellous body of knowledge . . . Shamanism may be magical, if that means powerful, effective, and beyond explanation. It is certainly practical . . . If you find that this magic tests your limits of credibility or excites and inspires you, then you need to experience it directly. I invite you to read on. Experience!' John Perkins, author of *Shapeshifting*

'If you've ever been drawn to Shamanism then this book is for you. Ross Heaven tells us of the path and practice of the Shaman, not just where it comes from and how it works but, most importantly, how it can be applied at the start of the 21st century . . . This is definitely a book for the start of the new millennium – new ideas, new ways of seeing the world, and written in a way which will encourage you to explore (for) yourself. And yet it is based on practices as old as civilization itself . . . If you're ready for a real 'journey of a lifetime', this could be your starting point!' Keith Beasley, Reiki Grand Master and publisher of *Sailing with Spirit*

'A book that will open peoples' eyes to the wonder that is life. Written with an obvious knowledge of the subject in words that speak directly to the reader, the book gives many pointers to practical wisdom, making the sacred accessible' Nick Wood, editor of *Sacred Hoop Magazine* and author of *Voices From the Earth*

THE
JOURNEY TO YOU
A Shaman's Path to Empowerment

ROSS HEAVEN

BANTAM BOOKS

LONDON · NEW YORK · TORONTO · SYDNEY · AUCKLAND

THE JOURNEY TO YOU
A BANTAM BOOK: 0553 81323 4

First publication in Great Britain

PRINTING HISTORY
Bantam Books edition published 2001

1 3 5 7 9 10 8 6 4 2

Set in 10½/13pt Sabon by Falcon Oast Graphic Art

Bantam Books are published by Transworld Publishers,
61–63 Uxbridge Road, London W5 5SA,
a division of The Random House Group Ltd,
in Australia by Random House Australia (Pty) Ltd,
20 Alfred Street, Milsons Point, Sydney, NSW 2061, Australia,
in New Zealand by Random House New Zealand Ltd,
18 Poland Road, Glenfield, Auckland 10, New Zealand
and in South Africa by Random House (Pty) Ltd,
Endulini, 5a Jubilee Road, Parktown 2193, South Africa.

Reproduced, printed and bound in Great Britain by
Clays Ltd, St Ives plc

DEDICATION

Our children are our greatest teachers, and our future. And so this book is dedicated, with love and thanks, to the two most wonderful children I have the honour of knowing – Jodie Heaven, for her natural compassion, unlimited kindness and for the adventure in her soul – and Amelia (Millie) Heaven, for her humour, openness, and otherworldly wisdom. *Namaste*, I salute the god in both of you.

'Ibashe Onile; Ibashe Omo Aiye'
I celebrate the children of the world and the Earth which supports us all.

This book is for Millie and Jodie, who are the real reason I do anything at all – and for all our children.

CONTENTS

FOR THOSE WHO SHAPED THE DREAM
ACKNOWLEDGEMENTS AND THANKS

I have journeyed to this book and its readers many times while writing it, and I feel like I know many of you already – seekers after truth, sensitive to spirit, challenging, intelligent, wanting evidence and answers, not empty words and lack of substance.

Welcome to this book and thank you for the contribution you have made to shaping it by telling me in these journeys what you wanted from it. I have tried to include the evidence you asked for, and obviously, there are many people I need to thank for their contribution to this. Without their work and their support, I would not even have got close. All of these people are powerful teachers and healers in their own right and, where appropriate, I encourage you to seek them out and to explore their own work more fully.

This is especially true of one author who has been a source of inspiration in his writing and in his explorer spirit and approach to the world – Michael Talbot, whose book, *The Holographic Universe* (HarperCollins, 1996), has done more to demonstrate the new direction taken by science in recent years than I could ever hope to. Michael's book has been a wonderful source of inspiration for my own work and I encourage you to read it for yourself in order to fill in the considerable gaps that I have left and to learn about the nature of science and reality from an expert who also has a real talent for poetry and plain talking.

At the risk of sounding like an Oscar winner, I also wish to thank . . .

Nick Williams, director of Alternatives and author of the inspired and inspiring book, *The Work We Were Born To Do* (Element, 1999), and his partner, Helen – for being my friends, for believing in this book, and for buying me dinner when really I should have paid.

Dina Glouberman, director of Skyros, founder of Imagework, and author of *Life Choices, Life Changes* (Thorsons, 1995), which is *the* definitive book on Imagework. The exercises included in my own book are possible only as a result of Dina's pioneering work in this field and through the training I have received from her personally and in workshops. I would also like to thank her for her contribution to this book in reading through it, and the chapter on Imagework, and for her helpful comments and suggestions for improvements.

Leo Rutherford of the Eagle's Wing Centre for Contemporary Shamanism, whose honesty and straightforward approach is a model. Sometimes a single word can make a difference. A few years ago, I was lucky enough to share with Leo a sweatlodge which he ran. (This is one of the most ceremonial of shamanic practices.) His warm and genuine prayers and his honest confession about his fear of ceremony speak volumes for his authenticity and impeccability as a teacher and a warrior, and for his relationship to Spirit.

Ruth Dawson, archaeologist, anthropologist, counsellor, Imageworker and friend, who submitted herself uncomplainingly to many of the techniques in this book before I would include them in the text.

John Perkins and Dr Eve Bruce of the Dream Change Coalition. Not only for the words of wisdom and compassion that are embodied in John's books, but for the words of encouragement and support John and Eve have given me – and for caring enough about the issues of global warming and rainforest destruction to do something about it for all of us, and for the children. No-one *had* to take responsibility for making a difference in the world. Thank God someone did.

My friends, Santeria Priest, LL, Vodou Priestess Mambo Racine Sans Bout, *Roots Without End*, Vodou Priest Bon Houngan Yabofe, and my kanzo brothers. All of them were with me during my initiation as a priest in their tradition and were generous with their time and wisdom in teaching me the ways of Vodou, Palo and Santeria, during the writing of this book. There is a Haitian saying, *Se bon ki ra*, good is rare. I was fortunate enough to find it in these people.

My agent, Andrew Lownie, who has been a guide for me through unknown territory for us both and whose quiet sensitivity is a rare joy in today's business world, and my editor, Brenda Kimber, for her honesty, humour and genuine interest in shamanism as a timeless route to self-development. Thanks also to art director, Liz Laczynska, for her enthusiastic support.

I also thank the students and clients who have shared this path with me and taught me endless truths about the nature of the soul and the meaning of compassion.

This book was written between 1998 and 2000. During this time, the world was lessened by the death of Carlos Castaneda and the serious illness of Michael Harner. Without these two pioneers of shamanism, our knowledge of this world would be much less complete and I fully acknowledge my debt to them both.

I also offer thanks to my spirit guides, who have worked with me throughout this book. It is their words you will sometimes hear directly, and their wisdom and humour which has many times made me laugh when I would have preferred to pull my hair out, and to look at myself honestly when I would have liked to look away. If there is anything good in this book, it is really down to them, not me. To Growler, DarkForce, Scarlet, Beatrix, Power, Whisper.

Gabrielle Roth, Sandra Ingerman, Felicitas Goodman, and the many other female shamans referred to in this book are evidence that shamanism is not just a male preserve. Indeed, many of the most powerful shamans are female and, in many societies, including that of the aborigines of Australia, female 'medicine' is considered the most powerful of all. To avoid the unwieldy convention of referring to all shamans as 's/he', however, and the confusion of mixing genders in the text of this book, I have tended to refer to shamans in the male gender. Please accept my apologies for this. There is nothing sexist intended and, in fact, my own daughters are the most important shamanic teachers in my life right now.

And, finally, a confession. Unlike thousands of other people, I came late to the works of Gabrielle Roth – but at least I finally got there! Gabrielle has a wonderful down to earth style and an honesty, compassion and truth which comes from real experience, and I think it is really appropriate to quote these words from her book, *Maps to Ecstasy* (Thorsons, 1999) as one of the guiding principles behind the book you are now holding:

The maps I've given you are only guides for your journey through the territory of your psyche; they aren't the territory itself. They are simply an aid to you as you travel through the mysteries of an ever-changing self. The journey is yours to take. It won't look like mine or anyone else's. And if you don't take your journey, no one will.

The same is true of this book. The journey is yours: I have merely given you one direction in which to walk.

AUTHOR'S NOTE

And what is good, Phaedrus, and what is not good
– need we ask anyone to tell us these things?
  – Robert Pirsig, *Zen and the Art of Motorcycle Maintenance*

Our scientists and our shamans agree that, behind our masks of civilization, we are living in desperate times.

The Dagara medicine man, Malidoma Patrice Some, wrote recently that, 'at this moment in history, Western civilization is suffering from a great sickness of the soul. The West's progressive turning away from functioning spiritual values; its total disregard for the environment and the protection of natural resources; the violence of inner cities and their problems of poverty, drugs and crime; spiralling unemployment and economic disarray; and growing intolerance towards people of colour and values of other cultures – all of these trends, if unchecked, will eventually bring about a terrible self-destruction. In the face of all this global chaos, the only possible hope is self-transformation.'[1]

These are words which we might expect, I suppose, from a shaman seeing the world from a quite different perspective to our own. Except that Some is also an extremely well-educated man, with PhDs from American and European universities, and immersed in our Western culture.

And nor is he alone. The celebrated American scientist,

Carl Sagan, just a few decades ago, made almost exactly the same point. 'On our small planet,' he said, 'this moment in history is a historical branch point as profound as the confrontation of the Ionian scientists with the mystics 2,500 years ago. What we do with our world in this time will propagate down through the centuries and powerfully determine the destiny of our descendants and their fate, if any, among the stars.'

The point of both men is simply this: *We all of us have a choice to make in our lives right now – do we want to live or do we want to die?*

It is a serious choice. If we carry on the way we are going, producing all of the misery and separation that Some points to, the outcome for our species is beyond scientific doubt. If that is what we truly want for ourselves and for our children, then that is exactly what we will get since we all of us have the power to make it so. *Our will be done.*

But if it is not, then each of us must consider, without guilt or pressure, exactly what we are prepared to do at a personal level in order to transform ourselves and to change things. The evidence of history – and of the moment – is clear that we are deluding ourselves if we expect our governments, our corporations, or any other institution, to take meaningful action on our behalf. The future is down to *us*.

You may not appreciate it, but you have already made a difference to the outcome by purchasing this book since the author's royalties are being donated in their entirety to an organization called the Dream Change Coalition, which was established for the preservation of our rainforests through the POLE project. The money you paid for this book could help to protect approximately one-third of an acre of this precious natural resource.

POLE – Pollution Offset Lease for Earth – is the annual lease of an area of rainforest capable of absorbing 1.5 tons of CO_2 – well in excess of the 425 pounds that you, I, and every single one of us contributes to the atmosphere each year – simply by breathing.

The rainforests are the lungs of our planet. If we are to reach the stars at all, and to solve the problems of our civilization, we must start in our own backyard – by preserving this world so that future generations can live to begin their own journey. By purchasing this book *you* have helped to make that journey possible. I thank you for that, and so do the children of the world whose future you are safeguarding with your actions.

POLE was developed after a meeting with indigenous Elders in the rainforest. Dr Eve Bruce of the Dream Change Coalition (DCC) tells how when they were asked how we could help them to stop the devastation, they said: 'The world is as you dream it. Don't come and try to help us, go to your people. It is the dream of the industrialized world that is destroying the forest.'

They pointed out that even if we bought every acre of forest with the intention of preserving it, it would still fall to destruction unless the *dream* of the Western world – our vision of reality – is changed. If we view the rainforest as a commodity to be bought and sold, that is precisely what it will become – not an aspect of the world that we are all intrinsically a part of, but something to be *controlled*, shaped, moulded, and used, by those who assume mastery of the planet. This realization was the beginning of Dream Change Coalition and of the POLE programme.

To the shamans, we are all one. They honour the forest in a very deep way, with a very deep connection. The POLE programme was devised to bring in money to the indigenous people of the rainforest, so they could continue to act as its caretakers, a lease for one year at a time. In this way, there is no disempowerment on either side since there is no ownership. Everyone can choose each year whether to continue or not.

But POLE is much more than that. It is taking responsibility for our own CO_2 emissions, for raising consciousness, for honouring the keepers of the forests, and changing the dream of the industrial world to one that is more Earth honouring.

If you would like to learn more about the work of the Dream Change Coalition, or to sponsor a POLE in your own name and receive a gift from the rainforest along with a taped message read by John Perkins, author of many books of shamanic wisdom based on his wide-ranging experience with the shamans of the Amazon, write to PO Box 31357, Palm Beach Gardens, FL 33420, USA or visit the web site at *www.dreamchange.org*

FOREWORD

by Leo Rutherford,
author of *Principles of Shamanism*

I fell face down. Deep, deep, deep relaxation. I felt held in the arms of the Bear of the West. Then found myself in the mouth of an enormous cave – hundreds of torchbearers – flaming torches – like a Mayan temple – huge steps leading upward. I was climbing them alone and wondered if I was the sacrifice. Met a huge figure with a vast eagle's head. He asked me why I had come and what I wished. I replied, 'I wish to dance in the realm of the gods.'

He took me to a stone slab, where I lay down. My head was chopped off and out of my throat flew bats. These flew off into the darkness of the void and I was one of them. Then from a bat I turned into a crow. Then I was human and crow. I was told that my power and energy came from the womb – the void . . .

Then in a crow-like manner – still flying but in human shape – I saw myself giving birth and out of my vagina was spinning energy that seemed like new stars and galaxies being born, but very much the awareness was that I was giving birth to myself.

Then I felt myself coming down to re-enter this me. I was floating down to the left side of my larger being. As I came back to this 'me' I felt I brought with me a lot of wholeness and completeness and power of the larger part of the being that is me. It made all the mundane problems of my life dissolve into insignificance.

A shamanic journey long ago in a far wilderness? No, a trance-dance session in a church hall in 1990s London!

Shamanism is our ancient roots wherever we live and whatever sort of culture we have grown up in. It is our spiritual heritage. Look back far enough in time and all of us come from shamanistic cultures. Long before such historically recent concepts as organized religion, humans sought understanding and knowledge of the wider universe using a variety of experiential ways and tools which are just as applicable today. These practices are still in use in a surprisingly large number of places in the world and many shamans of indigenous cultures are now teaching Westerners.

The shamanic journey, trance-dance, the vision quest, these are ancient but eternally relevant ways to contact the timeless reality that exists parallel to and just out of sight of the world we so mistakenly call the 'real world'.

It is here in the everyday that we experience the reflections of who we are, of our actions, our deepest beliefs, our 'dreams', but it is in the non-manifest world of the spirit that the hidden causal interactions take place. Hidden, that is, until we begin to open the doors and 'see'. And that is the ultimate purpose of shamanism.

The struggle to make sense of life in the third-dimensional space suit we call a body is just as important today as at any time. One could almost say even more so now that in the 'developed' part of the world we are polluting our home planet and upsetting the balance of our atmosphere as never before. A path that can bring us back into contact and communion with the primal elemental forces of life can show us the way to come back into alignment with the forces that shape and hold our world in balance. This is the way of the shaman, 'one who walks with one foot in the everyday world and one foot in the spirit world'.

The way of the priestess and priest, in original intention, was to guide and aid humankind to connection with the divine, but too often the 'organized' religions have their own agenda, which leads to power being taken away from the people and held by those that represent the concept of the religion or belief system. The original in-spiration for many religions reflects the ancient ways, but in the West these have long been hidden or changed to serve the conceptual ideology of the patriarchal culture of 'controlling' how humans experience the divine. In contrast, the aim of the shaman is to serve: to help and guide the people to gain their own sense of power, their own connection to Mother Earth and Father Sky, to the divine realm of cause, and to 'walk in beauty' and 'walk their talk' as increasingly self-empowered, self-actualizing people.

The revival in the West of shamanistic ways since the 1960s is reflected in the proliferation of alternative psycho-spiritual books, workshops and courses which has flourished into a vast grassroots university. Although most of these are not shamanism *per se*, they are nevertheless largely shaman-istic in their approach in that they reflect the ways and teachings of the ancient cultures. This movement towards self-development and spiritual awareness, and potentially a more community-oriented way of living, represents a great step forward for those cultures which have been the most predatory towards others and towards the Earth in recent centuries.

Shamanism, 'good medicine', is like tapping into a vast fund of ancient timeless knowledge which can be practised anywhere under any conditions. It is about helping us humans to heal the effects of past traumas, to live in an inner state of balance and harmony in spite of the vicissitudes of life, to develop the best in ourselves no matter what challenges come our way, and it is about the quality of how we relate to each other and to the Earth. All this is as important now as it ever has been or will be. Ross Heaven's *The Journey To You* is a splendid contribution to this ancient body of knowledge and brings home its relevance to life today.

Leo Rutherford is the director of the Eagle's Wing Centre
for Contemporary Shamanism

PREFACE

by John Perkins,
author of *Shapeshifting*, and *The World Is As You Dream It*

In the darkness of a jungle night, my hands guided me as I moved my mouth close to the hearing aid in Sally's ear. We were deep in the Amazon rainforest. The Shuar shaman's voice rose and fell in the distance as he chanted over the patient he was healing. My lips felt the fleshy softness of her ear, then the hard plastic device inside.

Although Sally's time with the shaman had ended an hour earlier, the work he had begun had grown steadily more intense for her. Now she was journeying back to the time when, as a teenager, she had gone deaf.

I spoke directly into the hearing aid. I could feel the heat of her body, as though she had taken on a fever – or the shaman's energy.

In the past, the hearing aid had amplified certain sounds, but it had not helped her understand the words of a human voice – except at very close range. She had become proficient at reading lips; here in the darkest of Amazon nights it was a talent that brought no comfort.

Slowly I pulled away. I kept talking to her, asking questions and responding to her answers. I did not raise my voice. But my mouth moved away from her ear. Still she heard me. She was journeying back to that time when things were being said that were too painful for her to hear. She was telling me about it and replying to my questions.

It suddenly struck me that I was sitting up. I reached over to the other bed, searching for Judy, Sally's room-mate. I found her knee and squeezed it, letting her know that I was a good five feet away from Sally's head.

The shaman had seen something in her ear, a blockage – more in the line of what we call 'spiritual' than physical. He had sucked it out and regurgitated it. Afterwards he had staggered off into the jungle. I had followed him, a man I've known for years, a great shaman, teacher, and friend, Daniel Wachapa. 'Tough,' he had said, dropping to his knees. 'At first it refused to come out. I had to struggle very hard.' In the moonlight, I saw him open his hands and dig his fingers into the jungle soil. 'I'll be OK.' He chuckled and glanced up at me. 'Nunqui, Mother Earth, heals me, gives me energy.'

Now Sally was hearing me, listening and understanding words not spoken directly into the device inside her ear for the first time in nearly two decades. She was realizing her dream. I encouraged her to continue her journey, to understand the message of her deafness, assured Judy that I would be nearby in case she needed me, and stepped outside. The moon was nearly full. Silently I offered my thanks to the spirits of the night, Nunqui, the elements, and the magic of the shaman.

As I walked slowly to the area where Daniel Wachapa was continuing his work, I thought of all the healings – all the 'miracles' – I have witnessed and personally experienced since I first came to the Amazon as a young Peace Corps volunteer fresh out of business school in 1968. I thought also about all the changes in our culture and its perceptions of things like shamanic healings. It occurred to me that ten years ago business executives like Sally and Judy would never have thought about coming on such a trip. Medical doctors who wanted to continue practising would not have dared even to consider the possibility of 'miracles' like the one I had just witnessed.

I entered the room where Danial Wachapa was conducting his healings.

Dr Eve Bruce was sitting on a stool next to the shaman, assisting him. Eve is an MD, surgeon, member of the American Board of Surgeons and the American Society of Plastic and Reconstructive Surgeons, dual board certified in both general and plastic surgery, director of a clinic near Baltimore, a doctor who in her early forties is at the pinnacle of the medical profession. She is also a Dream Change Coalition trip and workshop facilitator. She has lived and studied extensively with shamans from many cultures. She is the first non-Andean woman ever initiated into the highest circle of Ecuadorian shamans. A week before leaving on this trip to the Amazon she and I had lectured together to an audience of over 200 at the University of Michigan's prestigious Medical Center – about the role of shamanism in modern medicine.

I told her what I had just experienced with Sally. She was ecstatic. After a while she expressed a desire to 'check on the patient'. I took over her work of helping Daniel Wachapa. Eve left the room. Perhaps half an hour later she returned. 'I did the same thing you did,' she whispered. 'Sally heard me perfectly when I was sitting at the other end of her bed.'

That night there were several impressive healings. People talked about them all the next day as we hiked in the jungle, swam in the streams, ate lunch with a Shuar family in their home, and took dugout canoes down the fast-flowing head-waters to the Amazon.

The healings continued with a different Shuar shaman the second night. With equally impressive results. This time Sally was the caretaker and Judy, an executive with a major international company, had her own healing. It was very different from Sally's, dealing with another type of problem, one that had afflicted her for over thirty years and is relatively common in our society: chronic depression. It was an amazing night for her. She would later describe it in a letter to me as 'the most wonderful and powerful thing that ever happened to me, a shapeshift out of a long life of misery'.

During the decade that Dream Change Coalition has been taking people to live with, learn from, and be healed by the shamans, we have seen people shrink their tumours, lose weight, alleviate back pain, migraine, and chronic fatigue syndrome, drop addictions, climb out of depression, move into new 'dream' jobs, relationships, and lifestyles . . . the list of cellular, personal and institutional shapeshifts is nearly endless. Each one has been observed by many people from all walks of life, including scientists, medical doctors and psychotherapists.

Why has our culture found it so difficult to accept shamanism? Why have societies that pride themselves on the scientific method rejected a basic science that has been used successfully for thousands of years by people from all over the world? These questions are very valid, especially now that the pendulum is swinging in the other direction. They are the types of questions raised by Ross Heaven's book, *The Journey To You*.

Each of the healings described above involved the application of a vast body of knowledge that is focused into a technique we know as the shamanic journey. *The Journey To You* opens new doors for learning about this marvellous body of knowledge. It offers a forum for participating in your own shamanic journey, for – as Ross says – 'after all this "academic" explanation, you need to experience journeying for yourself . . .'

Shamanism may be magical, if that means powerful, effective, and beyond explanation. It is certainly practical. I personally have used it to heal myself and others and to turn failing businesses into extraordinary successes. If you find that this magic tests your limits of credibility or excites and inspires you, then you need to experience it directly.

I invite you to read on. Experience!

John Perkins is the founder of
Dream Change Coalition

1

THE INNER AND THE
OUTER JOURNEY

*Every sorcerer has to prove everything
with his own experience*

– don Juan

You are about to take an incredible journey to one of the
most amazing, exciting, powerful and unexplored places on
Earth, a place that beats and pulses with the energy of the
universe. It is a place of colour and music and magic, where
miracles happen and futures are woven, the past is undone
and the present is healed. That place is the very centre of
yourself.

Using the techniques of shamanism, you will prove –
through your own experience – that there is a world of
potential and possibility beyond the one we inhabit in the,
sometimes bleak, mundanity of our modern cityscapes and
the techno-dreams we weave.

You will learn that YOU have control of this world,
indeed, that YOU are the sole creator of the world you
occupy – and that YOU have the power to change it, to make
a better world for yourself, and for us all.

For the approach of shamanism is immensely liberating,
energetic, and offers the real prospect of positive change and
growth, a whole new world to be part of. The way of the

shaman may be anything up to 400,000 years old but it is still as valid, powerful and very much needed today.

In this book, we move out of the jungles of Peru and the plains of North America into the urban jungles and city streets. We acknowledge the birth of modern, techno-shamanism, which owes as much to quantum physics as it does to the ancient pioneers and voyagers to otherworlds. It is an approach which makes shamanism meaningful and accessible to the world outside your door *right now*.

In the Western world, our scientists and surgeons have become our saviours and saints, exorcizing our modern demons with wonder drugs and the suburban ritual of the games console. There has been no place in our skyscraper lives for the sacred. Our high-rises have taken us closer to the gods, but our culture has made us blind to them.

And then, very recently, something wonderful happened. The findings of modern science began to echo those of more mystical, deeper, shamanic experience, and now we are entering a new New Age, where the unity of science and shamanic practice is revealing an up-to-the-minute truth, endorsed by the wisdom of ages. We now know, through the discoveries of the physical sciences, that the nature of reality is no simple affair. It is complex, evolving, strange, not at all like the mechanical, external, planetary 'fixtures and fittings' we have been asked to consider as 'reality'. Now, in fact, it seems as if *there is no reality* – unless we choose to create one and to maintain it through a conscious act of faith.

The worldview of the ancient shaman is entirely consistent with the findings of these new scientists. Here, at last, is a place where faith and theorems can meet.

We will be hosting scientists and shamans around the dinner table of this book and hearing what each has to tell us and where these two worldviews come together. While even just twenty years ago the two factions might still have been arguing over the after-dinner mints, we'll now find them shaking hands over the aperitifs.

But first and foremost, we won't be taking anyone's

word for it; we will be seeing for ourselves.

For shamanism is an *approach*, not a religion or a science, a philosophy or theory, and one of its key tenets is that true knowledge can come only from direct experience, *our own experience*, of entering the energy-world of the shaman and sharing this reality in full. It is a truth which cannot be learned from textbooks or doctrine or pulpits.

So there is no set of beliefs to be blindly accepted in this book, no vows to swear, no rules to follow, no tradition to uphold or sacred commandments to defend. Only the natural, universal power within all of us to be awakened and employed, and simple guidelines to direct this awakening. And so, firstly, this is a *practical* book which will show you how to use these techniques for yourself.

NEW WAYS – OLD WAYS – THE SAME WAYS

The first rule of shamanism is: **there are no rules,** but there are certain principles which illuminate the shamanic way; principles which the physical and psychological sciences agree with in full. They are:

1. **Matter and energy are one.** Everything is connected through the energetic matrix, the great web of life, which makes all things possible.

    For the shaman, this has never represented a fluffy, new age philosophy. It is a cold, hard, fact which brings with it the technology of empowerment and, at the same time, personal responsibility for everything we do in the world. When we are given choice, we must exercise it consciously.

    It is an approach which is now fully accepted by the new science, which sees us all as connected at the most intimate level, and all of us as creators of reality who must be responsible parents to our own creations.

2. **Inner realms of reality affect what we experience in outward reality.** Our allies, helpers, guides, are energetic forces in

their own right. Spirit is real. And what we experience inwardly through our connection with these forces can have a massive, profound and manifest effect on our lives.

The human sciences, and especially psychology, now accept that this is fundamentally true, and we will look at a number of studies which prove the point.

3. **This energy can be transformed.** One definition of the word 'shaman' is, in fact, 'one who works with heat and fire, *a transformer of energy*'.

Shamanic techniques provide a methodology for change by transforming our own energy and the energy of the universe we are a part of, allowing us to blend, channel and direct it into the areas of our lives where it will have most beneficial effect for us and, through our connection to all living things, to the potential unfolding within the whole universe right now. For nothing is yet finally mapped and we are all cartographers of change.

4. **The journey, not the destination, is the basis of all knowledge.** The modern world wants to get from A to B and to get there as quickly as possible. The destination is the thing. Yet, we are part of a universe in flux, with no clear destination to reach for and no known end in sight. What we know today with certainty will be quaint and misguided tomorrow. We have only known for certain that the world is not flat since 1968, when the first members of our species to stand on another planet beamed back pictures of our blue celestial sphere to a waiting world. And in truth, only a handful of people, those who stood there on the surface of the moon, really know that for sure. The rest of us must take it on trust. Our worldview is a paradox: we accept our science as an act of faith.

Shamanic knowledge is fundamentally, immutably, true. It must be, because it comes from the very core of ourselves, the place within us where all truth begins. But as the world around us changes, we must learn to *apply* this truth in new ways in order to create what we desire.

If we truly knew the meaning of life, life itself would be meaningless. Uncertainty is what makes it bearable. Change is to be welcomed as part of the shamanic way. Indeed, it is one of the *aims* of the shamanic way.

Native Americans have a saying: 'Does it grow corn?' which means, roughly, 'Does it work? Is it right?'

The shamanic voice is one of trust in our abilities, of recognition that we are all truly gods – with all the responsibility that entails – that we create our own worlds. It is the voice which says 'Look at those perfect hands you have, look at those strong arms. Go out, plant corn and it will grow.'

The voice of the modern world is the one that steps in and says 'So, you want to plant corn? OK, you'll need to go to school and learn how to use your hands in the "right" way, then you'll need a PhD in corn management from the World Academy of Corn and five years' practical training in corn methodology. Then you'll be ready to plant corn.'

The shamanic world is experiential, not theoretical. It has no time for such academic nonsense. Who handed out the first qualifications? Who empowered the people who now grant us these diplomas and gracious validations? The monumental achievements of our scientists stem ultimately from the discovery, aeons ago, of fire and of the wheel. Do you imagine the great pioneer behind these innovations had a degree from Cambridge or the Sorbonne? The only truth that matters is our own.

'You cannot engage an experience without feeling it in your body,' said Dick Olney, therapist, teacher, shaman, in the inspired book, *Walking in Beauty*.[2] 'Just to understand an explanation of something is not enough.'

And so shamanism remains filled with a sense of wonder, acceptance; it knows how corn should be planted and its entire *raison d'être* is to show you how to plant it for youself. Shamanism has faith in something *being* right because it *feels* right, a contrast to our science-led society, which relies for its certainties on hierarchies, evidence, proof, and has a scepticism about the natural abilities and potential of human beings which can only be assuaged by producing what it sees as the proper credentials.

Our children are natural shamans. They experience the world from a position of trust and knowledge of their own abilities because they have not yet been fully exposed to this scepticism. My eight-year-old daughter doesn't know what a PhD is and has no idea what happens in a university. But she can grow crystals and she can grow plants and I have no doubt that, if she wanted to, she would grow corn too.

Our children – flesh and blood as well as the children we all keep within us – are our greatest teachers precisely *because* they already live in the shamanic world, our natural landscape, the birthright which, sadly, many of us have now left behind, but which is available always for any of us to rediscover and to reconnect with.

The core technique of shamanism in all cultures and across all time has been the shamanic journey. It is a technique which I have used for many years in my own adventures of discovery, with workshop groups and with private clients. Every person I meet has their own reasons, their own needs, and embarks upon their own unique adventure when using this technique. Invariably the experience is powerful, trans-formative and healing.

This book takes a step-by-step approach to the shamanic journey and sets it in a modern, urban context to demon-strate its enduring relevance for the world we live in *now*, and the importance it has for enabling you to meet yourself and to see your life more clearly. In doing so, it also has the following specific objectives:

1. To enable you to question the basis and assumptions of the reality we are ordinarily accustomed to ('everyday life') and to see that it is not the only reality available to us; that the otherworld destination of the journeying shaman offers a model which is just as valid as an interpretation of the universe we live in and the energies we have access to. This is the purpose of Chapter 1.

2. To explain how it is possible that these multiple and equally valid realities might exist alongside each other. To do so, we look at the latest scientific model of reality, the 'holographic universe' paradigm, which explains how different versions of reality can exist simultaneously since, in the words of Robert Monroe, 'The world of space and time is only a projection', something we *apply to* the world rather than something which 'just is'. This is the subject of Chapter 2.

3. After this 'academic' explanation, you need to experience journeying for yourself so you can make up your own mind about the existence of these other realities, the potential they offer you, the effectiveness of the journeying technique and whether it will work for you. You will only know the truth – *your truth* – through your own experience. This opportunity forms the heart of this book.

4. The approach of the shaman is a powerfully effective one, which produces *real* changes – physical as well as mental and spiritual – in ourselves and in the world around us. The human sciences, such as psychology, have now produced a considerable body of evidence to explain how these changes are produced and to hint at the, perhaps limitless, potential within all of us. We look later at the psychology of the shaman's otherworlds. Through consideration of what happens in the brain and the body during journeying, we discover how a new reality can be created by individuals using trance techniques such as these.

5. I need also to support your own experiences by showing you what takes place during the journey in terms of the thoughts, feelings and sensations you are likely to encounter. This will help you to understand that your own experiences are paralleled in those of others. Throughout this book, therefore, sections are included which cover my personal experiences of the shamanic trance and the reflections which follow the journey into the otherworld.

6. Finally, a technique with no application is not worth having

and so Chapters 6 (which concerns 'energetic trans-formation') and 8 ('Infinite Journeys') provide, respectively, a context for using journeying to effect concrete life changes, and a design for daily living using shamanic techniques and insights to guide your relationship to yourself and your interactions with others.

There is also another purpose to this book, that of personal empowerment or, as the shamans express it, of stalking power.

THE WAYS OF THE SHAMAN

There are essentially two paths in shamanism – the Way of the Healer and the Way of the Warrior, also known as the Way of Power. In fact, the two are arbitrary divisions since by healing others we are actually re-empowering them, and by reclaiming our own personal power in the Warrior Way, we also heal ourselves. Then, through our actions in the world, we, in turn, heal others and empower them too. The ultimate effect is the same whichever path we choose. Through healing or through the pursuit of power, we are transforming energy. Since we are all connected at the deepest level of being, this makes its impact felt on all parts of the web. By changing ourselves, we change the world we live in.

In *The Journey To You* we follow the Way of Power, which will show you first and foremost, that the shaman's practices for reclaiming and effectively using his own personal power are methods we can all use.

To *be* powerful, we must first learn to live according to our *own* definitions and sense of what is right, otherwise we make ourselves slaves at the outset to the worldviews of others. This book is a journey and each of the chapters is a step along this way. The first steps we will take together will explore the issue of 'reality' and what we mean by this term. We begin by 'deconstructing' and renegotiating the agreements we have made about this reality system. Through this process of enquiry, we will discover that there is far more to life than the worldview we have been taught to accept.

Our next step is to view these agreements from a new perspective and to construct a new framework with which to engage the world. The view of reality held by the new physics is a liberated one, which sees the world as less rigid and less fixed than the old, linear-scientific model of a world 'out there'. It is a view, in fact, which demands that we think and act creatively in the world for it to exist at all. It is also a view which leads us back towards the ancient landscape of the shaman and recaptures the sense of adventure and enquiry we left behind as children.

As you embark upon this journey of discovery you will encounter Imagework, a technique which enables us to access the shamanic state quickly and powerfully, and to journey in 'real time'.

These chapters represent practical steps which you will take, and which will lead you directly into the world of the shaman. Unless you experience it for yourself, you will never know if it is real; it will remain just one more interesting idea.

The final step in this journey, and the last chapter of the book, offers you a framework for the application of this shamanic knowledge in your daily life so you may remain connected to your power. It also introduces some of the enemies we will meet who will try to impede our onward progress, and suggests how you might deal with them in order to continue on your way.

But there are no rules to reading this book and you do not have to read it chapter by chapter in a linear way. You can create it for yourself instead, according to what interests you. In this way, it is very much like life.

Spiritual development is a long and arduous journey, an adventure through strange lands full of surprises, difficulties and even dangers. It involves a drastic transmutation of the 'normal' elements of the personality,

an awakening of potentialities hitherto dormant, a rais-
ing of consciousness to new realms, and a functioning
along a new inner dimension.
Robert Assagioli[3]

Life *is* a journey. And you *do* have the answers. I hope this
book will help you discover them for yourself.

2

INITIATION: WAKING FROM THE WESTERN DREAM

We only come to dream, we only come to sleep.
It is not true, it is not true that we come to live on
* Earth.*
Where are we to go from here?
We came here only to be born.
As our home is beyond, where the fleshless abide,
Perchance, does anyone really live on Earth?
The Earth is not for ever,
But just to remain for a short while.

– Traditional Mexican verse for the dead

I am naked, dancing in a landscape of rock and dry bone. Heat rises in waves from the mythic soil of this small Greek island. My body is brown and I am burning, but the sun here does not hurt.

Sweat rolls down my face, my back, my chest. I feel like a tribal warrior, in strange contrast to this Mediterranean setting. Maybe Lakota or Hopi. I am part of a sacred ritual, something like a Sun Dance, for enlightenment and visions.

Before me is my guide, a shaman who says he has been 'living in Wolf for too long'. His intention in offering this ceremony is to connect with other, less fierce aspects of himself by giving instead of defending his habitual stance. He will guide me through this ritual as a celebration of himself and of me.

I am dancing to connect with my Warrior and Goddess selves, he says. He has picked a place of power very carefully for this journey. Before me, in the distance, is a mountain; behind me is a cave. Nothing is spoken of the symbolism here but, to my Western mind, it is apparent. This ritual has been designed for my deepest self, to connect at a level beyond words, where everything is noticed and becomes part of the whole, and nothing needs to be said of it. It is my deepest self which answers.

Once I have found and made contact with the Warrior and Goddess aspects of myself, my guide will officiate over a spiritual marriage between the two. I will then always have access to their power, he tells me, and be able to draw upon their individual and collective strength.

My guide asks if I can see them and if I can find a name for each. I discover that I cannot speak to answer him. I nod. Yes.

He tells me to find the qualities they each represent and to take these inside myself. 'Find a gesture or a symbol which will remind you of their power,' he says. I find a symbol which has meaning for me but I need a tangible external object too, one that I can touch and feel. I reach down, pick up a rock. One end is sharp and pointed like a knife, the other is rounded, almost heart-shaped, a perfect blend of the masculine and the feminine. I place it against my chest. It is warm from the sun.

The dance continues, with new instructions and directions given every few minutes. I am acting out a battle, a warrior tired of fighting, sick of war, but finding superhuman strength to continue in the fight for what is morally and spiritually right.

Now, I am returning from war to the peace of my home-land. I am with my wife. We are making love. I am a warrior making love to my wife and, at the same time, a goddess making love to my warrior husband. I move between the two images until they become one single, powerful force *of love and strength, pure will and pure compassion.*

The ritual ends and I stand alone, breathing deeply and feeling the sunlight on my skin. My eyes remain closed, with the images of my journey now flickering beneath my eyelids. The images become one – a vision of the cave behind me. Just inside the entrance something sparkles, catching the light.

I turn, open my eyes and walk to the cave. Without pause, I reach inside and pick up a piece of quartz crystal . . .

The Shuar people of Ecuador have an expression, 'The world is as you dream it', which means that we can choose to see in the world and in ourselves whatever we want to see.

Here in the West, we live in a linear world of scientific causes and effects and, of course, it is not possible to be called to a cave by a crystal. In the linear world, the 'proper' way of things is to see the crystal first and then 'take' it. Just as day follows night, maturity follows childhood, old age follows adulthood, and death follows life. The progression is forward, mechanical, like the lurching of a giant, unstoppable machine. Other life forms cannot call to us – particularly not the dead carbon of an insentient crystal – just as life does not follow death and time does not reverse itself.

At least, this is what we are taught from the moment we are born.

This linear model isn't true, of course. The latest research into quantum physics has demonstrated this. You have only to dip into Fritjof Capra's *The Tao of Physics*[4] to discover that, at a subatomic level, particles do die and are then reborn, they can be in two places simultaneously; time does move backwards. The impossible happens with every heartbeat.

As human beings, however, we have made an 'agreement' to view reality in a particular way in order to control the chaos which would otherwise result, to give meaing to the otherwise meaningless, and to give ourselves a common agenda to work from. This scientific worldview is the model we have chosen as our operating system.

Yet, as many ordinary people know, through strange but meaningful coincidences in their lives, through ESP, precognition, information which has come to them in unbidden synchronicities or dreams – and as science is itself now telling us – the world doesn't *actually* operate in this way. We just act, for convenience, *as if* it did. It is a myth we have agreed to accept, a blunt model which allows us to get by in the normal world of everyday reality.

Shamanic teachers – like Castaneda's don Juan – have been advising us of this fact for years.

> *People tell us from the time we are born that the world is such and such and so and so and naturally, we have no choice but to see the world the way people have been telling us it is.*
>
> *Seeing happens only when one sneaks between the worlds . . . only then is one capable of knowing that the world we look at every day is only a description . . . Things are real only after one has learned to agree on their realities.*[5]

In fact, the idea that we do not experience reality *as it is*, but as an *image* of reality constructed in the mind is hardly new.

Plato argues in *The Republic* that the objects we see are not ultimate reality, but merely a reflection of that reality. The real world is one of ideas and essences; eternal, perfect concepts which exist in a place outside of time and space, a place which he refers to as 'the cave'; just as the Lakota holy man, Black Elk, reflected that the world we occupy is merely 'a pale shadow' of the true reality to be found in the otherworlds of the spirits and the shaman.

The philosopher, Immanuel Kant also made a distinction between what we see and what is real. All we ever know is what happens in our minds, he said. The world 'out there' may create our perceptions and we may take these to be real, but they are merely sensory impressions of the world. We are aware only of what our senses give us and the interpretations we place on these. We are slaves to our minds and may never actually see 'reality' in its 'true' form – whatever that is.

Time and space, our fundamental human co-ordinates, are not inherent qualities of a physical world, but things our minds have invented so we can categorize our experiences more easily, just as we have decided to agree our worth in terms of money, another human invention, and now all work for paper rather than purpose.

Time and space and many other aspects of our world are only frameworks we have created to guide us through our lives. They appear as qualities of a real physical world only because we have forgotten their origins as an expression of our own power. And now we find it hard to remember and we cannot see the world in any other way.

And so the reality that we see is just one way of looking at the world. The fact is that we are not passive consumers of the world around us, sponges for experience, but are *active creators* of it, and other worlds are possible and open to us right now.

Should we choose to hear the calling of a crystal, its song will surely be heard.

THE LIMITS OF LINEAR THOUGHT

The fundamental questions we all ask and which have been passed on through the generations from seeker to seeker – *Why are we here? What is this all about?* – have never been and can never be answered by the linear model, operating as it does on the basis of consensus. These answers can only ever be found in personal, and never collective, truth. Collective truth merely gives rise to dogma and consensus acceptance and we end up with a scientific 'proof' which gives us no answers at all.

We are told, for example, that the human species began its evolutionary journey as single-celled creatures – a random accident of chromosomes animated by a cosmic explosion –

and crawled from the primal soup, driven only by the compulsion of its selfish, survival-fixated and pre-programmed genes.

Where in that description is there a *purpose* evident, a *reason* for our being here? The 'answer' does not even begin to address the question.

Dr Stephen Hawking refers to unified field theory – the scientist's holy grail which would explain all of the questions of the universe within one elegant super-equation. Not only are we still some way off from that, he says, but the solution itself would not provide an answer.

> *Even if there is only one possible unified theory, it is just a set of rules and equations. What is it that breathes fire into the equations and makes a universe for them to describe? The usual approach of science of constructing a mathematical model cannot answer the questions of why there should be a universe for the model to describe.*
>
> *Why does the universe go to all the bother of existing?*[6]

That is the real question – not *what it is*, but *why it bothers*, and the role we are supposed to be playing in this.

DOUBT

Philosophy is about as far as free thought can go in our society before science steps in and claims the question as its own territory, and Descartes is one of its most famous sons.

Descartes was a seeker after absolute truth. To explore the nature of true reality, he invented the method of universal doubt, his logic being that anything which could in any way be doubted could not be an absolute and incontrovertible truth.

Using this technique, Descartes found he could doubt the existence of anything and everything – any social theory, religious dogma, legal truth, accepted morality, the evidence of his own eyes. He could even doubt his own mind – perhaps he was mad and his entire life a deluded fantasy. But he could never doubt the fact that he *was* doubting.

This approach reveals one absolute certainty, one truth: that everything we are and all we are aware of in our lives cannot be supported by any final evidence – except one thing: doubt itself. By doubting, we are thinking. If we are thinking, we must be capable of thought. And to think at all, we have, at least, to *be*.

Cogito ergo sum. I think, therefore I am. I exist.

The act of thinking is absolute proof of existence; experience is an undeniable fact of life, and *personal experience* is the most important thing in making sense of the world. *I* think, therefore *I* am.

There is nothing in this world that you cannot question from this perspective – no government dictate, or legal requirement, or social moral – because all of it, quite literally, exists only because you accept that it does. Everything comes back to us and what *we* choose to believe in the world.

Descartes' proof can tell you nothing about *me* or *my* experiences, or about the world at large. His method doesn't even acknowledge the independent existence of this world beyond the attention you give it and your awareness of it and me. But if *you* can experience something, it must, by its very nature, be real. And we are all in the same boat. My world only exists because you have built it for me. But yours only exists because I have imagined *you*.

Now all we need to know is what we are supposed to be doing with this experience. *Why* are we here? And what's next?

THE SEARCH FOR HUMAN CONSTANTS

What is the essence of humanity? What does it mean to be human? Sociology and psychology, the sciences of human society and human mind, suggest some answers but they too have their limitations.

One of the most fundamental things to affect all of us is our health – physical and mental. Without these, we are at a disadvantage for learning and developing throughout our lives. What can psychology and sociology tell us about health and illness, and how they are viewed in the linear world?

Not surprisingly, the linear model sees illness as based on constants, a progression of disorders, each of which contributes to the total picture of the patient. These can be quantified and measured progressively. When enough symptoms have been accumulated at a sufficiently high level, a diagnosis can be made, from which a treatment follows, with a definite end goal – the continuation of the body itself and the maintenance of life. It is an approach, for example, which keeps coma patients chained to life support systems, forever unconscious in soulless exile – sometimes even against their express wishes. For, in this worldview, spirit, if it is recognized at all, and even our rights as human beings, are all relegated to second place beneath the supremacy of the body, its chemistries and functions.

The shaman's view is different – human life is part of an infinite process which also includes death, and each person must be seen as a single, wonderful expression of that and treated uniquely and holistically, taking into account their spiritual, emotional and mental as well as their physical needs. Getting hung up on the precise functioning of one part of the body, one aspect of our existence, is a little like fixating on the car when we want to understand the driver, and destroys the natural balance of the whole person.

What the linear model tells us is that illness is caused by chemical imbalances and biological defects to bodily organs, that illness is a problem a person 'has' which is totally outside their control. At one level, of course, we all know this isn't true – what about the time you were sick because you knew you were going to have to perform in the school play? That wasn't a physical problem, at least not purely physical, it was produced in part by fear, and fear is an emotion – but it still made you *physically* sick. The seductive power of the linear medical model, however, suggests that such examples are somehow aberrations, that the biological 'nuts and bolts' approach is correct, despite inconvenient evidence like this to the contrary.

HEALTH IS A STATE YOU'RE IN

Since the 1960s, a lot of medical research has been published which shows conclusively that some life experiences can themselves cause, or at least substantially contribute to, physical and mental illness, so that physical symptoms might only be the later stage of much deeper emotional and spiritual problems.

Psychosomatic illness is a case in point.

ANOREXIA AND CULTURAL STEREOTYPES

Once looked at exclusively from a biochemical perspective, nowadays any analysis of anorexia nervosa will always include the effects of social pressure in its consideration of the problem. In the West, it is considered a good thing to be thin. This is not a universal view; in developing countries, the opposite is true. In some cultures, a well-rounded figure denotes high social status and power because it demonstrates very clearly that this person has sufficient wealth to be able to buy food while others in that society may be starving. Fat is a Financial Issue.

CANCER AND BEREAVEMENT

Studies show that cancer rates are higher among widows, widowers and divorcees than among the single or married. In one study of several hundred cervical cancer patients, around a quarter had recently been bereaved, compared with an average of just above 5 per cent. Bereavement and not susceptibility, genetics or social habits appears to be the significant factor. Cancer is a physical condition, but seemingly without a wholly physical cause.

BLOOD PRESSURE AND JOB LOSS

Research demonstrates that job loss causes high blood pressure as well as a greater likelihood of contracting common illnesses like colds. For Western men, work itself often defines the male role, status, self-esteem and lifestyle. When a man loses his job, he loses a major part of himself, and the sad truth is that men tend to die, on average, only four years after they retire. They have lived their entire lives within the Western dream and its definition of their role and, when they retire, they find that there is no-one left to be – so they simply cease to be. Traditionally, women have had multiple rather than singular roles – those of 'wife', 'mother' and 'daughter' are some of them, in addition to their more recent roles as 'worker' and 'provider'. Consequently, they have invested in a richer identity and a wider network of emotional and social support and tend to survive their partners by an average of five years. It seems that we are – or become – what we present to the world and sometimes even blood-pressure-related illnesses can be a symbol of our status and our role in life.

RUMOURS OF ILLNESS

On a similar note, Mika Kivimaki of the University of Helsinki has produced research which shows that even the threat or rumour of 'downsizing' at work can have a major and long-term physical and psychological impact on employees, to the extent that anticipated gains to employers are far outweighed by the detrimental consequences of any actual, subsequent redundancies. Kivimaki followed the progress of 764 men and women, ranging in age from 20 to

62, who were municipal workers in Finland during 1990–95, a time of severe economic decline. The results of this longitudinal study found that the threat of redundancy was associated with an increse in smoking, marital problems and greater workplace sickness and absenteeism, with a sickness absence rate twice as high after major redundancies, among workers who remained. The cause of these complaints was a feeling of insecurity, powerlessness and lack of control over their own destiny, but the disturbances were real and physical. 'It seems crucial that employees keep a sense of control in spite of the restructuring,' Kivimaki said in an interview with Reuters Health. 'This may also be a way to promote open communication in the organization, which, in turn, can reduce feelings of insecurity and rumours.'

HEART ATTACKS AND CULTURE SHOCKS

Researchers have found that immigrants to a new country experience profound 'culture shock' to the extent that a higher incidence of heart attacks occurs among first-generation immigrants. Surprisingly, changes in diet and living conditions are not as significant as social pressures and the cultural and lifestyle changes immigrants must adapt to.

What all of this evidence begins to demonstrate is that at a very real, physical level we create our own reality, even our own illnesses, by our reactions to and interpretations of, the events and circumstances we find ourselves in.

In other words, there is something between the cause (unemployment, for example) and the effect (illness), and that something is our worldview. It is how we see the world around us and our place within it that is important, and not the thing-in-itself. The world carries on to exist 'out there', but our interpretation of the messages it sends us determines our reaction to it.

Recent research by Dr Johanna Mooy of Amsterdam's Vrije Universiteit adds credence to this suggestion. Her study, of more than 2,000 people aged between 50 and 74, shows that the onset of one form of diabetes can be provoked entirely by particular life events, totally irrespective of any family history of the disease, excessive use of alcohol, or other factors commonly associated with diabetes. It is as if the potential for the disease remains dormant until it is triggered by an event such as the loss of a loved one, financial problems, or the end of a long-term relationship. This causes an emotional response, which then activates a physical re-action. In this study, people who had undergone such emotional and life-changing situations were 60 per cent more likely to have diabetes. Presumably – although the researchers do not say this – by changing our emotional reaction, therefore, we might also control the onset of diabetes in the body.

OUR INTERPRETATION OF STRESS

Mooy's study, quoted above, looked at emotional events in terms of the stress they caused, concluding that the results are consistent with other research which demonstrates that stressful events cause bodily changes such as an increase in the hormone cortisol, and a decrease in testosterone. Both of these have an impact on the action of insulin in the body, which regulates blood sugar levels and is therefore of crucial importance in the incidence of diabetes. Quite complex and subtle changes in the body can arise from our reactions to events taking place in our lives.

I remember being taught a whole module on 'stress' as part of my undergraduate studies in psychology. It is interesting to me now, when I look back at this in the context of our Western worldview, and also as a symptom of our modern age, that it should have been stress. Why not 'the psychology of love' or 'peace' or 'compassion'? The world, after all, is as we dream it. Be that as it may, one of the things our teachers showed us is that the same amount of adrenalin is released whenever we enter a stressful situation. It is our *reaction* to the situation, not the adrenalin itself, which determines the effect that stress has on us. In one experiment we were shown, the results demonstrated that if two groups of people were given injections of equal amounts of adrenalin and one group was then put into a situation designed to produce anger, the other into a situation designed to create euphoria, people interpreted their reactions *not* according to the adrenalin rush itself, but according to the *situation* they found themselves in. One group experienced joy, the other experienced anger.

Personal interpretation was the key. Stress, we always seem to be told these days, has a marked effect on our health, leading to a number of physical, mental and emotional problems. But the reverse is also true. The reality is that stress can be a source of great happiness if we imagine it so. We are masters of our own fate and how we see ourselves in any situation is more powerful than the situation itself.

A study, by Dr William Malarkey of Ohio State University, goes some way to supporting this. Malarkey and his colleagues found that emotional upset reduces the power of the body's natural healing process. In his study, thirty-six women completed detailed psychological questionnaires to determine their level of stress and the number of stressful conditions in their lives. They were then given 'wounds' in the form of small blisters on their arms which were produced medically in a relatively painless way and, as they began to heal, fluid was extracted from the wound and tested. The researchers found that interleukin-1 and interleukin-8, two body compounds important for healing, were much lower in samples from women who were more stressed. One of the study's co-authors has concluded from this that the immune system is extremely sensitive to emotional health, and suggests that appropriate therapies should be used prior to surgery, for example, in order to reduce or, perhaps, help the patient to reinterpret, the emotions they are experiencing, as post-surgery healing will be much improved by pre-surgery support.

HEALING OURSELVES WITH SUGAR LUMPS

Placebos are tablets with no known pharmacological value – they could be sugar lumps, and often are. But they have been used to cure all sorts of medical problems. Angina, backache, insomnia, arthritis, even leukaemia, are just a few of them. One group of people was even given a placebo and told it was a metabolic stimulant. They started to sweat, feel sick, and experience a range of other reactions entirely consistent with metabolic increase – for no physical reason whatsoever.

Their own belief in the potency of the placebo had created a physical reaction – a real case of mind over matter – which suggests the power we have to heal or harm ourselves through our own faith in a particular description of the world.

OPERATING WITHOUT PAIN

Hypnotism also works on a physical as well as a mental level, though there is no reason why it should if the mind and body are totally separate and if personal interpretation plays no part in our reactions. Yet research has shown that asthma can be controlled entirely by auto-hypnosis and, more recently, full surgical procedures have been carried out without anaesthetic, relying entirely on the power of hypnosis to prevent the patient from experiencing pain.

BLOOD FLOWS WHERE ATTENTION GOES

Even the autonomic nervous system (ANS), that part of our body which controls 'automatic' functions such as breathing and blood flow, and which was always thought to be beyond conscious control, is not, in fact, immune to the power of our minds. Migraine sufferers have been taught to consciously alter their own ANS, for example, to direct blood flow away from the head to reduce pressure and alleviate the pain.

Dina Glouberman, in her book on Imagework, *Life*

Choices, Life Changes,[7] dismisses the idea that the ANS is beyond our mental control. 'This only means that we cannot affect them [our autonomic responses] with words. Images are another matter,' she says. 'Try telling yourself: "I want to salivate". Does it work? Now try an image: imagine vividly sucking on a big juicy sour lemon, rolling it round your mouth while your whole face screws up. Any saliva?'

Imagery has, in fact, been used successfully in a number of healing contexts in order to receive information from the body about what needs to be healed, and then to empower it to transform the functions of the ANS to combat the physical problem.

Dr Carl Simonton, director of the Cancer Counseling and Research Center in Texas, works with cancer patients in exactly this way, using their imagery to determine how quickly their tumours are growing, and then to help shrink them.

Simonton asks his patients to imagine themselves winning the war against cancer by seeing their white blood cells as a powerful army destroying the invaders. Statistical studies of his patients show that those using his techniques live *twice* as long as others and that many recover fully through spontaneous remission, a result which is otherwise unexplainable.

The studies of health and well-being we have looked at here are just the tip of a vast iceberg of impressive evidence which has now been accumulated. All of them are really about belief – what we believe, or decide, to be true about the world 'out there' and about our own role in it. The over-riding conclusion is that we can choose any reality we want, including being ill or being well, no matter what disease confronts us.

In the realest possible sense, there is no objective reality. It is our image of the world that is the key to our experience of it.

Even before we are born, we are unconscious consumers of the world we will be born into. If you were conceived in the West, even while you were in your mother's womb, a WASP world was going on around you.

A WASP – White Anglo-Saxon Protestant – culture tends to have certain structures and values associated with it. The culture you enter will be white-male-dominated, relatively wealthy, middle class or middle class aspirant, science-based, with an international, industrial economy. It will have a unique set of values and beliefs, and its own place in time and evolution. All of which will make a difference to who you are and who you will become.

We absorb this information all the time. Directly in terms of the food our mothers eat and the nutrients we take from it (if you were conceived in Africa during the famine, you can imagine how your early life might be different to your current one), in the emotions our mothers experience at certain times and the reasons for them (anxiety will release more adrenalin into your shared bloodstream, for example), and indirectly in the sounds and sights and feelings you experience even in the womb.

As soon as we are born, we are exposed directly to this information in the form of social values passed on by our families. These are reinforced through education, through the predominant religion of our culture, through the political system which sets up the institutions we are a part of, and through the unwritten rules – and ultimately, the legal system – which moderate our responses and punish our transgressions.

This is socialization – learning indirectly to be a part of the society we are born into. The Eskimos have thirty-odd different names for snow because it's important in their culture; we have thirty-odd different names for a burger because it's important in ours.

If you had been conceived in a different country or a different time, your world would have been a very different place. If you had been born in the 1600s, for example, you would never even have experienced childhood. Children are a modern invention.

Philippe Aries, in his book, *Centuries of Childhood*,[8] studied the wills left by family members in the 1600s, and concluded that friends were more important than family and usually came before blood relatives (and certainly children) in bequests of property and other material goods.

The concept of the family was very different too. It *didn't* include relations who lived outside the home, but it *did* include servants and other people who lived under the same roof, even if they weren't even remotely connected by blood.

In the Middle Ages, children were seen as replaceable commodities. It wasn't a good idea to grow attached to them because infant death rates were so high. So, there was no acknowledgement at all of a child up until the age of seven. From then onwards children were treated as small adults.

It wasn't until the 1700s that architectural changes took place to give the family separate rooms from servants. Until then, there was no real concept of the family as separate, distinct and important in its own right, and not until the eighteenth century does any concept of the 'home' as a sanctuary for the family begin to emerge.

In the eighteenth century, too, the formal education system began to develop and only then can we really say that there is a growing recognition of the importance of childhood and a desire to extend it beyond the age of seven and cherish the uniqueness of our children.

Things began to change in the twentieth century when Freud, Piaget, Spock, Bowlby and other innovators emerged and began taking an interest in childhood in its own right. Only then did we finally begin to acknowledge childhood as a separate state of being and to try to understand the world and the reality of the child. Yet, even as late as the 1950s in America and the UK, new parents were being advised not to expend too much love or energy on children in case they should 'spoil' them.

It may be very different today, but remember that in all of these periods of history, *this was* the reality of the world, the only reality there was, and for those who lived it, it was a reality as valid as our own.

Being in your right mind

Mental health is another area where the definition of 'reality' plays a crucial role. The person described as 'mentally ill' or 'insane' has become easy to identify because he or she has taken on a very distinct and separate worldview to others, characterized, depending on the 'severity' or 'extremity' of the condition, as a (total) disregard for the rules which the social majority have chosen to live by.

Western societies have a history of dealing with their mentally ill in a very direct and insensitive way and this has had very serious consequences for the person so labelled. Separated from society at large, mentally ill patients are often incarcerated in a mental institution; or freedom of thought and emotions are removed through a programme of drugs or, in extreme cases, lobotomy.

Today, the rules on the treatment of patients may have changed but the focus is still on making our mentally ill as 'invisible' as possible. The approach taken now is one of 'Care' in the Community, even though the 'community' is never defined and no guidance is available as to how this care should be given. By dispersing the mentally ill throughout society, however, their impact is diluted and so, politically, the problem can be seen to have gone away. Meanwhile, the people affected have no commonality of identity or location and so wander the streets in increasing numbers without help or support, presenting a potential danger to themselves and the people they encounter.

For society to justify its actions and make sure it takes them only in appropriate circumstances, it had better be very clear what it means by 'abnormal' and, by association, what it means by 'normal' behaviour. If you were to try to define mental illness, however, you would be struck by the lack of a consistent agreement about what this actually is. Depending on who you listened to and in what period of history, you would hear it described as a biochemical problem, a social construct, possession by evil spirits – or that it didn't exist at all.

There is no such thing as an objective consensus on the subject of 'mental illness', beyond a vague understanding and a middle-ground compromise definition of what mental 'illness' or mental 'health' is in a particular time and place.

The twentieth-century medical view is that madness is due to some biological defect or psychopathology of the individual – it is a 'disease' – while the approach of humanistic psychiatrists, and of the shaman, is that the condition is a psycho-spiritual problem – a 'dis-ease'.

Until the seventeenth century, madness was allied to witchcraft and seen as a form of spirit possession. The 'witch' was normally burned, drowned or dispatched in some other way. In contrast, even today in some tribal cultures, people we in the West might describe as mentally ill are revered as 'wise ones' precisely *because* of the special relationship they are thought to have with the world of spirit. They may be elected as tribal leaders or respected as authority figures who are thought to bring special gifts to the clan.

In some societies, there is no such thing as mental illness – it is merely behaviour taken out of context, which therefore does not make sense to others. Michael Harner, who has done much for the cause of contemporary shamanism, tells a story from the rainforests of the Amazon.

Walking one day with a wise man from the indigenous Shuar tribe, he observed a man having an animated conversation with a tree. The Shuar are a highly spiritual people and one in four of their tribe is a shaman. Since he was in a culture so steeped in shamanism, a belief system which sees meaning and a living, conscious, energy in all things, Harner naturally assumed that the man in question was a wise and powerful shaman. Oh no, said his guide, this man is crazy. Had the same man been involved in the same activity in an appropriate ritual setting, he *might* have been a great shaman. Out here talking to trees, he was obviously just plain nuts.[9]

A Western scientist, Thomas Szasz, made the point succinctly when he observed that 'if you talk to god, you are praying; if god talks to you, you have schizophrenia.'

I recently took part in a Vodou ceremony, where the Mambo (priestess) made a similar point about the crucial importance of context. Vodou – what we in the West call 'voodoo' – believes in a vast pantheon of gods and spirits, all of whom must be approached in precisely the right ceremonial manner. Often these supplications are intense and elaborate but the priest is insistent that they should in no way be changed or adapted. To do so would be to invite a 'bad head' – insanity – since the initiate would be completely unable to disentangle reality from personal invention. It is precisely the elaborate nature of these formulaic rituals which gives them a framework and context to ensure that when the gods speak, it is *their* voices which are heard.

The Western 'anti-psychiatry' movement has put a similar emphasis on the exploration of context. In so doing, it has abandoned the notion of mental illness, believing instead that people respond in a 'mad' way to cope with a mad situation.

GHOSTS

R. D. Laing is probably most often quoted in this respect. Laing, one of the founders of anti-psychiatry and a foremost authority on schizophrenia, believed that insanity was 'a perfectly rational adjustment to an insane world' and saw society itself and the family in particular as a root cause of this need for adjustment and coping.

In The Ghost of the Weed Garden,[10] Laing tells the story of a young female patient he worked with in the 1970s, who could no longer see herself. She believed she was invisible as a human being and could recognize herself only as a tennis ball being hit between opponents on a court.

Clearly mad? The linear medical response would say so and would set about treating her symptoms. Laing, however, was interested in determining the cause, not dealing in isolation with its effect, and so looked at her behaviour in the context of her life as a whole and her interactions with others.

Within her family situation, for example, Laing found a mother and father who were at 'silent war' in the home, refusing to talk to each other directly and rarely communicating at all. At the breakfast table, the family would sit together and the mother, turning to her daughter would say, 'Tell your father his tea is getting cold.' The child would do so and the father would reply, 'Tell your mother I'll be late home from work tonight', or words to that effect. The child was used as a go-between by her parents – like a ball being hit between opponents over the tennis court of the communal table. Meanwhile, no-one was talking to her or taking her needs into account. She was, in effect, invisible.

Her response was a very accurate reflection of her circumstances. Creative and imaginative, yes, but real, not mad.

Laing's response was to address the whole situation, not just the 'patient'. By empowering the person caught in the middle of these sad games of power rather than trying to 'treat' her, he was able to change the behaviour of everyone involved and reach the best available outcome for all. His entire approach to treatment was, in fact, extremely unorthodox – even shamanic – on occasion, and often startlingly effective.

Laing was once asked his opinion about a young girl diagnosed as schizophrenic, who had been locked in a padded cell in a special hospital. There she sat naked, rocking backwards and forwards, and had spoken to no-one for many months.

As the other doctors watched, Laing stripped off completely and entered her cell as naked as she was. Then he sat with her, rocking backwards and forwards to her rhythm. After 20 minutes of this, she began to speak.

Emerging from the cell some time later, Laing put his clothes back on, looked at the other doctors and asked simply, 'Did it never occur to you to do that?'

This is an example of the triumph of the spirit over cold science. By recognizing the connection between all of us, this girl was treated – not as a 'case' to be studied and observed – but as a human being. She had problems and she needed the kind of compassion and support that made her feel part of society, not isolated and separate from the world around her.

While recognizing the effectiveness of Laing's methods, however, there were sadly few of his peers who were prepared to emulate them. It was not the 'proper' way of 'the profession'. And so the patient was allowed to go back to her silent world until she was deemed, some time later, to be 'cured' by more orthodox methods.

One of the paradoxes of our approach to the treatment of mental illness is that we require our patients to acknowledge the 'fact' that they *are* mad before we are willing to consider them on the road to recovery, even though we ourselves have no real definition of what we mean by 'madness'.

The fragility of the concept was brought home to me by an amusing story I heard as an undergraduate, of a sociologist who set out to study what Erving Goffman has called the 'total institution' of the typical mental asylum.

The sociologist in question got himself admitted to just such an asylum – very easily, in fact – by telling his doctor he was hearing voices. All went well for his study and he managed to accumulate lots of data – until the point, a few weeks after his incarceration, when he decided he had all the information he needed and tried to confess to the psychiatrists who he really was so he could return home to write up his notes.

The doctors were having none of it. They had already defined his note-taking of the last few weeks as a form of obsessive-compulsive behaviour, and now he seemed to be having some type of identity crisis too – and it must be pretty extreme as only somebody really sick would see themselves as a sociologist, right? His confession of the truth was labelled as an unfortunate deterioration in his condition and the doctors agreed that their patient's stay should be prolonged. Only by admitting to his delusion, they told him, would he finally be able to break through the mental barriers he was erecting against his treatment so that a cure could finally begin.

The doctors were, effectively, unable to distinguish *one of their own people* from someone 'genuinely' mentally ill and it took a number of frantic calls by the sociologist to his university head of department to get him released at all.

The more humanistic perspective Laing represents can still be regarded as the 'alternative' view to the accepted mainstream medical perspective, but its impact is growing. Just as we have moved from a view of children as not really there at all, to a child-centred universe, the more 'people-focused' psychiatrists today would like us to accept that other views of reality – even if people do want to label them 'mad' – are valid expressions of where a particular person is at on their journey through life. In doing so, we move towards a more shamanic view of the universe.

Liz Tomboline, a psychiatric nurse turned shamanic healer and therapist, has this to say:

There are vast cultural differences in what is deemed to be socially acceptable behaviour.

Modern day living poses many challenges to our mental health and most of us are probably not living as we truly are and [instead] present extremely sophisticated personas to the world. What we lack in this society is a sense of community, of family and the wider, personal support that our ancestors enjoyed. We have few Elders to turn to, few spiritual guides – for goodness sake, it is often really difficult to get a baby sitter these days, let alone any deeper support unless we are very lucky![11]

THE TRUTH AND THE MATRIX

In the Keanu Reeves film, *The Matrix*, when the character Neo is woken from the dream he has been living, into the reality of another world outside of the vast computer program that is the matrix of the title, he asks his benefactor, Morpheus, for an explanation of this construct.

'The matrix is the world that has been pulled over your eyes to blind you to the truth . . .' says Morpheus. It is all around us and in everything we see and sense and feel. It is there when we pay our taxes and agree unquestioningly to fund the system, or vote for the political candidate of our choice – the assumption being that *there is no choice* apart from subscribing to some political party's view of reality. It is there when we open a book and read someone else's truth, or pray to our god, or make love to our partner, or kiss our child goodbye at the gate of the school. The reality is all in our heads. It has been quietly placed there by society, by the matrix, since the moment we were born. The 'linear' model of reality *is* the matrix.

But the Western urban dream is at best only an agreement between us to accept a mythological view of 'the world out there'. It is not the only model. Nor can it answer the truly important questions for us – indeed, it struggles even with its own internal consistency in matters of physical and mental health. Ultimately, questions which concern us as individuals must always, and in all times, be answered by ourselves. 'No-one can tell you what the matrix is,' says Morpheus. 'You have to see it for yourself.'

The matrix is a comfortable world – although or, perhaps, *because* – it deprives us of our freedom and makes us slaves to the worldview which sustains it. Within it, we no longer need to take responsibility for our own actions, to find a sense of purpose for ourselves, to develop the personal moral strength to guide our human interactions, to explore the world around us and figure out our role within it, or even to truly engage with it. As long as we do not rock the boat, we are quite at liberty merely to go through the motions of *playing* the role we are programmed for and continue with our comfortable existence, unaware even that we are part of a dream or that there is the potential for another world, one that we ourselves might create.

And so it is with our dream of society too. In the linear world we have created, we have generated many specialisms and given birth to a long list of 'experts'. Now we do not need to heal ourselves as we once did, or to take personal responsibility for our own well-being. We turn instead to doctors who we expect to 'heal' us, to policemen, lawyers and politicians who will enforce the social dream for us according to the ethics our society has, almost randomly, chosen to live by. We do not need to exercise our own sense of what is right. Our psychiatrists and scientists define what is real and what is fantasy. Our TV sets and journalists interpret the wider world for us. And our priests stand before us to decode the words and the will of god if, indeed, She is deemed to exist at all.

We have placed a million intermediaries between us and our direct experience of life in all of its manifestations – and every time we turn to one of them, we give away our power and accept the dream of someone else.

And what can these 'experts' really do to help us that we cannot do for ourselves? We have already seen that, in matters of physical and mental well-being, it is our *belief* in our own power which cures and defines us – and surely, we do not really need a politician or a priest to tell us right from wrong?

I was amused and also saddened recently when I was asked by a national newspaper to take part in a debate between shamanism and mainstream religion on the nature of the soul. 'What is soul?' the journalist wanted to know.

Apparently, she had phoned Lambeth Palace, our seat of accepted religious belief, before coming to see me – and was met by stunned silence at the other end of the phone. Nobody had ever asked this representative of the Church about the soul before, and he had to check his ecclesiastical dictionary for a definition. 'The soul is sacred,' he finally concluded, after reading her a verbatim description '– but please don't quote me on that!'

These intermediaries and experts that we invest our power and faith in – to whom we trust our very souls, perhaps – what do they really know about the human experience? About as much as you or I, it seems, since they are human too – and in some cases, maybe considerably less than most of us.

I was also struck, a few days later, by a report in another paper about the people who arrive each year in Jerusalem, one of the holiest cities on Earth, and are touched by the presence of the divine that they find there. It is a miracle in itself that people *can* still find the spirit of god in this place so torn by division and bigotry, by religious intolerance, hatred and war, but some do.

Once we called these people pilgrims and offered them alms to support them in their quest. We blessed them and wished them well on their journey to the Holy Land to commune with god and to feel the ecstasy of the spirit. Now, we call them 'mad' – there is even a clinical name for the possession of the Holy Spirit. It is called the Jerusalem Syndrome. What does that say about our own dream of the world and the place of spirit within it?

Under the headline SAD PILGRIMS WHO THINK THEY MAY BE JESUS, writer Karin Laub talks of the 'deranged tourists' – around 150 a year, but perhaps increasing by up to 60 per cent in recent years, aged from 17 to 70 and 'of above average intelligence' – some of whom feel 'inexplicably compelled' to wear white and 'preach rambling sermons' upon their arrival in Jerusalem.[12]

Once we might have called such people visionaries and listened in awe to the word of god that was channelled through them. In the new religion, we call them 'sufferers', their words are 'rambling'; they are the mad. They are also the reason for the expansion of the Givat Shaul psychiatric clinic in Jerusalem, which now houses and 'treats' them. We have a whole institution devoted to these visionaries, where the voice of god is a drug-induced slur. Our experts are the agents of the matrix and we find ourselves now living their dream. If, in this new millennium, Jesus Christ has returned to Earth, as many of our religious leaders predicted, perhaps he is now explaining his own 'identity crisis' and delusions to the doctors of Givat Shaul. For how would we even recognize the Messiah from the mad in a world with no understanding left of the sacred?

I do not intend disrespect, I am merely highlighting the contradiction, and underlining why we must always find the answers to life's great spiritual and philosophical questions for ourselves. When it comes right down to it, there is nowhere else to look, no consistent external reality we can subscribe to which is unchanging and universally true, and no-one else who can answer for us. Whether we look for answers in the physical, emotional, mental or spiritual world, we are only ever what we believe ourselves to be, or else we are the dream of someone else. As Castaneda tells us in *A Separate Reality*: 'The world is whatever we perceive, in any manner we may choose to perceive.'[13]

THE OUTSIDERS

Living with the knowledge that there is no objective reality is not an easy option for some people, and it is a lonely world for many. Colin Wilson, in his book, *The Outsider*, estimates that only 4 per cent of people can live with the tension of being both a part of and outside of society at the same time, living within the matrix but knowing there is more, sensing that there is something wrong with reality but not knowing what it is.[14]

If they can manage to do so, these people fulfil a vital function for us all as the innovators, the pioneers, the creative individuals, the urban shamans, who are able to shift our collective consciousness through the power of unorthodox thought and a willingness to explore new realities. But many – the drop-outs, the burnouts, the isolated, the teenage suicides – fail to cope with the colossal existential task of recreating and redefining their lives and their world each and every day. And even those outsiders who succeed for a while – Gandhi, Martin Luther King, Van Gogh, Hemingway, James Dean, Kurt Cobain – risk literal as well as psychic death in doing so. It is a perilous path we embark upon when we choose to live our own personal truth.

'When a man embarks on the paths of sorcery he becomes aware, in a gradual manner, that ordinary life has been forever left behind; that knowledge is indeed a frightening affair; that the means of the ordinary world are no longer a buffer for him and that he must adopt a new way of life if he is going to survive,' says Castaneda's don Juan,[15] for whom 'sorcery' is the process of attaining the personal power which will help us to live with the contradictions and the psychic struggle of remaining an outsider, an authentic human being living truthfully apart from the world's agreements.

People who live their lives with an awareness that there is no objective reality, that the world is, indeed, as we dream it, can follow only one of two courses. They can either opt *in* to society, throw up their hands and call the world unknowable (though occasionally they will still find themselves asking 'Why am I doing this?', 'What is it all about?'), or they can keep searching for meaning in their own lives.

Those who continue the search are engaged in one of the oldest quests known to humanity – the Journey of the Hero.

For the psychoanalyst Carl Jung, the Hero is a symbol of transformation. His journey begins when he awakens from the trance of childlike innocence where there simply are no questions to ask and the world just is, to the realization that the rest of the world does not operate this way. Then, he must embark upon the quest to understand this contradiction – or decide to look away for ever.

A person becomes a Hero when he decides to take the journey, painful and disturbing though it may sometimes be, in order to discover the new truths that will help him to create meaning in *his* world. The Journey, in fact, is what makes him a Hero, instead of someone who ignores the calling of the quest and opts *in* to the social mythology of the majority worldview.

Having taken the journey, that person, fully transformed into a Hero, is able to integrate what he has learned and return to normal reality, often with the gifts of new knowledge and insight, which he will share – indeed, cannot help but share – with others, since this is his new truth. The world he finds upon his return is maybe not so very different from the one he left – but everything has changed. It is an experience captured elegantly by T. S. Eliot in the poem, 'Little Gidding':

> *We shall not cease from exploration*
> *And the end of all our exploring*
> *Will be to arrive where we started*
> *And know the place for the first time.*[16]

The Hero's quest is a motif which underpins the initiation into shamanism. The first stage is always a separation from the group – the rules, norms, and conventions of society – where the shaman-initiate will voyage, psychically and literally, deep into the wilderness to seek for and explore new realities. This is the shaman's awakening from the dream of his society into the quest for his personal truth.

Shamanic tradition sees this stage metaphorically as a dismemberment of the initiate. He may be captured by the spirits and, in their world, have his body ripped open, his skin torn off, internal organs pulled out, his bones pulled apart, which he will watch and contemplate as his body is destroyed. In psychological terms, he is stripping away all he has been taught by society about how to view the world, all that he has internalized about this worldview, while he contemplates the new realities and mysteries which remain.

In the tradition of initiation, the empty body of the shaman, his eyeless sockets, the cavity of his skull, are often then filled with quartz crystals, symbolic of greater clarity, wisdom and purity. He will absorb these new truths, uncover the wisdom of the universe and empower himself with new knowledge and technologies for healing.

The final stage is his return, bringing with him for the benefit of others the insights, learning and greater consciousness he has uncovered. Often this increased power is accompanied by new psychic abilities – to divine the future, to heal the sick, to offer new interpretations and insights into the events of life and the destiny of the tribe he serves.

The Vision Quest of the Hero, the journey into inner and outer solitude to discover new truths and new ways of seeing, is a theme which runs through all spiritual and religious literature. It is the meditation of Jesus in the desert for forty days and nights; the contemplation of Buddha beneath the bodhi tree; the entombment of the Voudoun initiate in the seclusion of the sacred *djevo*, the sacred inner temple; the mountain isolation of the warrior-sage. The journey may be lonely, difficult; temptations and challenges may arise, but from facing each of them the Hero returns victorious with greater wisdom and power as his bounty.

'Heroes take journeys,' says Carol Pearson,[17] where they

> *confront dragons, and discover the treasure of their true selves. Although they may feel very alone during the quest, at its end their reward is a sense of community: with themselves, with other people, and with the Earth.*
>
> *Every time we confront death-in-life, we confront a dragon, and every time we choose life over non-life ...*

we vanquish the dragon; we bring new life to ourselves and to our culture.

It is a quest which you, too, are now embarked upon, and it is fully heroic in nature. If you sometimes catch a glimpse of the matrix in the anomalies that break through the structure we have imposed on the world and, at those times, feel that maybe there is something more, that you have given too much away – you are right, and you have. We all have. And now it is time to take it back.

So let's go on a journey together beyond the dream and see what the universe really looks like . . .

EXPLORATIONS – LIVING WITHOUT LABELS

Your life is not an exam and you do not *have to* complete these or any of the exercises which are included in this book. They are offered only for their practical application and insights into the contents of the sections they follow.

Just as the society we live in has a dream of its own reality, so we too have a personal dream of ourselves, which is the blueprint or pattern for the way we behave and present ourselves in daily life. We may actually work as accountants or housewives or doctors, or anyone of the thousand different personas open to us, but underlying it all is the dream we have of ourselves – as 'villains', 'victims' or 'lovers', or many different expressions of the personal script we have had written for us. But are any of them truly us?

Often, as children, our dreams are woven for us by parents and other significant people in our lives. You are told you are 'just like your grandfather', for example (who may have been a scurrilous rogue or a great leader of men), or a 'chip off the old block', 'the black sheep of the family', 'in a world of his own' or many other seemingly innocent expressions which set the scene for our later development into a particular role. And so the script is written for us to slip into character as Villain or Victim, respectively, whenever an appropriate situation arises.

1. Understanding your dream of self

What was the most frequent description your parents offered you? Did you believe it? Look back over your life from the perspective of this description of yourself. Does any pattern emerge?

Sometimes we resist the labels which life hands us, and then begins what Laing called the Good–Bad–Mad progression of applied labels and sanctions. The 'Good' girl is one who accepts the original part that is offered. The 'Bad' girl rejects it and the family then do all in their power to bring her back in line by punishing the behaviour which does not fit the dream they have of their daughter. The 'Mad' girl is the one who will not even respond to this punishment and holds fast to her own sense of self. Then, clearly, there must be 'something wrong' with her.

We all have an original blueprint handed to us to a greater or lesser extent. But the very notion of one single role is illusory and we all play many parts in a single day.

Take a few moments now to think back to a significant time in your life, something which has had a real impact on you, whether positive or negative – or even one you're not sure about; you just know it has some particular energy associated with it. Jot down the key details on a sheet of paper. It doesn't have to be a long description: bullet points will do.

What implications has this had for the way you have lived your life until now in the context of the event you have described?

How does your perception of this event change if you now rewrite the story from the perspective of:

- The Hero of the piece?
- The Victim?
- A bystander on the scene?
- And now from the point of view of your 'higher' spiritual self in touch with all aspects of this event?

How would it benefit you to change your personal dream of this event? Can you allow yourself to live *as if* the outcome had been better, more empowering for you – and if not, why not? What are you doing to prevent this, and why?

2. Who are you today?

The truth is evolutionary and may even change second by second. The 'past' begins the moment you reach the end of this sentence. And right now you are already in the 'future'.

As you reach the end of this sentence, 100,000 of your cells will have died – you will be someone else. You can recreate yourself in this moment if you truly want to, leave the past behind, and the part you have played up until now.

We all play many different roles every day – mother/daughter, father/son, boss/employee, lover (active)/loved (passive). We can use these roles creatively in our own empowerment by choosing a persona which best reflects our needs in any particular circumstance. As long as *we* know who we truly are and stay true to our authentic selves at heart, there is nothing 'wrong' in using our natural abilities for self-preservation. The first, and perhaps the only, moral principle of life is the survival of the true self.

But often the role overrides the context and we may find ourselves acting as the powerless son of an irate father when faced with an angry boss at work, for example. Particularly in moments of heightened emotion, such as angry scenes or places of deep passion, we find it easy to slip into these roles.

The next time such a situation arises for you, recognize the part you are playing and ask yourself who is the 'real' you. If all of these people are equally you and the way you present yourself in the world (your 'truth') changes with each persona you adopt, there may be something you are not admitting to yourself. For there is only one core truth, one authentic self within any of us, and we can act either in or out of accordance with this. If you *feel* uncomfortable with some of the things you allow yourself to do and say, is it perhaps because your true self is trying to make itself heard to you?

3. Stalking the true self

When shamans talk about 'stalking' they are referring directly to the activity of hunting. A good hunter will know his chosen game well. He will watch its habits, try to understand its needs, record its appearances in a certain place at different times, in order to build a complete profile of the animal he is dealing with. Once the hunter is aware that a particular animal appears always at a specific watering hole between 6a.m. and 8a.m. every morning, trapping it becomes a simple matter of timing and location.

We can set similar traps for the self.

You will need to set aside at least a full day for this, and preferably a whole week. During this period, make a conscious effort to recognize yourself 'in character' as a role-player during an average working day – as mother/daughter, wife/husband, employee/head of department and so on. Reflect on the way your mental processes, physical posture, way of 'being' and presentation of yourself change in each role. Use a diary to record your insights so you can reflect on this later.

When you do so, hold this question in mind: 'With all these actors in my head, who am I – *the essential I* – really?'

As strange as it may seem, make a conscious effort to

act 'out of character' during at least one of these role-playings. If at work you are in charge of a division, for example, act instead during your next departmental meeting as if you were having a friendly parental chat with your son or daughter (this need not change the content of your meeting). Or as you would if you were 'in character' as the champion of the local soccer team or the most able yoga student in your class or as 'the person your parents always wanted you to be' before you disappointed them/proved them wrong/or whatever.

What is different? How do you feel and what physiological changes take place in you?

As importantly, what changes for other people and how do they now view you? Do they feel confused or uncomfortable with this 'new you' or do they accept it as a positive move? Be aware of the subtle movements of energy between you.

At the end of the week, look back over your notes for this period and see when the different characters you play begin to emerge. What are the triggers? Do you become a 'little girl' in times of stress, or a 'warrior', or a 'teacher', showing others how to behave by your own actions? You can, if you choose, act 'out of character' at any time if this serves you better.

With practice, you can simply become aware of the trigger and where it would normally lead you, and decide to go elsewhere or become someone else instead.

3

THE SCIENTIST'S DREAM OF A SINGLE FISH: ENTERING THE HOLOGRAPHIC UNIVERSE

*The most difficult part about the warrior's way
is to realise that the world is a feeling.*
– don Juan

Crystals have been used since ancient times to present futures and offer communion with spirits and otherworld energies, a reflection of a deeper crystalline affinity with, and technology of, communication.

The French explorer, Auvergne tells of an experience in turn-of-the-century Tibet where he witnessed a Che-Sho priest use crystals and the sound of a gong to create light.[18]

'The priest raised the mallet and struck the gong once. I was startled to see half a dozen lights of a strange green colour come into vision. They shone dimly at first, but within a minute, the lights had grown in intensity, perhaps attaining some five hundred candle power each . . .

'When I approached one of the lights, I found that it was . . . common stone crystal about four inches in diameter on a plate of stone of some kind of grey metal. Over and around the plate ran an ornamental tracing of thin lines of gold hieroglyphs resembling cave writing.

'The priest informed me that the sound of the gong

penetrated the metal plate from which a vibrating force emanated [and infused] the crystal particles with a bright luminous glow, gradually growing to a certain intensity in accordance with the volume of vibratory sound . . . Had the gong been struck with a metal hammer . . . the glow would have been so great that the human eye could not stand it.'

Sound experienced as light through a crystal intermediary.

'The word synaesthesia, meaning joined sensation, denotes the rare capacity to hear colours, taste shapes, or experience other equally startling sensory blendings,' says Dr Simon Baron-Cohen.[19] 'A synaesthete might describe the colour, shape, and flavour of someone's voice, or music whose sound looks like "shards of glass" . . . Or, seeing the colour red . . . might detect the "scent" of red as well.'

Synaesthetes – like the Russian novelist Vladimir Nabokov, who perceived words in colour – are also prone to 'unusual experiences' including déjà vu, clairvoyance, precognitive dreams, empathic healing and psychokinesis, almost as if their talent for seeing the world in a different way is linked to an inherent ability to handle the stuff of the world differently too.

And yet, according to Baron-Cohen, 'We are all synaes-thetic', with the capacity to fully experience the miraculous – sound as light, colour as shape – before our minds tell us otherwise. We all experience the totality of all there is, in all its forms, before selectively filtering information and channelling it through the senses, in a grand division of labour and functionality, so that 'Only a handful of people [the synaesthetes] are consciously aware of the holistic nature of perception', but 'We are all unknowingly synaesthetic'.

Sound becoming light. Something we are all capable of.

There are infinite echoes here. New theories of reality, holographic universes and holotropic minds. Ideas which, in turn, reflect the more ancient wisdom of the shaman that we are all one, all more capable of miracles than we believe, and all of us intimately connected by the seamless web of life.

The crystal is a metaphor for these connections, reminding

us that communication is what unites us – communication with ourselves and with others – and of the need for all of us to retain the capacity for magic in our lives.

Mankind has always known the magical quality of crystals. We have found collections of quartz among remains dating from 70,000 BC and, even today, Hopi medicine men use them to gauge energy flow in the body, as an acupuncturist uses the body's meridians, while the Aborigines of north Queensland use quartz to provoke rainfall. Among the Huichol people of Central Mexico, they are the means by which the ancestors are reborn, as rock crystals which contain their essence as they move on to a higher vibrational realm of life. Crystals transmit radio waves, control tele-communications, and store vast quantities of information – which may go beyond raw data to include consciousness itself: experiments are said to have captured human thought in crystal and then transmitted it as an image.

All of life is carbon-based and so we should not be surprised to find that we are all brothers and sisters under the skin. Sound as light. Knowledge in crystal. We are fundamentally connected, all part of the web . . .

On 30 January 1999, at about 10.30 a.m., I got off the BART (Bay Area Rapid Transit) system at Powell Street station in San Francisco to walk the mile or so to Haight-Ashbury, birthplace of the 1967 Summer of Love which helped to create a change in global consciousness.

As I walked, I was thinking about this section of the book.

We began this journey by looking at the linear-scientific model and its preoccupation with sequential events and compartmentalized meaning. What we saw in the last chapter is that this social model of reality does not work when it comes to philosophical concepts of personal truth and ultimate reality. It does not even work on the physical level, when we consider the issues of mental and bodily health. In these areas, *the* truth is *our* truth.

But what about the laws of physics? Surely we must be able

to prove reality at a deeper level? Can we at least say, for example, that the wood and bricks of these Haight-Ashbury houses, the kids on the corner and the cars now passing occupy a solid space of reality, that they exist – even if I am not here to experience them?

According to the latest thinking in science, the answer, almost certainly, is no. The new physics offers us more of a shamanic than a scientific explanation. The perspective of new science is one which sees all events, the whole fabric of reality – you, me, these houses – as ultimately linked in a holistic, interconnected system, a 'reality' which does not exist at all until we choose to see it.

As I walked towards Haight, I was thinking about the differences between these two worldviews. Just then, I rounded a corner and noticed some acetates which had been thrown out, presumably following a presentation of some kind, one of which had fallen from a trashcan onto the sidewalk. I picked it up. The heading on the sheet was *Perception of Time*.

The content (referenced as 'adapted from Edward T. Hall') mapped the difference between monochronic (linear) and polychronic (non-linear) time, in the following way:

Monochronic	Polychronic
Linear, consecutive	Non-linear
Concrete, in short supply	Abstract, abundant
One thing at a time	Multi-tasking
Event and goal-orientated	Process-orientated
Perceived in small increments	Perceived in large increments

I have no idea who prepared this slide or for what purpose, and at the time I had not even come across Hall's work, but I still have the acetate and it makes the point for me about some of the differences between the linear, social world, and the non-linear reality of the shaman and the new scientist. And, as an instance of synchronicity in itself, it does so in the perfect way for this chapter since Hall, as I subsequently discovered, has written extensively about the difference between the cultures of the world and their perceptions of reality.[20]

One of his books, in fact, was given to all Peace Corps volunteers as part of their preparation for working overseas in cultures new to them. His findings suggest that different cultures use time and space in totally different ways. In the West, we are focused on the linear, the sequential, the moment-to-moment, and on our physical interaction with the 'things' of the world. However, in some cultures people are actively involved in the world of *their* experience and have no concept whatsoever of a world which exists outside of themselves. Hall's 'monochronic' perception of time is the one we use as adults living in Western societies; the 'polychronic' perception is the experience of natural, tribal living and pre-civilizations, connected to the cycles of life, of nature and of maturation, rather than the panic to get from A to B. It is the world of our children and the world of the shaman.

In the monochronic world, things move only forwards, one after another, like marching men, in an event-orientated way based on cause and effect. In polychronic time, we enter non-linear reality, where abstract thought and simultaneous events are possible and the process of action, rather than the cause or the outcome, the flow instead of the form, are the most important elements.

In monochronic time we are still in the dream of what is possible. In polychronic time, we enter the holographic universe of pure potential.

THE BIG BANG OF THE HOLOGRAPHIC UNIVERSE

The holographic model which has developed in recent years among scientists tells us that reality is far more complex than our old, but still current, scientific worldviews suggest. It pioneers a new reality which is in large part formed by our own individual consciousness. Mystics, spiritualists and shamans have always told us that the reality we experience is an illusion, 'maya', 'a dream', and we, of course, have accepted this as a poetic description of a very real world. But things have changed. Now it is not even *scientifically* possible to say that objective reality exists. Instead, it exists only in the mind of its observers, and the world of our experience is really the world of our own creation.

Michael Talbot has written a brilliant book, *The Holographic Universe*, which explains why.[21]

A multitude of scientists, academics, psychologists and authorities from many other disciplines now accept the basis of the new holographic model and its far-reaching conclusions, which might even 'change drastically our image of human nature, of culture and history, and of reality', as Dr Stanislov Grof puts it in Talbot's book.

Talbot's findings, after extensive research into the new scientific evidence now emerging, are in many ways revolutionary. He concludes that the only way of making any sense of 'reality' is to see our world and our lives within it as a projection, and the universe as a 'kind of giant floating hologram'. And this is not shamanism talking, or the words of the poets and the mystics, it is science.

'Our world and everything in it,' says Talbot, 'from snowflakes to maple trees to falling stars and spinning electrons are also only ghostly images, projections from a level of reality so beyond our own it is literally beyond both space and time.'

For Talbot, the holographic story begins in Paris in 1982, with an experiment at the Institute of Theoretical and Applied Optics, by physicist Alain Aspect, which yielded some very surprising – in retrospect, even Earth-changing – results.

Aspect found that some of the subatomic particles he was studying seemed to be communicating with each other – and doing so instantaneously. Each particle was aware of the actions of its cohorts, no matter what distance separated them, and would take action complementary to it, so that they were synchronized in their movements. This had nothing to do with magnetic fields or other obvious forms of connection. There seemed to be little to explain it.

We might imagine a football game where one player begins a run and his team mate moves up to support him. The actions of the two are not identical, but they are totally in sync and supportive of each other.

The existence of seemingly sentient energy and thought forms in solid matter at a subatomic level seemed strange enough and quite contrary to our normal expectations – we do not expect our TVs and our toasters to have a life of their own. But what Aspect's results also suggested was that these particles were responding to each other faster even than the speed of light across distances which were immense to them.

Now, this is not comfortable to science; in fact, it presents it with a real problem, since in doing so, they are violating Einstein's theory that nothing – communication included – can travel faster than the speed of light. And Einstein's theory is what supports all life on this planet and underpins our reality.

The C (which stands for Constant) in Einstein's now famous equation, $E = MC^2$, refers to the speed of light. The fact that it is a constant underlines the fact that it cannot be exeeded or superseded: it is the one sure thing in the universe, and energy (E) and mass (M) – you and me and everything we do in the world – are entirely dependent upon it.

So you can appreciate Aspect's concern at these results. If he was right, the particles he was studying were not only breaking the time barrier – that was the least of their transgressions – they were acting in a way totally contrary to nature. It is a worrying thing when subatomic particles – the building blocks of all life – start acting up.

And then, how do you tell the scientific community that everything it has held sacred for the last fifty years is wrong – presumably just before you yourself fly off into space, implode, or dissolve into a parallel universe of other energy forms?

Not surprisingly, Aspect found his results difficult to explain and that might well have been that: a quiet record of aberrant experimental results crushed against the behemoth of Einstein's long-standing and highly respected explanation of our universe – if not for the intervention of University of London quantum physicist, David Bohm.

His entrance was hardly a silent one: he interpreted the Paris experiment as implying that objective reality as such simply did not exist. What we think of as a solid universe 'out there' is a trick of the mind, all an illusion, said Bohm. Instead, we need to see the world as a vast and complex hologram if we are to make any sense at all of Aspect's findings. What is actually happening, said Bohm, is this . . .

DREAMING WITH THE FISHES

In Bohm's vision, Aspect's subatomic particles are able to work together over incredible distances and to do so in instants not because they are communicating via some mysterious cosmic messaging service. *They are not communicating at all* – they are *one and the same* particle.

For Bohm, there is a level of reality beneath the one we are conditioned to sense and see, which he calls an 'implicate order'. It is a place, like Plato's cave, where all particles, all things, are not individual *entities*, *things* (plural), but expressions of the same fundamental *entity* or *thing* (singular).

Bohm's idea is easier to understand if we use his analogy and imagine that we are looking at an aquarium of fish, but that we cannot see it directly, and receive our information about it instead via a couple of TV screens. These are linked to cameras, one of which is aimed at the front of the tank, while the other covers the action from the side. It is these which supply our information to us and allow us to see the comings and goings of the fish in the aquarium itself, which we now perceive to be two different tanks since this is how the cameras present this submarine world to us.

Since we have never received our information about these fish in any other way, we naturally believe that what *we* see is also *their* reality, as the occupants of two separate tanks. We never even suspect that there could be a different world of interaction here with a deeper level of meaning beyond the TV screens we see it through.

And so, as we watch the fish on our television screens, we first assume that they are all completely separate entities, individual fish in two different tanks. Over time, however, we notice that there seems to be a curious relationship between the two sets of fish, perhaps a form of communication, even telepathy. Because whenever one fish moves one of the others in the second tank always seems to make a corresponding move. Just like our football players, we cannot say that there is a *direct* relationship between them, perhaps, but there is certainly enough to establish a pattern, so that when one fish turns to face forward, the other faces the side of the tank, or one swims upwards and the other down, and always at exactly the same moment.

This synchronized swimming display is fast – faster than the speed of light, in fact, when measured – so maybe we *are* looking at a form of telepathy here, or an enduring form of cosmic synchronicity. Anyway, it seems clear that the fish are interacting in some way across their respective tanks or there could not be this coincidence of movement.

While we are busy trying to explain this swimming drama from our own human perspective, what we do not see, as observers outside the tank, is that no communication is actually taking place between the fish because, at a much deeper level of reality – what Talbot calls 'the reality of the aquarium' – the 'two' fish are actually one. We see them as two because our way of looking at the world – through two TV monitors – only presents us with this worldview.

There is no way we could know that the real world is any different or that the two fish are one. To do so, we would need to be standing outside the habitual reality we have imposed upon ourselves and which we now share with the fish. We would have to break out of our perceptual prison and become one with Baron-Cohen's synaesthetes, taking in information from the flow of pure cosmic energy before it reached the point where we *interpret* it according to our habitual ways of seeing. Only then could we truly 'see' the fish, the tank, the TV screens and the connection between them all.

In the same way, the communication taking place faster than light speed between Aspect's particles is not actually communication at all because the particles themselves are not separate, they are one. We merely sense them as different because our minds are designed to view 'reality' and assemble the data it presents to us in that particular way. We are victims of our perceptual habits, trapped inside the matrix, exactly as Immanuel Kant predicted a couple of hundred years ago when he realized – without the benefit of million-dollar scientific instruments – that our *minds* and not the world 'out there' were the alpha and omega, the starting and the end-point of reality.

The holographic model becomes even more interesting when we look at some of the other properties of holograms.

A hologram is a three-dimensional image built from laser light. To produce one – putting it very simply – an object must be caught in a laser and a second beam then directed at the light reflected from it. The interference pattern where these beams meet is captured on film which, at this stage, looks like a chaotic Jackson Pollock splash-art visual noise of light and dark lines.

But if a third laser then illuminates the film, a magical transformation takes place and the information it contains becomes identifiable as the image of the original object. This can then be studied in three dimensions from all angles and explored in the fullness of all it represents. If it is cut in half, instead of getting two parts of the single image, as we would with a normal photograph, we get two separate, whole images, each just as complex and complete as the original. And the process continues – if the halves are divided again, the new films also contain complete and intact images, smaller versions of the original – on and on into infinity.

Since everything is made up of the same subatomic material that Aspect was studying, if the universe does exist holographically, everything in it must have the same ability to be infinitely dissected; every single thing in the universe – including ourselves – is an expression of one larger, unified whole. The universe in its entirety shares the characteristics of Aspect's particles, with each part representative of the whole.

Or to put it another way, 'everything is the center of the universe', as the shaman Black Elk remarked almost 200 years ago.[22]

We are all the infinite divisions of the original film, the sentient whole, all participant-observers in a hologram of our design, and all things are intimately interconnected, just as the dissected parts of a hologram reflect and, indeed, are, smaller parts of the entire picture, strands of the cosmic web.

For Talbot, only one conclusion can be drawn from this. If the universe is holographic, then every cell in our bodies contains information about the entire universe because we are all made of the same thing, all StarStuff made conscious. If we knew where and how to look, the mysteries of the cosmos would be revealed in the cells of our own eyes; the swirling starscape of the Milky Way reflected in the whorls of our fingerprints and in the shapes of the tide in the sands of the beach. And we need only look within ourselves to find the answer to all things. Each cell is sentient, everything is alive and connected. We are all one, all aspects of the Earth. We are One and She is Us.

'Despite the apparent separateness of things . . . everything is a seamless extension of everything else,' says Talbot. Even 'time' and 'space' become arbitrary terms as man-made concepts which position us somewhere in physical or temporal space. But there is no 'here' or 'there', no past, present or future since we are all of us connected to all things. There is only Here and Now, this moment in this place where we choose to see and experience. Everything reflects the infinite – as if entering one grand wardrobe of 'all that is', we can choose to 'put on' and be any moment, any place in our lives, lived or, as yet, undiscovered.

The universe is exactly as Black Elk saw it in his grand shamanic vision of the connection between all things: all of nature is one giant, sacred, hoop, an infinite circle of life.

PUTTING PEOPLE IN THE PICTURE

While Bohm was making waves in the fish tank of the scientific community, Stanford University scientist, Karl Pribram, was quietly going about his business of turning the world of neurophysiology on its head.

Pribram's studies led him to the conclusion, quite independently, that our brains also interpret the world holographically, which gives us vast free rein for individual interpretation of what we regard as 'objective reality'. What we see as a tree, for example, is not a tree to the brain but a pattern of codes and frequencies, electrical impulses, onto which we then project meaning. A tree does not have to be a tree; for many traditional cultures, in fact, it is not: it is an extension of spirit, energy in a particular form. More mundanely, your experience of a tree in a park in London or San Francisco is very different to what someone in the rainforest will see. To you it may be a pleasant reminder of nature around us and a symbol that we can get away from the smog and speed of the city; to the people of the Amazon it is a source of life and protection for their world.

As Judith Hooper and Dick Teresi put it in *The Three-Pound Universe*:

> *The image in your head is not a straightforward copy of anything. Palm trees and Ella Fitzgerald's high notes are represented in your brain by abstract codes.*

There are no colours, no sounds, and no smells in your neural tissue.[23]

Pribram arrived at his own holographic explanation after many years of puzzling over the exact location of memory in the brain.

One of his research motivations was the results of research carried out as long ago as the 1920s, which showed that, no matter what part of a rat's brain is removed, its memory of how to do certain things, like run a specific course in a maze, remains. Since these tasks were carried out *before* brain surgery, there is absolutely no reason why its memories should stay with it – in fact, we would expect the opposite according to contemporary models of the brain, which assume that memory occupies a particular brain space – since, to all intents and purposes, for the rat now, the learned event has never happened.

Pribram's explanation was that, instead of being captured in one specific area of the brain, one 'brain-lump', memories are a giant lattice which crosses the entire brain like the light-work swirl on the holographic plate, enabling us to pull in reflections and associations from a vast range of locations and sources. The key to memory and the understanding that comes from it has little to do with where it is located in the brain and, once again, everything to do with our inter-pretation, and the acceptance or rejection of images, metaphors, symbolic messages and other shorthand code from the universe, all of which may or may not be meaning-ful depending on our current needs and context. For Pribram, what this meant is that objective reality – the world of crystals, clouds, starlight and Christmases – could not exist at all because there is no consistent, cohesive reality 'out there', only the reality we choose to create. What does exist is a universe of 'frequency domains', a holographic world, which presents us with its data, which we then decode, interpret and reflect back to ourselves as 'reality'.

The reality we subscribe to is merely the brain's

interpretation of this data and the world itself, if it exists at all, does so in a very different form from the one we give it. And so, once again, it has taken us 200 years from the works of Immanuel Kant to get back to the works of Immanuel Kant.

Where does this information come from before we begin our interpretation of it?

Both Bohm and Pribram suggest that beyond our world of interpretation there is another, like a 'superhologram' containing the essence of things as we see them, which we could regard as a representation of things at their crudest and most 'unformed'. This is the shaman's spirit world, the energy domain of the universe from which all things stem. Beyond this there may also be other 'super-superholograms' – the essence of what the Vodou tradition calls the 'god-vibration' – until we arrive at the very essence of all there is. Science is still in the business of finding these new worlds for us.

In the 'implicate order' of things, there are new worlds in their own right which contain all that we do not see, simply because our minds have not been conditioned to receive this type of information. Our eyes present it to us, but we do not process it, although we may register it unconsciously. It does not occur to us, never crosses our minds. We can change that, the shamans would say, by making new decisions about our world, by an act of conscious will which would allow us to explore realities that otherwise we could not even imagine.

And so we find ourselves back in the world of the shaman for, in the terminology of Castaneda's don Juan, the explicate order is no more than what the Toltecs called the 'tonal' – that which we see – while the implicate order of reality is the 'nagual' – all that is currently unknown to us.[24]

THE HOLOGRAM OF THE SHAMAN

The tonal (*toh-na'hl*) is what we know and believe about the world. It is the order and the structure of existence, which even includes the unconscious since this, too, is part of us and can be understood, even though many choose not to explore it.

The nagual (*nah-wa'hl*), meanwhile is the vast pool of formless, nameless energy within and around us and throughout and beyond the universe. This is a force we can never control and never truly know, although the shamanic journey is one way for us to become a part of it and to understand it for ourselves.

The tonal, says don Juan, is 'The social person ... the organization of the world. On its shoulders rests the task of setting the chaos of the world in order. Everything we know and do as men is the work of the tonal. The moment we take the first gasp of air, we breathe in the power of the tonal ... [it] is what makes the world ... There is a personal tonal for every one of us and there is a collective one for us all at any given time.'

The nagual, meanwhile, is that part of us for which there is no description – 'no words, no names, no feelings, no knowledge. It is not mind, it is not soul, it is not a state of grace, or Heaven, or pure intellect, or psyche, or energy, or vital force, or immortality, or life principle, or the Supreme Being, the Almighty, God – all of these are items on the island of the tonal ... It cannot be talked about [but it is] there, surrounding the island of the tonal.'

We cannot embrace the nagual because, like Bohm's implicate order, it is a slippery fish which maintains a space outside the aquarium. As soon as we try to understand it, to name the sensation, we paradoxically make it tonal, the known, what can be held and named. The nagual is mysterious and elusive, not because of any inherent characteristics – it has none – but precisely because, as soon as you think you have understood it, you find that you have created something else. In understanding it and naming it, you have given birth to a new force which is an expression of the tonal since it is now part of you.

This is precisely what is happening at Bohm's explicate and implicate levels – once something is taken out of the implicate, the domain of potential, and brought into conscious awareness, it becomes something else, that which is known. It seems as if we have no choice here, our minds are simply set up to view reality in a particular way and we are usually not even aware that we have a choice of seeing things differently.

But it only seems that way. Shamanic tradition is very clear that we do have a choice. One of the ways we can learn to experience the nagual, for example, is by journeying, an experience which encompasses the nagual world of the shaman and the holographic universe of the scientist.

Before we embark upon our journey together, however, we need to explore another shamanic practice which gets us close to this experience of the infinite by freeing our minds in the moment. It is an exercise which don Juan called 'not-doing', and it will help to open us up to the possibility of new possibilities.

THE NOT-DOING OF ORDINARY REALITY

We create reality by focusing on the interplay of opposites – light and dark, hot and cold, good and evil, boy and girl – and by choosing to give more attention to one of these attributes at the moment when we interpret it. We may often define our whole lives in terms of our jobs, for example – they are 'what we do' – and, as there are certain norms, practices and expectations associated with any job, these in a way *become* our lives. A businesswoman wears a suit and sits behind a desk, while a labourer wears overalls and perhaps digs ditches. Each goes home to a very different world. Such expectations and patterns of behaviour are the way of our habitual reality.

The 'not-doing' of this pattern would be to reverse the roles, choosing, perhaps, to leave our desks, take off our suits and offer ourselves for voluntary work, digging irrigation trenches in a Third World country for a few weeks, as a 'holiday from ourselves', instead of the traditional two weeks in Barbados, or wherever. When we do this we break the pattern of our lives and create a gateway for new experiences of life to enter.

Of course, we don't have to go to these extremes. There are many ways in which we can break the pattern of habitual reality, as Leo Rutherford has pointed out:

> *Disrupting our routines helps us to stay awake. Get out of the other side of bed, go to work a different route, eat when you are hungry, not because it's lunchtime, get into some different social activities, listen for the spaces between sounds, look at the shadows rather than the foreground, challenge your addictions and habitual behaviours, eat less and enjoy becoming lighter.*[25]

One of don Juan's examples of 'doing' is the way we see (or create the reality of) a plant by viewing it as a configuration of leaves and stems. The 'not-doing' of this creation is to ignore the leaves and fix our attention on the shadows between them. In this way, we 'stop the world' and shift our attention so that we become more aware of the presence of the nagual as well as the tonal in our lives and the interplay of the two, bringing one into the other, without words or explanations.

The liberal philosopher, John Stuart Mill, once said: 'The tendency has always been strong to believe that whatever received a name must be an entity or being, having an independent existence of its own. And if no real entity answering that name could be found, men did not for that reason suppose that none existed, but imagined that it was something particularly abstruse and mysterious.'[26]

Well, the nagual and the implicate order *are* the 'particularly abstruse and mysterious', the 'no real entity answering that name'. They are beyond our description since by naming them and knowing them we create something else.

'You are the unspeakable. That which cannot be named,' Dick Olney once said, describing the power of the nagual within all of us. 'If you name it, you turn it into one more concept.'[27]

Whilst we cannot speak it, it is certainly possible to experience this strange new world.

THE DOMAIN OF POTENTIAL

What we are in the here and now is part of the explicate, the clear image, the tonal; what we can be, our human potential, is embodied in the vast realm of the implicate, the interference pattern, the nagual. Accessing this vast pool is simple – we merely have to change our minds.

'If we got rid of our "lenses" [the 'filters' through which we interpret 'reality', the sensory stimuli presented to us] we'd experience the interference patterns themselves,' says Karl Pribram. 'We would be in the pre-frequency domain.'

'What would that domain look like? Ask the mystics. Though they have trouble describing it too. Space and time would be collapsed or, as I prefer to say, enfolded . . . There's no space and no time.'[28]

In fact, it may not just be the mystics who have the answers. Dr Simon Baron-Cohen's synaesthetes may also offer us some insights into the nature of this world.

We normally think of perception as a 'one-way street, travelling from the outside world inwards', says Baron-Cohen. 'The process is metaphorically like a conveyor belt running through stations in a factory, until a perception rolls off the end as the finished product.'[29] If we are watching TV what we see on-screen is the image as it rolls off the programmer's conveyor belt. But if we could interpret the transmission at another point between the television camera and the screen, we would have access to an infinite number of totally different experiences and realities that these basic data also contain. The synaesthete is, metaphorically, able to tap into the data stream at another transmission point and does have access to these other worlds.

All people receive the same information from the outside world, says Baron-Cohen – the same data from the TV studio. And so we are all equally capable of a wider, more synaesthetic experience. Our brains disentangle the information of the world, filter and channel it 'appropriately' and make conclusions for us about what constitutes sound, what is image, what is taste, smell, good, bad, indifferent.

We categorize our world in the moment, although the basic data are the same for us all. Like a holographic plate and the nagual which exists outside of ourselves, this jumble of information remains indecipherable until it is interpreted by the mind. The universe just 'is': it is we who give it meaning.

There is an echo here of earlier conclusions by Dr John Lilly based on his experiments in the 1970s, where people were left in a meditative, womb-like state in the body-warm saline solution of a floatation tank. For many, this produced life-changing visions as well as the emergence of an ancient wisdom.

A floatation tank is a meditative space created from a waterproof and lightproof box, part-filled with warm, salty water, in which the body floats. For the person so suspended, there is no distinction any more between 'inner' and 'outer' in this dark, relaxing space, the body losing much of its recognition of separateness and merging with the waters which surround it.

Lilly originally designed these environments to study what happened to the mind in a state of deep relaxation. He was surprised to discover that, rather than 'closing down' in response to the lack of stimulus from the environment, the person floating was able to tap into a vast pool of cosmic wisdom which the everyday world actually *prevented* him from seeing *because* of the excess stimulation it supplied. The natural state of the mind is not an empty 'black box', but one of amazing and innate creativity, and deep visionary connection with all that is.

In *The Centre of the Cyclone*, Lilly summed up his overriding conclusion from these experiments: 'All and everything that one can imagine exists. Literally. One is tuned into the cosmos with all of its infinite variations.'[30]

It does seem that, once the white noise of the city is silenced and the Filofax of the mind is closed, we find it quite easy, in a short space of time, to access this infinite wisdom of the universe which flows through us at a cellular level. There are infinities within the mind, says Lilly.

What one believes to be true, either is true or becomes true within certain limits, to be found experientially and experimentally. These limits in turn are beliefs to be transcended. Hidden from one's self is a covert set of beliefs that control one's thinking, one's actions, and one's feelings. The covert set of beliefs is the limiting set of beliefs to be transcended.

No space and no time.

BODY ECHOES

Some of these limiting beliefs arise from memories of our past 'failures' and 'shameful' actions. But, looked at holographically, the whole subject of memory becomes interesting and problematic too – because there is some evidence that 'memories' as such do not exist at all, and certainly not in the form in which we have come to understand them, as biochemical reactions to external events. Rather, it seems, we recreate ourselves and the event in the moment – we re-member it instead of remembering it – and can choose either a limiting belief pattern as the hook for our experience, or a more liberating interpretation of the same event. Putting it bluntly, even our deepest, darkest secrets do not really exist.

Talbot quotes the results of experiments by neurologist Wilder Penfield, which suggest that memories are not confined to specific areas of the brain, as we have been taught, but are dispersed throughout it as an 'energy form' which occupies the abstract space of the 'mind', instead of the lump of solid matter which is the brain.

Our mental processes refuse to be ascribed to convenient parts of the brain. Our whole mind – potentially, our whole *body* – may be capable of what we call memory and thought.

There is no space.

In the old model of reality, Penfield's results leave us only with a mystery because if everything really is compartmentalized, linear, solid, 'concrete' instead of energetic, and 'mechanical' instead of flowing, then memories should have specific locations in the brain and rats should not be able to run mazes after their memories are cut away. Yet, even though brain is removed, memory remains.

There is no time.

The holographic explanation is that memories do not need to be filed away in precise and specific areas of the brain, because they are not solid things but patterns of energy which cross the entire mind, just as laser light covers the entire holographic plate. The human brain is part of the hologram and so it contains the whole picture. The information we need exists everywhere at once within our minds. We give a particular meaning to this energy only when we apply meaning to it. Thus, any limiting belief we carry forward from our past can be deliberately changed if we choose to re-member it differently and reinterpret the event which gave rise to it.

And the implication may be more far-reaching even than that. For perhaps this energetic potential and its interpretation do not necessarily arise only in the brain. Perhaps the whole body is a holographic plate for information, so that we can access our truth from the very essence of our whole being.

Paul Pearsall has studied this idea extensively and, in *The Heart's Code*, offers study after study to show that heart donors give more than just flesh and blood to their recipients – their energy patterns come with it too, so that people who undergo surgery often develop new tastes, new skills, new expressions, new patterns of speech immediately after the transplant operation, with no prior knowledge at all of the donor.[31]

In *The Work We Were Born To Do*, Nick Williams pursues this theme. 'I met Clare Sylvia when she was promoting her book, *A Change of Heart*, at Alternatives. Clare was a dancer and actress who had been extremely ill, and her only hope was a heart and lung replacement operation, if a suitable donor could be found. When one was found she was rushed into hospital and the operation was carried out successfully.'[32]

During Clare's recovery, she noticed thoughts, ideas and actual bodily sensations which were strange and unusual to her, like a craving for beer and for certain foods that she had never even thought of before.

Then one night she had a powerful dream – what shamans call a 'Big Dream' – of a young man who called himself Timmy, who told her, 'You have my heart.'

Clare was curious and began to investigate who her donor was, since the medical authorities will not comment on matters such as this. She found a newspaper from the time of her transplant, which mentioned a young man named Timmy who had been killed in a road crash and, as a result of her investigations, discovered that Timmy had indeed been her donor. She even arranged to meet his family, and found that many of her new ideas and cravings were actually those of Timmy. His experience of life, or some of it at least, came with the territory of his heart and lungs.

When Clare spoke about this, thousands of people came forward to report similar experiences after organ transplants. 'The cells in our bodies carry memories,' says Nick, 'and pass these memories on to the new cell before they die.' This they could only do, of course, if 'memory' is a form of energy instead of a physical thing. And energy can be changed.

Even more interesting in the context of memory is the holographic notion that we are all connected to the entire energetic pattern – and by 'entire', I mean the full potential of the whole universe in all of its forms. As Dick Olney has pointed out:

> *According to the holographic model . . . every cell in your body would be doing the thinking . . . But what if it's all happening on the outside? . . . What if you are just one microscopically small cell in an organism which is incredibly bigger and you think you are doing the thinking just because it's all a big hologram, where every tiniest part contains the whole thing? So that the centre of everything is everywhere and yet not anywhere at all.*[33]

What if the Earth has a dream of us too and, at a deep level, we all really know it because we remember our connection to the whole? How should we act towards the Earth and towards each other, knowing that we are one?

WHERE DOES THE BRAIN GO NOW?

If reality *is* holographic, we can no longer claim that the workings of the 'rational' brain are somehow paramount and responsible for our experience of consciousness. Instead, our consciousness creates our myth of the brain's importance – along with everything else around us. Objective reality ceases to exist and human potential, rooted in the implicate, becomes infinite. We are everything and capable of anything we want to be.

'Prior to the development of quantum physics and the holonomic model of the brain [the idea that the brain itself is designed to operate on holographic principles], people based their notion of who they were and how their minds worked more on the Newtonian classical model of physics, and would deny their spiritual experiences, or not really feel connected with that part of themselves,' said Dr Jeffrey Mishlove, in recent dialogue with Karl Pribram.[34]

'Very definitely,' said Pribram in response. 'And that recalls something De Tocqueville said . . . "Maybe I've been interpreting it the wrong way, because I've been doing it in terms of classical mechanics, with cause-and-effect relationships. But when the human being acts, this is not a cause; this is a challenge".'

Bohm's reinterpretation of reality and Pribram's reassessment of our fundamental biology have profound implications for our understanding at all sorts of levels, not least our view of our own personal reality, and the healing processes we subscribe to.

If the physical and psychological self is not a 'given' but a reflection of our personal consciousness, then we have infinite power over our own well-being and can choose our futures – and our pasts. And the forms of energy medicine and shamanic healing which have previously remained unexplained, or have even been mocked by those who subscribe to the linear worldview, become not only explainable but extremely helpful tools in our daily lives and our quest for empowerment and meaning, producing alterations in consciousness which have a real, physical and beneficial effect in our lives. In this new model of reality, we can enrich ourselves by simply choosing a different pattern for our world from the infinite whirl of lines and shapes, the Magic Eye picture of the cosmos. Visions, miracles, mystical and magical effects become absolutely possible and within the capabilities of us all.

Cerridwen Connelly, high priestess of the Tuatha Druid tradition, in her study, 'The Cosmic Computer', modernizes the language of ancient 'magick' to draw out the parallels and similarities between the practitioners of the Celtic Druidic path and the skills of the modern computer programmer.[35] Her view is that the magickal tradition has always used the holographic potential of the universe in order to work its effects and to change the fabric of reality – not in a woolly, 'new age' way, but in a highly effective, concrete way which has delivered real and powerful results.

My ancestors used principles of quantum mechanics and other 'modern' scientific concepts such as fractals, to work 'magick', more easily understood as realms of energy, manifesting, when the programs/spells are successful, into matter.

The universe is an interactive program. To be a witch/shaman/druid/programmer, whatever-you-choose-to-call-yourself is to exercise control over these forces to achieve goals . . . We are all pieces of the matrix, which is not separate, superior or external to its parts.

Once again, this modern computer terminology is reflected in the more ancient wisdom of the shamans – 'Our world is only one in a cluster of consecutive worlds, arranged like the layers of an onion . . . Even though we have been energetically conditioned to perceive solely our world, we still have the capability of entering into those other realms, which are as real, unique, absolute and engulfing as our own world'[36] – and in words which do not sound so dissimilar to those of David Bohm, University of London physicist, writing with all the power of state-of-the-art technology to assist him and seventy years of experimentation in quantum physics to support his views.

'In a universe in which all things are infinitely inter-connected, all consciousnesses are also interconnected,' says Bohm. 'Despite appearances, we are beings without borders. Deep down the consciousness of mankind is one.'

The holographic model offers powerful validation of the shamanic journey by confirming that other realities are not only possible but can be accessed through a change in perspective alone. 'In the implicate order, as in the brain itself, imagination and reality are ultimately indistinguishable,' says Talbot. 'It should therefore come as no surprise to us that images in the mind can ultimately manifest as realities in the physical body.'[37]

Let me repeat: *images* can manifest as *physical realities*.

In quantum terms, according to John Lilly, we live every second in 'alternity' (a compression of *alternative* and *eternity*). When our brains describe 'reality' to us, we merely choose between possibilities to create *'one alternative future'* by selecting from the range of those available. The universe we share is a formless zone of pure potential. It offers us myriad possibilities and options, any one of which will only become manifest when it is seen, or imagined, by us as conscious beings taking responsibility for our choices.

'The universe bifurcates ... becoming many branches,' says Amit Goswami in *The Self-Aware Universe*, 'until, in one of the branches, there is a sentient being that can look with awareness and complete a quantum measurement. At this point the causal pathway leading to that sentient being collapses in space-time reality.'[38]

The universe becomes real only when reality is applied to it.

Ultimately, this is an incredibly liberating and enriching conclusion. 'Each and every single one of you, as an individual, will experience yourselves becoming the whole dimension,' says Talbot.[39] 'You will all have the same experience because the universe is holographically structured. That means that any point of view can exist equally, everywhere within creation. And that all points of view are relevant and are true.'

Which is exactly what the shamans have always maintained – we are all one and all equally valuable pieces of the whole.

Nowhere is this better exemplified than in the shamanic healing practice of soul retrieval.

CALLING THE SOUL BACK HOME – THE SHAMAN'S JOURNEY OF HEALING IN THE HOLOGRAPH

If we are all holographically connected and everything exists right now, in the infinite experience of the moment, then it should be possible to enter the hologram in this exact moment, to revisit a past hurt and change it. And then to feel the effect of that immediately since, applying a linear timeframe to the event, the past has been changed and no longer exists. We are reborn in this moment without the baggage of the past. This is exactly the experience of shamanic healing.

Whenever we are traumatized, abused, hurt or neglected, says the shaman, parts of our soul split off and take refuge or become lost or trapped in the otherworlds and we must find them again to be truly, completely whole.

Physical accidents, emotional trauma, abuse, childhood neglect, assault, and rape are a few of the more common motivations for the people who have visited me to recover their own missing soul parts. But I have found, paradoxically, that love can also be a culprit.

Sometimes an ex-partner will not, or cannot, return our soul parts to us when a relationship ends. In our Western marriage services we even encourage this, using the words 'Till death us do part' to enforce the bond between lovers, which gives us little freedom, energetically, if the marriage should subsequently end, and is a significant contributor, I am sure, to the ill-will between ex-partners who once used to care deeply about each other, and who still feel they have a promise to honour in some way. Sometimes we are also inclined to give ourselves too freely in the first place. 'All that I am I give to you' are words from the same marriage vows, which are often made lightly in the optimism and joy of the moment, without any consideration of what these words really mean or their possible impact in the future.

Our soul parts, faced with this hurt, simply take flight, just as we might avoid or run away from a situation which is painful to us in daily life. In itself, this is an action of positive healing and self-protection. It is only when the loss of this energy begins to have detrimental effects that the soul part needs to be returned.

Then, the task of the shaman in all cultures has been to enter the hologram and search the otherworlds to find these fragments. Once found, the shaman can reunite them with the person who has lost them, or guide the client so that he can recapture them for himself. It is the return of these soul parts which explains the immediate feeling of wholeness on the part of the client, who is re-united with the energy of the lost self and so, for the first time, actually can see his world in a fully holistic way and appreciate his real place and his true role in the universe.

When this happens, when we once again experience connection with ourselves, with the universe and the oneness of all things – when we finally get beyond theory and therapy to enter the hologram for ourselves – the results can be powerful and rapid.

Fiona first came to see me in January. A successful, well-paid accountant, living in a beautiful house in an exclusive area of town, she seemed happy in her relationship and had a seven-year-old daughter whom she loved very much. To many people, she seemed to have it all. Her problem, as she explained it, was a vague feeling of being 'stuck', a feeling she could not name and which, on the surface, should not even exist, given the trappings of her life. She described it as a 'sense of paralysis' and her life as like 'swimming through treacle'.

Our first session together lasted an hour. During this initial journey, I first guided Fiona to meet with her empowered self, which in shamanic tradition is often visualized in animal form. Shamans call these spirit-entities power animals and maintain that we are all born with at least one such spirit which is our protector throughout our lives, rather like the Western concept of a 'guardian angel'. The Salish people of America and Canada, for example, believe that all illness stems from a loss of power which usually takes place when we lose our natural connection to this protective being.

The first stage of Fiona's healing would be to meet again with her power animal, to recover this energy, and then to journey together with this protective and empowering spirit to recover the soul part or soul parts that she most needed in her life right now.

The session went well and Fiona met with her power animal very easily as she entered the otherworld. She was not immediately sure exactly what animal she had met with, describing it only as 'a small, warm creature'. Later, she thought it might be a marmoset or meerkat.

Her feeling of connection to it, however, was profound, and its significance as a helping spirit made obvious when they journeyed further together to locate Fiona's missing soul parts. Within the cave that they came to, the soul part that she needed was out of reach, on an outcrop of rock high above her, at the top of a sheer wall she was unable to climb. She asked her ally to help her to retrieve the missing part (which, for Fiona, was itself a breakthrough since she had always found it difficult in her life to ask another for help of any kind), whereupon the creature simply skipped up the wall and came back with the soul part she needed.

Together, they brought back a rather unusual aspect of herself, which she described as looking like 'jagged metal, somehow connected to my heart'. At first this made little obvious sense to her, but she accepted it and agreed just to work with it to allow its meaning to emerge gradually.

As we sat talking following the retrieval, I gave Fiona a beautiful white stone to hold, which I had picked up on a beach in Turkey a few years before, to help her ground the new energy returned to her.

When she left, I began to tidy up my shamanic tools and picked up the stone she had been holding. During the 30 minutes she had held it, it had changed colour from white to jet black.

A few days later I received a letter from Fiona. Everything had become clear to her almost as soon as she had left me. She had spent her life accommodating others, working within a system she did not truly believe in for a cause she did not really accept and 'going along' with the lifestyle that her career suggested, rather than living in the way she wanted. 'I feel I have sold my soul to my job,' she said. The metal symbol connected to her heart had become clear to her as the power to be 'harder', its jagged edges the permission to be 'less soft, less willing, less pliable, less available for others and their expectations of me'. She sounded tougher and a great deal more focused, even on paper.

Within days she had put her house up for sale and given up her job. She is now taking time out to decide what *she* actually wants to do with her life.

I recently met up with Fiona again when a national newspaper in the UK interviewed me about the nature of soul retrieval and wanted a client of mine to be there so they could hear at first hand about the effects for someone who undergoes this shamanic healing process. Fiona kindly agreed to be present and it was fascinating to hear, four months after the retrieval, of her reflections on the event and her evolving experience:

'The journey itself was incredibly revealing in all sorts of ways – what my power animal meant to me, how it helped me in the journey, and my ability to ask it to do so, which before, would have been very difficult as I never like to ask for help but always try to solve my own problems. All of these things had real significance for me. And then, when Ross returned the soul part to me, I felt like I had been knocked 20 feet across the room, it was so powerful.'

As the soul part had continued to reintegrate itself into her energy body, she had experienced further revelations and understandings about her life, including a very powerful vision which changed her interpretation of the new soul part she now had within her.

She had been standing in her kitchen one day, not particularly reflecting on this event. Looking up from her work, she was amazed to see clearly, and in three-dimensional reality, her own heart there in the air before her. She watched as it transformed itself from a shattered, jagged, image to a fully whole, soft and strongly beating organ. The 'jagged metal, somehow connected to my heart', she realized, was, in fact, her own broken heart, now made complete. It had appeared jagged and frayed where it was ripped apart but now she felt the sense of its wholeness once again.

SOUL RETRIEVAL PRACTICE

In its Western usage, soul retrieval is often a three-stage process, with the client and practitioner meeting for three individual sessions, normally separated by a period of two to four weeks.

The first of these is a journey taken either by the shaman-healer, or by the client with guidance from the shaman, to recover the soul parts which they have lost and which most need to be returned to them so that they can deal with current life issues. Many of these issues – whether an experience of abuse of some kind or a disappointing love affair which still haunts the person – are fundamentally concerned with power or the lack of personal power.

This being the case, when I conduct healings, I normally encourage clients to take the journey for themselves, as this action is itself an expression of intention by them to re-empower *themselves*, a declaration to the universe that they are now taking back the power which they have given away or had taken from them. By contrast, if I journey *for* a client and return their soul parts, it is I who am re-empowering *them*; I am giving them back power rather than enabling them to seize it back for themselves. My feeling is that it is a more sacred expression of self-worth and more self-affirming for the client to make the journey herself.

The process begins with a smudging ritual, using special herbs to clear and sanctify the healing space, the energy body of the client, of myself and of the tools I will use.

If the client agrees to take the journey for herself, she then lies down in a particular trance posture. This is a traditional posture used by many tribal communities, and one which modern science, in endorsement of the shamans, has recently discovered to be a precise alignment of the body which facilitates the opening of specific neural pathways to encourage the experience of trance.

I use a drum to deepen the trance state, having given the client instructions on the intention for this journey, the stages to be encountered and the type of information to look for.

All of these elements of journeying we will look at later in greater detail.

When the client locates the lost soul parts she is seeking, she clasps them to her chest and brings them back to ordinary reality, a transition supported by a special 'call-back' signal from the drum. At this point, I take the soul parts from her and blow them back into her energy body at the areas of the solar plexus and fontanelle, before using a rattle to seal the energy body to prevent the soul exiting again.

The second meeting takes a similar form, but in this session the client journeys to release the soul parts of others which she, perhaps quite inadvertently, may be holding on to.

Our energy bodies are finite. We cannot cram more energy into ourselves. When we take in energy or soul parts from others, it will indeed fill the vacuum created when our own soul parts are lost, but we cannot use it since this energy is out of resonance with our own. The net effect is not a gain of energy – we have the same amount of energy – it is just that now we have a quantity of energy which is of no use to us. It is better to let this go by returning the soul parts of others so that our own energy can flow more freely and occupy this useful space.

In the third session, the client journeys to consult with the soul parts returned during the first meeting, to ask for an explanation of why these parts left, to recognize any wider patterns in her life and to help these soul parts to reintegrate effectively. It is not uncommon for long-forgotten or repressed memories to resurface during this session and for the client to realize things about themselves and their circumstances which they had never before noticed.

Beth is a store owner in her mid-forties who emigrated to the UK from South Africa twelve years ago. She had a difficult childhood, with a violent, alcoholic father, and this has made a lasting, painful impression on her. She was reluctant to take the first soul retrieval journey herself, so I journeyed for her.

I see a child of five or six, sitting in a small apartment, with her head down, crying softly and trembling. A large man stands over her yelling and waving a document of some kind, which could be a letter, in the face of the child. I have the feeling that this is somehow connected to school. It is always difficult for me not to intervene in situations like this: child abuse is something I will not tolerate, but I know that to be effective, I must simply observe and bring back the information to my client. None of us, no one of us, has full information about the unfolding of the universe and so we must carefully consider our value judgements and prescriptions in any situation, difficult as that may sometimes be.

Beth can accept the information I bring back for her, but does not feel any special connection to it. 'We did live in an apartment like the one you describe and it wouldn't surprise me at all if my father was there shouting – he was always shouting – but I can't remember an incident exactly like this.'

She feels able to take the next journey herself, to consult with the returned soul part of this five-year-old – and this time, things are different. Her first words are 'Oh no, I'd forgotten that ever happened.'

Later she describes the incident. She was five. It was her first day at school and, a sensitive child made even more nervous by the erratic and violent behaviour of her father, she had been so frightened at school for the first time that she had made a tiny mistake, really of little consequence, in her classwork. Her hugely unsympathetic teacher had sent a letter of reprimand home to her father, who had beaten her badly. The memory was so painful for Beth that she had completely repressed it and, to all intents and purposes, forgotten it ever happened. Now she had the five-year-old back and adult Beth was able to look after this sad, hurt child in a way her own father never could.

Part of the reason for the success of soul retrieval is its direct focus on the client in a totally holistic way. Soul retrieval supports the whole person and deals with every aspect of our personal mythology, spiritual needs, emotional well-being and physical selves, not just those of the body – the focus for conventional medicine – or the mind – the territory of the analyst.

In fact, there is very little analysis as such in soul retrieval; the emphasis is on action and results. The Western psycho-therapeutic model, indeed, has been likened by some shaman-healers to slowly flaying a person by digging and digging into the background of grief and apportioning blame for past hurts. By contrast, soul retrieval strips away the hurt and blame in one go, like a snake shedding its whole skin. This is similar to the way in which Laing was able to help his patients by simply entering their world and becoming one with the problem instead of endlessly analysing it and the person suffering from it.

The shamanic view is action-orientated and the goal is not to *analyse*, but to *understand* the situation and then *change* it. By understanding the true nature of an event from our past which is limiting and negative, we can acknowledge it for what it truly is and see beyond it to accept our own place in the universe, including the role that part has played in our journey. The event itself is never simply good or bad: these are descriptions we apply, it is just another aspect of our-selves and we have a choice over how we see it.

Through the intervention of the shaman, who will visit these past episodes for us, we are liberated, so that we are no longer stuck in that emotion or event, and we can then change by taking back the energy we gave away at that time. With the return of our energy often comes the memory of the events we have repressed through the splintering of our souls. *This* is the time for therapy and analysis, so we can work with the memories and emotions which return, and, quite often now in the West, soul retrieval is being used alongside therapy by more enlightened psychoanalysts, who recognize that it can be the quickest way to beneficial change.

Debbie's story is a good example of the shamanic approach at work and shows how this compares to that of traditional psychotherapy. I first met Debbie in 1998. She had lost her young son eight years before this, in a tragic road accident, and had been seeing a psychotherapist ever since. She had made good progress but still felt herself to be 'incomplete', even after all these years of analysis.

Her first guided shamanic journey lasted just 20 minutes and was taken as a precursor to a full soul retrieval session. On this initial journey she was introduced to her power animal, the spirit ally which we all have from birth and which remains with us as our guardian throughout life. Although shamans regard the power animal as a separate, spiritual entity, it is also an expression of our own empowered selves and represents our inner strength and courage. Shamans call this entity a 'power animal' because it most often appears to us in animal form when we take the journey (as we will do later) to recover this aspect of ourselves.

The impact of even this initial journey was, for Debbie, dramatic and immediate. 'For the first time in a long, long time, I felt that I could go on,' she said. 'I never got this from therapy. I feel like I have emerged from a long dark tunnel into a bright, warm light which is embracing and supportive. I have a future now.'

Years of therapy had been surpassed in terms of their effectiveness for Debbie in actually *living* her life in a single journey of just 20 minutes where, at last, a real, tangible, positive result had been produced for her.

Twenty minutes versus eight years.

But when we think of what is at stake here, the incongruity is not quite so dramatic.

The Western dream, perhaps summarized most effectively in the word *analysis*, is concerned with endless thinking and rational discussion, ascribing blame and talking for hours to a 'sympathetic' ear about who has hurt us and when and where and how and why.

Eight years of this. A lot of talk, some of it undoubtedly worthwhile. But no action, no intention to change things, and no progress.

Whatever else may happen for the client during soul

retrieval, it seems plain that she enters some other realm of understanding where her concerns are set in the context of a bigger, deeper picture of reality and where, for the first time, she can see her true role and her unique place in the universe.

There is another aspect of healing here too. The shaman's journey is an archetypal one, the quest of the Hero to find lost treasure, which, by its very nature, places the client at the centre of this drama, in a position of tremendous value. Just a few minutes into a typical soul retrieval consultation, the client – perhaps for the first time ever – has been listened to impartially, had her story believed and had a difficult and dangerous journey undertaken on her behalf by someone acting expressly in her interests. What the shaman-healer sees and experiences in the otherworld is often a clear and direct validation of the client's own past experiences, even if, like Beth, she has completely forgotten that they happened.

Perhaps the client has also shared in the journey by entering the hologram herself and changing the energy patterns which create the reality of her world, an action of personal empowerment which automatically signals that she *can* change for the better and *does* have the strength and resources to do so.

'Think of a child lost in a deep wood, cold, frightened and alone, who hears a warm voice singing a song of comfort and love, which he can follow back home and into the light', is the way one contemporary Western shaman rather beautifully describes soul retrieval.[40]

In holographic terms, the shaman enters the flow of pure quantum energy, which contains all the raw information about the event in question, and then takes action on behalf of his client to reconfigure it. And because all things are connected, it makes no difference at all that there is a temporal distance between the present and the event to be changed, or even a physical distance between the shaman-healer and the client he is working for.

Early in 1999, Karl, in Germany, asked me to help him with a long-term medical problem: his immune system was attacking the part of his kidneys that filters the blood so that proteins which would normally stay in the body were lost in his urine, leading to a serious weakness of his kidneys and a dangerous retention of water. When the problem first started, Karl put on 11 kilograms in ten days.

His doctors could not explain the problem, they had no idea how or why it had started or how to cure it. They gave him drugs which they thought might help with the inflammation, and to reduce the excessive action of his immune system, neither of which worked.

Karl remained in Germany and I in the UK while we carried out this healing. I asked him to lie down and meditate quietly in a room where he would not be disturbed while I journeyed for him to bring back the soul parts which, by their absence, were creating this problem for him by depleting him of the energy that he needed.

In my journey I saw a very hurt little boy of nine or 10 years of age, the splintered soul part which held the emotions of Karl at that age. He was alone in a world without support and subjected to the anger and aggression of a violent and abusive home life with parents who were at war. His father was always yelling and screaming while his mother remained passive and would not intervene on his behalf. Young Karl felt betrayed and let down by the adults in his life and quite alone in a world of misery.

When I asked this young boy to return with me, he was not keen and asked why he should. I explained that older Karl now had an illness that this child could help with. He wasn't impressed; after all, no adult had ever done anything for him.

I sat next to the child and put my arm around him, very aware of his sadness and pain, and explained as simply as I could that adult Karl did love him very much and was expressing that love by asking me to be here now. All things are connected, I said, and if adult Karl was cured, his child self would be helped too because he would never have to face this illness in later life. Instead, the soul-energy of young Karl would be returned to the adult so that the child could continue his life again at that moment and never know the physical suffering that his adult self had had to endure.

The child was moved that someone, finally, had cared enough about him to do something positive for him – but he was still very wary and wanted assurances that 'big Karl' would look after him if he came back with me. I explained that, at that very moment, 'big Karl' was meditating on exactly that – how to make the world a better place for him – and that he would be loved, protected and very much needed if he returned with me.

He became happier and more open on hearing this, a glimpse of the happy child he used to be before the trauma that had brought him here.

He began to play and asked if I would like to see some of his life. I said 'yes please', so he showed me some of the scenes of his home, very fast, just glimpses, but the overriding impression was of a very critical father and a mother who would do nothing to support the child, not exactly siding with her husband, but not doing anything positive either, as if she really didn't care or want to get involved.

I reassured young Karl that things would be different now and we played together for a while before coming home.

I e-mailed 'big Karl' that evening to explain what I had seen and done for him. His reply made interesting reading:

I must say that you hit the point! The main feeling of your vision is the real reflection of what I lived. I was moved by the fact that, in two sentences, you summed up perfectly what my childhood was: a very critical father and a rather absent mother. I know that my mother really loved me but she was so scared by my father that she never dared to fight him . . . I had to stand many humili-ations and I must admit that I have difficulties in loving people.

Immediately after the journey, Karl said that he was aware of 'bodily sensations . . . a warm feeling spreading from my belly and I had the feeling that I had done the right thing.'

That night when he went to bed, Karl experienced pain in his back, at the level of the kidneys, which he had never had before but on waking, fully rested for the first time in a long time – 'I used to be rather tired when getting up' – the pain had gone and he was feeling fine and very quiet.

He added: 'Something funny – my wife told me that during the soul retrieval, my cat went mad for about 25 minutes, running everywhere and very excited, then it suddenly stopped. Do you think there could be a connection?' Karl's soul retrieval had taken almost exactly 25 minutes.

I was delighted to receive an e-mail from Karl a few months later to say that he had been for a check-up at the doctor's and was told that the problem had gone.

Time and space are meaningless and all is possible when you journey into the hologram of the universe.

The shaman-healer, of course, has a very different explanation of soul retrieval from the scientist, and quantum physics does not enter into it. But the difference, I think, is a mere matter of semantics. Exchange the word 'energy' for 'soul' and 'hologram' for 'otherworlds' and we are speaking exactly the same language.

Shamans have themselves been called 'wounded healers', reflecting the fact that most practitioners have been through a healing crisis of their own as part of their initiation into shamanism. Their survival and self-healing is testament to their ability to guide the client through similar distress and to find an outcome which is effective. In Western societies it would probably be unique to find someone who had not suffered trauma, injury, neglect or abuse, or who had not given themselves away to others in a dance of power and office politics. We all become more fragmented every day. The agenda of the shaman-healer is to heal the wound by returning the energies we need so we can all contribute more powerfully to the healing of the Earth we are intimately – holographically – a part of.

And so the 'otherworlds' of the shaman, the 'miracles' of the mystics, turn out to be very like the descriptions of reality found in the new science. The lessons of the holographic model are (at least) threefold – and all of them shamanic.

1. The universe exists exactly as we decide upon it, as fragments of our own worldview, and we are all at the centre of our own experiential world. Beyond us there is only energy and we can choose from this any reality we care to live by – the one most beneficial to us or any other. We have a choice.

2. We are all connected, all indivisible parts of the same holographic entity, and all of us equally valuable, mysterious and infinitely powerful.

3. And, being one, we are all also aspects of the Earth itself – and She has perceptions and expectations of us too.

Consensus reality is just that, consensus reality. It is not the only reality. In shamanic reality [and in the reality of the new science], *every pebble, every rock by the wayside has significance.*[41]

Ultimately, you must draw your own conclusion about this, and that is entirely right. This is your world, no-one else's. If you experience it, feel it to be real, then it is real. In the end, this is all that science or mysticism can offer – and it is tremendously uplifting. It makes us free agents in a world of our choice.

'What we see in everyday life . . . is nature encoding reality in ways we can come to terms with under ordinary circumstances. Nature looks the way it does because of the way we are,' says Dagara medicine man, Malidoma Patrice Some. 'We could not live our whole lives on the ecstatic level of the sacred. Our senses would soon become exhausted and the daily business of living would never get done.'[42]

We can, however, taste this ecstasy and experience the sacred if only briefly through the shamanic journey, and often, this brush with the divine will be enough to open your eyes to new possibilities for a better world.

The techniques of shamanism are the engine room of change, enabling entrance to this world of choice and greater access to our true selves as a reflection, and essential part, of that whole. When we change ourselves, the universe changes with us.

In this world of uncertainty, self-knowledge is perhaps the greatest power of all.

EXPLORATIONS – ACCESSING THE DATAFLOW AT A NEW ENTRY POINT

1. Omens and synchronicities

The holographic theory tells us that reality is not in any way a 'given' but is created in our minds when we choose to pay particular attention to specific information presented to us *en masse* in the form of a stream of random data. You can access this datastream at any point and by doing so, you create a new reality.

Try this:

Decide for a day to pay real attention to the oddities and omens which you might normally notice but not really give much thought to.

In some tribal communities, the shapes of clouds are used to divine the future, the direction in which smoke blows can be significant, as can the shape and movement of flames in a fire. The people of Burkina Faso believe that the direction in which someone approaches you has significance in terms of the nature of their interaction and the impact this will have on your life. The north, for example, is 'the place where those who have something to say to the souls of others come from.'[43]

In the Western world, we are more or less familiar with

the concept of omens from Jung's writings on synchronicity. Synchronicity is the acausal connective principle behind seemingly random events which have an uncommon significance when considered together. Examples include the phone call that comes from a friend just as you were about to phone her, a particular name or number that keeps cropping up, the random opening of a book while holding a question in mind and the useful guidance revealed from the page.

We who have been raised in a linear society are unsure of such matters. We give limited credence to events such as these while, at the same time, millions of people check their horoscopes religiously each day (a divinatory method relying for its effectiveness on the alignment of the stars at the moment of your birth), perhaps use the *I Ching*, rune stones or the tarot, carry lucky gemstones, talismans or charms – or, indeed, enter the National Lottery each week using numbers selected from the birth dates and anniversaries of loved ones.

All of these, in holographic terms, are techniques for 'enfolding' the datastream at another place in its flow or, to use Baron-Cohen's analogy, of interrupting the transmission from the television studio at a different place on its journey to you.

So, just for today, choose to pay attention to the omens, the coincidences and synchronicities which surround you. Ask yourself what it is that unites these events. What if Bohm is right and all things are connected, like the fish in the aquarium, and it is all just a matter of seeing how the connections work? Does this explain these events?

Assume that it does, just for a day, and during that one day, act *as if* the information you are getting from synchronicities of this kind is entirely valid. *Use the information and act upon it.* Notice how you get on, what happens and whether the day goes well for you – at least as well as if you were acting only on 'normal', 'rational' information. If it does, what does this tell you about the value and usefulness of information received in this 'non-traditional' way?

2. Spiritual hide-and-seek
In the holographic universe images can have external reality and telepathy is entirely feasible.

Modern-day shamans use a technique to hone these natural abilities, which is somewhat like the childhood game of hide-and-seek – the only difference is that they do not move physically, they enter a landscape in their minds and find a place to hide there.

To play this game, ask a friend to imagine a place to hide in her personal otherworld. This could be a real place she knows from childhood, or somewhere she has made up entirely. In any case, it should be a place you would not easily expect to find her. A few seconds later, enter her mental landscape and attempt to track her. Take about five minutes. When you find her, tap her on the shoulder to signal the end of the game and tell her where you found her hiding. See how close you get to her own description of the reality she was a part of when you found her.

Playing this game with Suzanne, recently, I see a lush rural landscape which I understand to be Wales. A farmhouse stands on a hillside overlooking the coast. I enter through the front door and see a flight of stairs in front of me, a kitchen to my left and a lounge to my right, with a large open fireplace. I find Suzanne crouching in the fireplace.

When I tell her this she laughs. 'You have just described my grandmother's house in Wales,' she says. 'I loved that fireplace when I was a child, and often used to sit inside it just as you describe. But on this occasion that wasn't where I was. If you'd have gone a little further, past the house and out into the sea, you'd have found an old shipwreck, just off the coast, submerged in the water.

I was hiding in one of the rooms there.'

Some you win, some you lose! Do not expect to get every detail right, especially at first, but do expect there to be similarities in the landscapes and landmarks you both experience.

And expect to get better over time too. This technique of 'remote viewing' was used by the security forces, as the perfect tool for espionage, with trained agents as 'psychic spies'. For more than twenty years, the Pentagon worked to perfect this technique, using remote viewing to explore enemy locations and eavesdrop on their plans, and the results were so convincing that eventually more than a dozen security agencies, including the CIA, FBI, National Security Agency, the Secret Service, Army, Navy, and Special Forces, were all involved – because it works. Reports of these experiments show remarkable correspondences, as Jim Schnabel reveals in his book, *Remote Viewers: The Secret History of America's Psychic Spies*[44] – and they will begin to do so for you too as you become better at navigating the holographic landscape of the otherworld.

3. Conversations with stone

The lessons of the holographic theory are that all things are intimately connected and that time and space are merely constructs of the mind. Everything is actually taking place in the Infinite Now of 'alternity'. If that is so, then the answers to the secrets of the universe are inherent in all things and nature will reveal herself in an infinite number of ways.

One of these ways is the rock divination method used by the Lakota Sioux.

You will need a rock, roughly the size of a grapefruit, which has four sides or faces. When you collect this, be sure to remember where it came from as you will later return it to the exact spot. You should also approach the collection of the rock in a courteous and sacred manner

– remember: everything is alive and has purpose; we are all brothers and sisters – and ask permission of the rock for its use in this way, just as you would ask a friend for advice rather than demanding an answer.

Place the rock before you and hold in mind a question you need an answer to. 'Why?', 'Who?', 'What?' and 'How?' questions are all fine; 'When?' and 'Where?' questions can be more difficult as there is no time and no space in the holographic universe and all locations we occupy are really Here and Now. Questions which require a straight 'Yes' or 'No' answer are also less appropriate for this method.

It is important to be as precise as possible in the phrasing of your question. For example, your question may be 'What job would make me most happy?' This is a perfectly valid question as long as you are aware that a job which makes you *happy* may not make you *rich*, for example, which is why you need to be very clear about what you are asking.

Let go of the question once you have asked it and, taking the rock, look at its first face until four symbols reveal themselves to you. The symbols you receive could be anything – you may see birds or trees, faces or cars, houses or jungle in the contours and shading of the rock face. Write these down as you see them, then return to your question. You then respond to the question from the perspective of each of these symbols and, having heard the responses from all four, distil these answers down to make one final single statement of reply from that face of the rock.

I once consulted with a rock about some healing work I was asked to do at Machu Picchu, the sacred mountain of the Incas in Peru. An international hotel chain was planning to develop the site and to build a six-storey hotel complex at the summit of the mountain. I had been vocal in opposition to this plan and was leading a protest campaign in the UK. At the same time, I had been contacted by the hotel chain itself and asked for my advice on how to proceed shamanically with the development. The concern of the hotel group was, presumably, to protect its economic interests in the face of incredible grassroots opposition, by getting the environmental and shamanic community 'on side'. Still, whatever their motivations, they wanted, they said, to act as honourably as possible and to consider all sides. The net effect of this was to leave me in the difficult position of both leading a protest and, seemingly, working in support of the developers. My question concerned the nature of my involvement and the outcome of my taking on this healing work.

The first face of the rock revealed a turtle head, a phoenix, a snail and a withered face connected to death and loss and decay.

The message from turtle was to 'accept quietly the outcome', from phoenix, a bird connected with death and rebirth, the observation that 'things move in a circular manner', from snail that 'the journey will be a slow one' and from the death's head that 'life goes on no matter how it seems'.

My distillation of these four answers was the statement that 'all things must move in a circular way and according to a grand universal plan. What seems to be a major concern today is merely a snapshot in time of an infinitely bigger picture which is fluid and harmonious. So do not focus on an "outcome"; in the grand scheme of things, it does not matter.'

I still disagreed fundamentally with the Western arrogance which enables us to 'develop' sacred landmarks for financial gain, but I now also understood that human life is, in any case, just a passing phase on the planet and that all things will eventually return to their natural state.

To use this technique of divination for yourself, first find a rock which seems appropriate to you for your purpose. Then, just as in the example above, work with four symbols from each of the sides to develop one single statement from each side. The final stage then is to create a composite statement by combining all of the four. This is the advice from the rock.

In my case, the advice I was given on whether to consult or not with the hotel involved in the 'development' at Machu Picchu, was that 'the mountain has its own agenda and all will be well. The involvement you take is up to you and in the wider scheme of things is merely one event in time – like a drop of rain in a storm, an essential part but just a single part of the whole.'

My decision was to get on with other things, since my own involvement was hardly life or death.

4

INTO THE CAVE OF SOULS:
THE EXPERIENCE OF SHAMANISM

I want to know how God created this world. I am not interested in this or that phenomenon, in the spectrum of this or that element. I want to know His thoughts. The rest are details.

– Albert Einstein

In front of this cave is a pool of bones, arranged in a half-circle, an art form built by surgeons or sculptors. I sit among the symmetry of ancient bones, the debris of lives lived, thoughts expended, memories used up, all of it experience now dissipated, energy given back to the universe.

Where does it come from, this energy, where does it go? Are these old bones the natural outcome of life's entropy and chaos, or of energy changing form? Matter cannot be created or destroyed, thermodynamics informs us, it can only be transformed.

Chaos is a form of high order. Infinite complexity. A crack in the sky of the symmetrical universe where a new order of magic breaks through. Chaos is not comfortable to science.

And so scientists, like gods of alchemy, have learned to transmute energy, creating light and heat from matter, and now creating matter from collisions of light. A remarkable,

117

divine act, to create something from nothing, form from light, matter from energy.

But where did this matter come from? It is energy plucked from the universe and reassembled, all the expended energy and dissipated thoughts of these old bones, reeled back in from the void of space-time and recycled by scientists creating new physical structures from transcendent ideas.

Particle physicists have things to tell us about their dream of the universe. We see things, they say, and things are 'real' because particles of light – photons smaller than atoms – bounce off them.

Atoms are smaller than angels. The head of a pin contains 100 billion, and they are made of even smaller bits of matter, all of which has a history of 15,000 million years, beginning with an explosion so powerful that the universe is still dancing in our hair and in the air around us. Clumps of this matter formed in minutes, in a waltz of electrons orchestrated by gravity, atoms swirling and spinning together to form stars and galaxies.

And then, here we are, a mere 15,000 million years later, suddenly conscious complex molecules, creators of form, sentient energy dressed in stardust, occupying a universe six by eight inches in size, weighing just three pounds, the whole known universe of your brain.

And when life ceases, as it has for these old bones, then its energy is released again, becoming the stuff that is created from, instead of a created and creative form.

Sentient particles, globules of energy, drifting in space-time, waiting to be pulled into matter and re-engineered by scientist-gods and children modelling with clay. The dance of light, the web of being. We are all one.

Shamanism is one of the oldest psycho-spiritual practices known to humanity. That much we know, although its true origin remains tantalizingly mysterious to us. The shamanic approach to life and to healing is at least 20,000 years old and there is a reasonable body of archaeogical and anthropological evidence to date it back further, to 200,000 years or more.

In fact, quite recently, archaeologists working at Twin Rivers, near Lusaka in Zambia – a part of Africa where the first homo sapiens are known to have emerged – discovered evidence of paint grinding equipment and more than 300 pigment fragments dating back somewhere between 350,000 and 400,000 years. For Dr Lawrence Barham of the discovery team, the find is evidence of 'people who were using symbols far earlier than we expected'. And, indeed, where such use of symbols has previously been discovered – in cave paintings, such as those at Lascaux in France, for example, some of which are themselves 35,000 years old – it has usually been seen as evidence of shamanic and ritual activity. In the cave paintings at Lascaux, for example, shamans incline in trance to commune with the spirits of animals around them in order to 'call the beasts' in preparation for a hunt; others change form, actually metamorphosing into creatures which are half-man, half-animal, symbolic of the shaman's ability to shapeshift into new life forms and to communicate with other creatures.

So perhaps shamanism is as old, or older, in fact, than the dawn of the first protohuman.

What is just as interesting is that many different societies, separated from each other by vast geographical and cultural distances, seem to have arrived at a shamanic worldview at roughly the same time, quite independently of each other. Why it should be – and how it came to be – that an approach to the universe designed for the harsh, barren landscapes of Mongolia should also be appropriate for the vast rolling plains of North America, the snow-frozen wastelands of the Inuits and the heat-blasted Aborigine outback – remains a mystery which the sands of time serve only to deepen.

The shamanic worldview was embraced by these peoples as a technology for self-transformation which offered a way for all people to reconnect with the world of spirit, to under-stand themselves and their role in nature, and to clearly see their own relationship to the universe and the divine.

All things, say the shamans, are expressions of energy – sentient energy. Strip away the man, the roles he plays, the car he drives, the society he lives in, the world he is a part of, and eventually you will arrive at the essence of the person – an energy being, a creature of light, which simply occupies a material human form for this short passage on Earth.

Trees, dogs, rocks, clouds, skyscrapers, automobiles, insects, smoke, computers, atoms and old bones. All have different material forms, yet each is an expression of the same energy, no different, no less complex, no less aware and no less valuable than our own. All things are part of the hologram and all parts can reveal the whole.

The word *shaman* originates with the Evinki people of Siberia and came into usage English via Russian. It refers specifically to a 'man of power', '*one who knows*', but it has now become the universal term for a person exhibiting mastery of energy and of ecstasy. Even so, all cultures have their own unique name for the person within their community who plays the shamanic role. For the Huichol of Mexico, he is *mara'akame*; for the Navajo, he is *hitali*; for the Innuit, he is *angaqoq*. The Zulu call him *sangoma*; in Tibet, he is *llapo*; in Nepal, *dhami*. In Europe, perhaps, she is 'witch', while he, like the Merlin of Avalon, is 'wizard' or 'sorcerer'.

While technically more of a religious, priestly role than a spiritual, shamanic one, the Vodoun tradition of Haiti has its own terms for men and women of power who guide the ecstatic and deliver the spirits to the people – they are the *hougan* (male) or *mambo* (female) and their job is to make the unseen visible, the sacred, present.

Recognizing the deep historical roots of shamanism, the tradition was defined in the classic work by Mircea Eliade as 'archaic' and as a 'technique of ecstasy', ecstasy deriving from the Greek, *ekstasis*, meaning to be outside of oneself, a reference to the shamanic trance or out-of-body 'journey' that lies at the heart of the shamanic experience.[45]

A modern and somewhat Westernized form, known as

neo-shamanism or core shamanism has emerged in recent years. This uses the central tenets of shamanism in a way which makes them practical and relevant to the modern world. As part of this resurgence, shamanic practices have been incorporated widely into psychotherapy and counselling, as well as numerous healing practices. This is quite in keeping with the spirit of shamanism. Even in traditional societies, shamans usually have a particular magical speciality in addition to their core shamanic abilities, and this is often concerned with physical and mental healing. Knowledge of the magical and medicinal use of plants and herbs is part of the shaman's natural and learned repertoire of skills which the Western world has only recently been coming to embrace through the less direct methods of aroma-therapy, homoeopathy and herbal medicine. While the modern practitioner deals with the chemistry and physiology of the plant, however, the shaman engages its spirit essence or energetic form.

The difference may seem slight but it is not. A Dagara medicine man tells, for example, of the use of special herbs during the funeral rites of his grandfather. During the preparations for his grandfather's spirit to take its final journey to the otherworld, a last meal was prepared where the cooking pots and utensils sat literally suspended in mid-air, upside down from the ceiling of the hut where the body lay. 'There are secret plants in nature that are very powerful,' said the shaman. 'By using some of these plants, known only by healers and men and women in touch with the great medicine of Mother Earth, our cooks were able to produce, for a short time, an area free of gravity.'[46] Despite the undoubted powers of many modern Western herbalists, such magical usage of plant energies is well beyond their capabilities or even their understanding. Imagine the possibilities for healing, however, if we could tap, even shallowly, into the magical or spiritual possibilities inherent within these plants, rather than relying solely on their pharmacological properties. Sadly, we have lost touch with many of these powerful healing methodologies and even the work of reiki masters who channel the flow of universal energy for healing purposes, and feng shui practitioners who use this energy to create sacred and peaceful living spaces, are a pale reflection of the powers of the traditional shaman. They are bound by the use of symbols and artefacts to direct and channel energy, whereas the shamans of old were in immediate contact and dialogue with these forces.

Consider psychic or spiritual surgery, an aspect of the shaman's work which we, in the West, have no parallel for at all in the more mainstream alternative therapies. Here, the ability of the shaman to cut open his patient and extract the illness from him in the form of real surgery, all without anaesthetic, is difficult for the Western mind to accept, even though it is still practised in more traditional communities such as the Philippines. Even so, in recent years, remarkable success has been reported in the West with hypnotism and auto-suggestion which has been so effective in controlling pain that surgical procedures *have* been carried out without anaesthetics.

These 'magical' surgical techniques of the shaman were dismissed by early investigators as mere trickery designed to dupe the gullible 'savages', as they witnessed the shaman 'remove' tumours from a patient's body, which were later revealed to be the organs and sinew of animals. What they did not take into account, and which modern anthropologists, medical doctors and scientists are increasingly accepting – and the shaman has long known – is that 'rituals of healing' such as this play a vital part for the patient in most medical procedures. Even in Western medicine, a trip to the doctor or a hospital stay is a ritualized process which has its own dynamics and power, all of which contribute to the cure. In this the shaman's 'trickery' is no different.

Shamans themselves offer a quite different perspective on such 'trickery'. What they are extracting from the patient – sometimes by sucking it from his body – is a psychic 'intrusion', an 'energy form' (in shamanism there is no such thing as 'illness' *per se*, it is merely inappropriate energy trapped in a particular place). To remove this, they must offer a physical object for it to move into. Hence, the shaman may keep a piece of sinew or bone in his mouth and suck the energy from his patient into this receptacle, which he will then spit away. What early anthropologists saw as trickery from their perspective outside of the aquarium of the shamanic healing ritual, was merely the shaman's way of safely handling energy. *It was not the sinew or the bone which was important: it was the energy it contained.*

One tribal member who was witness to many shamanic healing ceremonies summed up the experience of such healing, in words which are hardly those of a 'gullible savage'.

I do not believe these things come out of the sick man's body. The shaman always has them in his mouth before he begins the treatment. But he draws the sickness into them, he uses them to catch the poison. Otherwise how could he catch it?[47]

Shamans also developed practices for lucid dreaming (where dreams are made meaningful through special techniques for interaction with the spirit world) and for what we now call out-of-body experiences. These practices enabled the shaman to engage reality beyond the limitations of time and space and to use his soul as a vehicle to enter deeper levels of existence, to visit parallel worlds, or other parts of this world which may be distant in both space and time.

Once again, early commentators were far too dismissive of the shamanic trance state, explaining it away as a form of fit, and in some cases alluding to a supposed history of epilepsy among shamans. If this is true, then the population of epileptics must be far vaster than medical science will admit since we are now aware that shamanism is a universal pursuit which has extended over tens of thousands of years.

The early psychoanalytical explanations of the shamanic journey were even more insidious. Geza Roheim, a Hungarian psychoanalyst, writing from a Freudian perspective in the 1940s, described the shamanic journey – what he called 'a flying dream' – in fairly typical terms when he defined it as 'an erection dream, in these dreams the body represents the penis'.[48] This is so wide of the mark to anyone who has practised journeying as not to be worth commenting upon – as you will come to see in your participation in the following exercises.

CARETAKERS OF THE SACRED

Traditional shamans were people of purpose – their role was to act as a bridge between worlds for the entire community and to bring back gifts of healing, foresight and divination and messages for the tribal group. In this way, the shaman was often healer, guide, psychoanalyst, priest and 'guardian' of the community he served. His role was multi-faceted but his job was singular: to serve the tribe by giving their lives a spiritual dimension and depth, and a sense of morality as caretaker of the sacred.

As is so typical of the West, which wants its spirituality in bite-sized chunks, taking only what it can devour and re-gurgitate with a different name today, the current vogue sees the shamanic journey as a voyage into the inner, mental landscape, a 'creative visualization' within the infinite chambers of the mind. For traditional shamans, however, the journey represents much more than this. It is a very real voyage beyond the limitations of the physical body, to meet real spirits who have a separate existence in a world quite different from ours, with its own rules and structure and logic. For the shaman, this is no imaginary inner world, a description which makes it sound more like a child's playground than the potentially lethal environment visited by the shaman of old.

The shaman's journey begins with the ecstatic trance – what Michael Harner calls the shamanic state of consciousness, or SSC – where the soul of the shaman is believed to leave his body and voyage to one of the three worlds –

upper (Sky), middle (Earth) or lower (Underworld).[49]

The shaman will consult here with his spirit helpers or allies, communicating with them directly within his journey, while all the time retaining control over his spirit body while he walks in their world, and his physical body which remains passive and immobile in ours. He walks between the worlds and is potent and powerful in both.

These spirit guides are viewed by Western science, which does not like its worldview to be rocked too dramatically, as aspects of the shaman's own psyche rather than actual spirits. The shaman is in contact with archetypal aspects of himself which speak for the tribe and are expanded and made clearer, more accessible, by the ecstatic trance. The shamanic journey itself does not take place outside of the body; it is a journey *into the self*, to a place where we are all connected through the power of the collective unconscious or the holotropic mind.

Who is right – the shaman or the academic? The truth is, it matters very little.

To academics it may be important to establish 'beyond doubt' (as if that were possible) that the shamanic journey does not take place in another world but within the mind of the shaman. But if we are concerned with *positive effect* rather than academic 'proof', then where that effect comes from does not matter at all.

We are entirely free to believe that our benevolent spirit guides are giving us the answers that we need, that we are truly journeying to other worlds, other enfoldings of holographic probability, or that we are accessing it through our connection to a universal consciousness and our own inner resources as a result of the trance state. It becomes simply a matter of choice and perspective if it is *meaning* in our lives which we are seeking, and the *effect* of the journey in enriching and empowering us. And, in fact, it matters little to the shaman which of these viewpoints you choose to adopt.

Shamanism is concerned with the interrelationships between all aspects of life and with the essence of all things, human, animal, plant, mineral or spirit. To the shaman, all things are alive and no one thing is more important than another. Though the shaman would see his spirit allies as existing outside of himself, he would not necessarily see this as any more important than if the reverse were true. He has simply chosen a way of relating to and interacting with these forces. 'All paths are the same,' said don Juan. 'They all lead nowhere . . . The question is "does this path have a heart?" If it doesn't, it is of no use.'[50]

The job of the shaman is not to make use, in an exploitative sense, of the forces he encounters on his journey, but to consult with, understand, and accept the wisdom offered through the otherworld connections that he makes. Shamanism and modern science both recognize that all things are fundamentally connected by the 'web' that is the energy of life and the holograph we are all a part of. Shamanic practice is therefore never manipulative and does not try to *control* these forces. To do so would be ultimately to manipulate all things, including ourselves, and to damage the balance of everything. Instead, shamanism honours these connections and co-operates with all forms of life in a mutually beneficial, spiritual adventure for self-development and growth.

THE SHAMAN'S COSMOLOGY

In the shaman's world, his journey of exploration is taken to one of three domains. Accompanied by the steady rhythmic tone of the drum, he will enter into a deeply relaxed state and from there will journey to the lower, middle, or the upper world, to meet with particular guides who occupy these realms and to gather information from them in order to better understand himself or the issues and illness of the client he is journeying for.

The importance of this journey in traditional societies is something largely overlooked by modern researchers and investigators. In traditional societies, the world of the tribe was often bounded, more or less, by the distance it was possible for a man to cover before his water supply ran out or he found another source – probably about three days' walk. The world was small and its dangers very real. To know in which direction game could be found or how to heal a sickness running through the tribe really was a matter of life and death in a community cut off from others and with no immediate access to the 'urban wonders' of hospitals and supermarkets. The shaman's role did not *just* have a psychological, sociological or spiritual aspect; it was a real service to the community in its practical matter of daily survival.

A charlatan unable to deliver the information required by the tribe would last about five minutes and, rather than aspiring to this position, many shamans saw their calling as a curse rather than a blessing because of the heavy responsibilities which came with it. So the shaman needed to know the otherworlds intimately in order to locate the information he needed to secure the survival of the tribal group.

Thankfully, most urban shamans are not in such a position of heavy responsibility. But still, as essential parts of the whole, our role is just as important to the evolving consciousness of our planet and for healing our own ills and those of others who come to us for help.

If we are to make best use of the worlds accessible to us, we need a detailed awareness of their topography. Although shamanism divides non-ordinary reality broadly into three levels or worlds, this is not the full story, and many shamanic cultures divide the upper world into an almost infinite number of other levels – like the 'super-hologram' Talbot describes, of worlds beyond worlds and deeper levels of reconnection to the essential source, the raw data, of all that is.

Some shamanic customs work with nine levels of the upper world, others with 11, 13, 27 or 33. I have personally visited four of these and have met others who have journeyed to nine; only the most experienced shamans seem to get much further than that or, indeed, need to. But even 33 divisions may not be the final total, and it is unlikely that the upper world has been fully explored, so the exact 'number' of worlds open to us is quite probably limitless.

THE WORLDS OF THE SHAMAN

The lower world is a place of instinct, where our animal-like powers reside and where we are given access to 'Earthy' knowledge and to practical help and guidance. It is the landscape you might visit to understand your own place in nature or to work with the spirit-essences of other life forms, such as animals and nature spirits, which are familiar to you from the more material forms they take in our ordinary reality.

The upper world is the home of more philosphically inclined spirit teachers and guides, the ancestors, the Elders and the wise ones who generally appear to us in human form but whose wisdom is universal and cosmic in its scope. This is the world you may visit to understand your own purpose as an incarnated being here on Earth. Some traditional communities believe strongly that each incarnating soul has a purpose in coming to this plane and the expectant mother, with the shaman, will journey to the unborn child to understand this purpose. The child is then named for its purpose in the world. The upper world is the ideal destination for spiritual questions of this nature – such as your own purpose in this life.

The middle world is the most dangerous of the three and is often treated as a 'shamanic no-go zone', especially for novices. It is the direct parallel of our ordinary reality, filled with the same feelings, power and energies. It may therefore seem very similar in architecture to our own world, although the connections made there will have a quite different content.

Because it parallels our own world, it is the spiritual home of all the negative energies of the world – the serial killers and psychopaths, Stalins and Hitlers who have 'passed over' – as well as the positive energies of the Mother Teresas, the

Christs, the Buddhas and the other great spiritual leaders that our own world also creates. The shaman requires special skills to navigate its terrain or he may get lost in the division between the worlds and is prone to attack from negative forces which have their own energy and may seek to take control of his body.

In some customs, such as the Vodoun practices of Haiti, temporary possession by the ancestors, who will then reveal their knowledge through the human who becomes their 'horse', is encouraged. But even so, its dangers are recognized and the houngan or mambo who officiates over the possession state will be careful to ensure that there is 'hygiene' between the worlds by maintaining strict ritual over the proceedings, and will drive out unhelpful spirits or those who stay too long.

Although we will not be journeying to the middle world in this book (we will be using Imagework to get there instead), it is the landscape you might enter to understand the spiritual dimensions of issues which you are currently dealing with in ordinary reality – issues connected with career, for example, or relationships, finances or physical health.

All of the three worlds are connected and the boundaries between them tend to blur as you become more familiar with journeying. Traditionally, the shamanic 'world tree' is the central pillar of energy connecting the three worlds. This can be visualized as a literal tree, with its roots in the lower world, its trunk in the middle world and its branches reaching into the upper world, the roots below and the branches above forming an exact mirror image of each other to represent the connection, balance and equality of all things.

The lower world is reached by descent into the Earth, which may be through a hollow near the roots of this 'tree of life', while the shaman may climb the branches of the tree to ascend to the upper world, perhaps being assisted by the use of a vine, a whirlwind, or some other form of climbing device beyond the branches of the tree, until he has the feeling of passing through a membrane and into the new upper world landscape.

By its nature, shamanism is an individual activity where each person finds their own way into these worlds and their own special meaning in the new truths they uncover there. Paradoxically, it is also a universally valid experience where individual truth tends to echo and reflect the truths independently arrived at by other explorers.

Each traveller experiences their own version of these different realities when they first start journeying. But once they have made a few journeys, it is remarkable how similar these worlds turn out to be. It is a little like taking a journey to a new city for the first time and then coming back to describe it to a friend who has been to the same city a few times, so is more familiar with it. Initially, your impressions will differ from those of your friend. You will have been to different areas, taken in different sights, gleaned information which maybe she hasn't, even though she has been there more often. Your feelings about the city will tend to be different because of this. Eventually, however, as you visit the same city more often, your experiences may come to parallel those of your friend.

Indeed, Michael Harner's Foundation for Shamanic Studies is currently undertaking a project to 'map' the shamanic landscape, by integrating the accounts of thousands of individual shamanic journeys through a computer program designed to identify similarities. Called MONOR – Mapping of Non-Ordinary Reality – this project has currently been ongoing for thirty years. According to Simon Buxton, founder of The Sacred Trust and the UK faculty member for The Foundation for Shamanic Studies, it is likely to be another thirty years before the results can be published. When available, they will give us a vast encyclopaedia and atlas of the otherworlds beyond our own.

In the meantime, my own online shamanic community, which links practitioners from around the world, has now taken a number of group journeys together: we synchronize our times of departure from ordinary reality so that we meet in the otherworld at a pre-arranged location.

In one journey, we met together to carry out Earth healing at a sacred site in a place distant to us all. Intent only on carrying out the work, I was surprised, particularly in view of the recent violence there, to be told that this healing did not need to be done. When I later shared this revelation with the group – all of whom had journeyed with the same intention – I learned that we had all been told that this work was not needed at this time because the place itself had its own bigger agenda. Part of this was to galvanize opinion and create a sense of community in the world by the sacrifice of itself in order to draw attention to its plight. Its actions were a deliberate and conscious act intended to raise global awareness. Such episodes are a powerful validation of the existence of another world which has its own purpose beyond our own, but which we can all of us share and return from with the same information, whether we journey alone or as a group.

And so the fundamental experience of shamanism, in whatever culture and at whatever stage of that culture's spiritual-religious development, and even between individual shamanic explorers, remains constant. It is as if the basic spiritual and healing needs of all peoples had been independently understood by a number of different cultures and effective techniques developed by each which are universally workable. This is the world of the shaman today, just as it was a thousand years ago.

THE CALL OF THE UNIVERSE AND THE SHAMAN'S REPLY

Traditionally, the shamanic vocation is heralded by a trauma of some kind, which may be a psychological crisis or a physical near-death experience. Even today, it is far from uncommon for people to come to shamanism in this way. One of my teachers, Howard Charing, discovered shamanism, or was discovered by it, after nearly being killed in a lift crash. My own initiation began at birth with an emergency medical procedure to free the umbilical cord from my neck and prevent my death. Other contemporary practitioners I know of have survived meningitis, emerged from childhood coma, or recovered after being hit by a car and floating between life and death for weeks of their young life.

Initiation into shamanism is traditionally sudden and dramatic, akin to the conversion of Saul (later known as Paul) on the road to Damascus, and normally accompanied by physical or mental anguish. Being struck by lightning, falling from a height, suffering a life-threatening illness, are all common. Frequent, too, is the experience of a lucid and terrifying vision where the initiate dies and is dismembered by spirits, with his bodily organs consumed, before his rebirth into a new form and a new way of life. When the spirits want us, they make their intentions very plain.

Black Elk tells of his own initiation. As a boy, he fell into illness and unconsciousness for twelve days and was saved from death only by the intervention of a shaman. When he returned to consciousness, 'he was not like a boy. He was more like an old man', said Standing Bear of his friend.[51]

Typical, also, is the experience of being saved, not by modern medical intervention, but by the hand of spirit. Howard Charing was able to recover fully and to go on to teach shamanism only when he began to listen to the advice he heard from his spirit teachers. Simon Buxton tells of a childhood illness where medical doctors had no more solutions available and he hovered on the verge of death, until a powerful shaman called at his parents' home one day and sang a spirit song of healing and well-being, after which he recovered completely.

Even where the initiation is elective on the part of the shaman, it is not without its risks. 'There is a test that one undergoes to find out who can become a shaman,' says don Agustin Rivas Vasquez, a modern-day Peruvian *ayahuascero* (a shaman who works with the teacher-vine ayahuasca, also known as 'the vine of souls' or 'the little death'). The procedure involves drinking a special mixture of tobacco herb and water which is treated in a ritual way and becomes toxic, a practice which must be undertaken only with strict supervision by a master shaman.

'This is a very dangerous practice,' says Agustin. 'In 10 minutes you go to bed and stay in a sleep state for three days. You learn a lot during those three days . . . My teacher told me "if you are lucky, you won't die, you'll resuscitate. You'll either live or die".'[52]

Surviving the trauma which accompanies the call to shamanize strengthens the shaman and enhances his ability to work more effectively on behalf of others since he will now have a better understanding of how to correct a similarly life-threatening condition in others, and a deeper appreciation of its spiritual and energetic causes, cures and the experience itself. He has already lived it – and lived through it.

The most powerful shamans were believed to be 'chosen' by the spirits, or were predisposed to shamanism as a result of hereditary transmission. They were literally given no choice in the matter: they must become shamans or die. Others, considered less powerful, but nonetheless capable of awesome feats, enter shamanism by personal choice and quest. This is the typical route taken by modern urban shamans and particularly by Western practitioners of core shamanic forms.

Even in the 1950s, Mircea Eliade quoted tribal leaders who bemoaned the 'decadence' of more recent shamanism, which was seen as far less powerful and pure than in previous ages, and practised by much less courageous shamans. 'According to legend, not long ago there were shamans who really flew in the sky,' said one such tribal leader.[53] Nowadays, the shamanic journey is more likely to be regarded as an internal 'flight' to inner worlds with messages returned from the deep reaches of the psyche rather than the vast cosmic kingdoms of the gods. But even if we choose to see them as inner journeys rather than connections with spirit, these are still powerful experiences, revealing potentially life-changing information to us about the way we create our realities, forge our destinies and hold ourselves back or give ourselves wings.

The core method of such revelations is the ecstatic trance which enables the shamanic journey to take place.

THE ECSTATIC TRANCE OF THE SHAMAN

The ecstatic experience of the shaman is entirely different from the prophetic and mystical ecstasy of the poets and the priests. 'The prophet believes he is the voice of god on Earth, while the mystic is lost – just as he is also found – within his sense of the divine,' is the way one Cuban shaman explained it to me. 'The shaman is far more practical and down to earth.' His trance is self-induced, purposeful, and has a definite objective. He is at one with, not in awe of, the gods. He is their equal and his mission is to commune with them, not worship them, to interpret their words, not to quote them to the masses.

In concrete terms, the ecstatic experience can be divided into three experiential levels, all of which take place simultaneously for the journeyer.

The first of these is physiological, where the mind and the body engage with the experience and begin to forget the ordinary world around them.

The second level is emotional and is often accompanied by a definite but strange sensation of feeling-but-not-feeling which we might call a sense of awe, an experience of being part of the great mystery. It may also be accompanied by anxiety, elation, fear, delight, or some other emotion which is not truly felt but somehow sensed. But it is really none of these things. The distinction, again, is between the tonal and the nagual. When we experience the nagual and are at one with the universe, no words or feelings are available to us to describe this adequately. It is only when we return that the words of the tonal must be found in order to explain what we have seen, and they will fall short, always. The actual feeling of being part of the flow of energy within the universe is a wordless but very real sense of connection with an unnamed yet powerful intelligence, an entity with independent existence that we are also all a part of.

The third level is intuitive: here this connection with that 'something beyond the self' is entirely obvious and apparent, combined with greater clarity, understanding and awareness of all that is unfolding in the experience of the universe as a whole.

Shamanic ecstasy combines all three of these levels of sensation and, for the most experienced, is more akin, qualitatively, to the latter, so that the shaman does not just *feel* his connection with the sacred, he is *part* of it and at one with the entities which occupy these other worlds.

At the same time, as a 'walker between worlds', he is quite able to control and fully direct his consciousness in non-physical reality. It is *through* this control, not through *loss of control* that he is able to visit new levels of existence, to communicate with spirits, to access hidden and arcane information, and to make subtle changes in the 'otherworld' which will have a real, physical effect in the world of ordinary reality.

Put simply, we enter the otherworld trance as physical, material beings, but what takes place there happens at an energetic level. When we return, we bring this energy back with us and reintegrate it within ourselves at a physical level. For example, we may enter the otherworld and, with the help of our spirits, deal with past issues of self-healing, such as the current impacts of a previous abusive relationship, and learn how better to cope with the situation we now find ourselves in. We are then able to use this information constructively and practically in our immediate and future interactions in the world, in our present relationships, and in all situations where power is the underlying issue.

While we are in the trance state and journeying with our spirits, we can more intensely see, hear, smell or feel the impact of the otherworld experience we are part of. With this greater knowledge and enhanced self-awareness comes a greater sense of personal power when we return from the journey, which then enables us to act differently, more positively and purposefully in the world that we return to.

BEING IN A TRANCE

Joseph Bearwalker Wilson – shamanic practitioner, hypnotherapist and author of *The Waxing Moon* – describes the ecstatic trance as an altered state of consciousness not unlike self-hypnosis.[54]

Light trance states, he says, are like losing yourself in the TV or a book, where you become so engrossed that you are not fully aware of your surroundings, but still completely in control of yourself. When the chapter ends or the adverts appear, you are quite able to get up from the sofa to make tea.

Deeper trances are like the experience you have when you first wake and are still between the world of dreams and reality. You may be aware that you are still 'dozing', even though you are also involved with the vivid imagery you are part of.

Achieving and controlling the trance state is simply a matter of practice – like learning to drive a car. First you will grate the gears and stall it as you learn to master the controls and to steer and watch the road at the same time. But within weeks you will be driving smoothly and shortly after that you will be coasting with one hand on the wheel, listening to the radio and driving on automatic pilot.

In fact, most of us are in a trance state most of the time – one where we blindly accept, without questioning, the linear world's dream of a reality which 'just is', where things cannot be changed by our actions, and there is no alternative to the consensus. In the shamanic experience, we are merely entering a different trance to swap one reality for another by entering the holograph at another point in the flow of information, before it is interpreted for us and the Western reality handed to us as a given.

As you enter any trance state, says Wilson, you progress gradually from ordinary, to deeper levels of consciousness – from Beta, to Alpha, to Theta.

Beta consciousness is normal, alert awareness. This gives way to a feeling of physical relaxation and drowsiness characteristic of the Alpha state. Your body feels heavier; you are reluctant to move, your breathing becomes slower and deeper; your pulse rate slows. In this light trance state you will feel less inclined to speak or to engage with 'rational' thought and your body may also feel somewhat detached from everyday awareness, as if you are not really there, as the division between your physical and spiritual self begins to become more obvious.

When you then enter the medium trance you may experience sensations of taste, smell or touch, without being physically touched or tasting or smelling anything. You will be more sensitive to variations in temperature and typically, you will feel colder. Visions will appear. You are now an active participant in the landscape of the otherworld.

In deep trance you are much less inclined to move physically at all, as the outside world and your surroundings have simply become less interesting to you. In very deep trance states, typical of the Vodou possession trance, you may even be able to open your eyes and still remain separate from ordinary reality. The gods will move through you, but you will have no recollection whatsoever of your actions and interactions. You may also be able to control automatic body functions such as heart rate, blood pressure, and the sensation of pain. In one Vodou ceremony, a person is required to plunge their hand into boiling oil, which is only possible with the magical or spiritual intervention which deep trance allows. At this level, you will also be in touch wth a deep place within yourself where old memories will resurface and you will be able to explore feelings, places, ages and sensations long forgotten. There is no time and there is no space.

In the depth of this experience, the shaman is living in the Infinite Now. He may cover a lifetime of sensation in minutes or he may be in trance for hours or even days. In many tribal communities there remains an injunction against disturbing the shaman while in trance because his soul is considered to have literally left his body and to wake him at this point would mean his certain death – his body may survive but it would wander soulless like the zombie of Haitian tradition.

'Each depth of trance has valuable uses,' says Wilson. 'In the light and medium trances you can learn to begin practical shamanic journeying so that you can see, hear, touch and smell experiences in the worlds which border ours. In those trance states, these journeys will feel similar to a fantasy or daydream and you may wonder if it is real, or just your imagination. As you train yourself to deepen the trance, the journeys become more vivid, until, in the deep trance, they look and feel as though they are taking place in physical reality.'

The experience of the shamanic journey through the ecstatic trance state is a powerful one which brings insights and new energies into our lives, creating immediate beneficial effects which mean that we, in turn, will have a more positive effect on the world we all live in.

JOURNEYING

Experience, say the shamans, is everything. Things can never be real because someone has told you they are real; they must be personally experienced. The shamanic journeys which follow will enable you to test the reality of the shaman for yourself.

The first section, below, is a general description of the technique of journeying – a technique which is valid for all journeys you may wish to take. I suggest that you read this through before trying out the technique itself, as the stages often include a descriptive narrative to illustrate the events you are likely to experience.

Normally, you will lie on your back to take a journey of this kind and it is, of course, important that you have arranged to be undisturbed during this time. You will need about 20 minutes.

Try not to get too comfortable, even though you lie in a restful state. You are aiming to enter Theta awareness, a 'medium' trance state, so a degree of alertness, which is promoted through remaining a little less than totally comfortable, is helpful in ensuring you do not drift off too far, into sleep and dreaming. The shamanic journey must be seen as a *mission* and intention is everything. In no way is the journey a form of meditation or an excuse for relaxation. Alertness is crucial.

It is recommended that you use a source of sound to help guide and focus you during the journey – a technique which neo-shamans call 'sonic driving'. Traditionally this is provided by a drummer, but in the urban form of shamanism there are now drumming tapes and CDs which can be purchased to do the same job.

The advantages of drumming – live or on tape – are that it provides a definite point of reference in case there is any temptation for you to get 'lost' in the journey, that it provides boundaries to the journeying experience, and that the tape you use will normally include a 'call-back' signal, represented by a different and much faster beat, to end the journey and bring you back to ordinary reality. The beat of the drum is hypnotic in its own right and will help you to achieve a deeper trance level, while the sound is an important 'carrier' for spirit and will help you to make contact with these universal energies.

If you cannot find a shamanic drumming tape, try at least to find some form of steady tonal background to help you go deeper into the shamanic state. Ideally, this should provide a pulse at 220 beats a minute but even the constant white noise of the TV or a mistuned radio, or the hum of some electrical appliances may help. I have also found it helpful to move the body at the 220-beats-a-minute rhythm, by pushing against a solid surface with the feet, for example, and others use the modern form of 'trance dance' to achieve a similar state. Movement like this can be helpful even if you also use a drumming tape as it involves the whole body in the sensory experience.

In scientific terms, the sound you use provides a focus for your journey and helps you to produce the ecstatic state by stimulating the release of specific neurochemicals in the brain, which activate the areas responsible for dreaming and for visions. The steady beat of the drum is closely attuned to the natural rhythms of the body and of the heartbeat – the natural pulse of energy – of the Earth.

The favoured position for journeying is the lower world posture taught to Michael Harner by the Jivaro people of Ecuador (now known more commonly as the Shuar). Many other trance postures are now known and recorded, thanks primarily to the work of Felicitas Goodman and Belinda Gore of the Cayamungue Institute in America, some of which are described later, but the Jivaro posture will serve you well for the journeys you are about to take. Though precise, it is also one of the most simple trance postures to achieve.

Lie on your back with your left arm across your forehead and the top of your eyes, with your hand slightly twisted so the palm faces forward and the back of the hand rests across your brow, as if you were shielding your eyes from a light which is being shone at you from a position behind you towards the top of your head. You may also wish to use a bandanna or scarf to cover your eyes.

Your other arm lies at your side, directly parallel with your body, your fingers extended along the line of your thigh. Your feet are together only at the heels and are allowed to fall open to create a 'V' shape, producing a sensation of slight tension in the legs.

It is important to approach the journey in a sacred manner with full awareness of the purpose and the challenge of what you are about to do. Many people use herb bundles called smudge (available from many 'new age' stores, or from some of the suppliers mentioned in the Resources section of this book) to clear the space before journeying or, at least, light incense as a ritual of purification.

STATE YOUR PURPOSE – *INTENTION*

The purpose or intention you have in mind for the journey and your clear statement of this intent are both vitally important if you hope to receive unambiguous, definite answers from the journey. It is preferable to have a clear, open-ended question in mind – a 'what if' rather than a 'should I' question.

As we saw with the rock divination exercise, 'what', 'why', 'how' and 'who' questions work better than 'when' or 'where'. 'Yes' and 'no' answers are to be avoided, as are 'shoulds'. Human beings are one small part of the whole, we do not have access to the full picture and, within the total scheme of the universe and the agenda of the spirit people, 'should' may produce a very different response to the one you might expect. 'Should I marry Joe?' for example, may well produce the answer 'no' when your real intention for this journey may have been to affirm the decision you have already made that you will get married.

Because your question does not invite information as to *why* you should or should not do so, you may never see the full picture on the basis of this question and may therefore miss some vital piece of information for this and future relationships. A better question might be 'What will be the outcome of my marriage to Joe?' which will give you more of an overview of the energetic forces at play between the two of you.

When you are clear on your intention and able to phrase it unambiguously, state it out loud three or four times in order to ensure that you are totally focused in your purpose. For example: 'I am journeying to the lower world to ask for guidance on the following matter. How best can I help Lesley in her need for healing?' Only begin the journey when you are absolutely clear about your intention.

I worked recently on distance healing with a client in France, who is also learning to journey. He wanted to know if he should still state an intention if he was simply journeying to explore the otherworld. The answer is 'Yes!' – even if you are journeying simply to explore, then your intention is to 'journey to the shamanic lower world to explore the terrain – to meet with my spirit allies – and become familiar with my surroundings'. If you do not state this intention, you will have no idea where you are going, or why, or what you have learned when you get back. Always keep a purpose in mind.

THE JOURNEY – *ATTENTION*

The otherworld is divided into three – the upper, middle and lower worlds – all of which have different purposes and are home to different sorts of energy in the form of spirit beings who provide different sorts of help and advice.

The lower world is entered through a hole into the Earth which you may visualize as a cave, the hollow of a tree, the burrow of an animal, a whirlpool; in any event somewhere that takes you *down* into the Earth Herself and, symbolically, deeper into you. Ideally, this should be a place you know from real life, somewhere that has meaning and significance for you, which gives it added power and a greater link to you and your experience.

My own journeys used to begin with my entry into one of two caves. One of these divided inside into two passageways. The right hand side was bright and adorned with crystals, and led out to a Mediterranean landscape overlooking a wide blue sea; the other was dark and led to an even darker chamber which did not appear to have a physical exit.

In shamanic journeying there is no attempt to control any aspect of the images that arise, though one can interact with the beings one meets and ask for information, so I never knew until I was in the cave which of these two passages I would take. Normally, before I met the division point, I was joined by my spirit helpers who discussed with me the best route for my present needs. I usually knew I was in for a journey of positive and direct learning if I was drawn to the lighter passageway, whereas the darker way usually meant a 'darker' journey where I would deal with current fears or psychic blocks which were holding me or my client back, or with issues of physical or mental well-being. I have learned over time, however, that the dark passage is also the route to deeper understanding and more positive and long-lasting transformation. In the landscape of the shaman, all things contain the seed of their opposite and all things, para-doxically, are one.

Wherever you are taken and whatever options you choose, you must give the experience your total, non-judgmental attention. Remember that everything has meaning here and try to remain open to it and aware of the subtle messages within it. Try not to let the rational, analytical mind intrude too greatly into your decision-making. Rational thinking leads to judgement, and judgement to doubt. At this point it is important to 'suspend disbelief' and to act from intuition, from instinct and 'gut feelings'.

MEETING YOUR ALLIES – *ACCEPTANCE*

On your journey, you will meet energy beings (spirit guides or allies) which may take the form of animals, people or, indeed, 'inanimate' objects such as trees or stones. In reality, there is no such thing as an inanimate object, since everything is alive.

The fact that these entities have come to you – whatever they are and in whatever form – or that you have, if you wish, created these particular images to represent the energies you encounter, is itself significant. There is an obvious differ-ence – symbolically at least – between a buffalo and a rabbit as a source of guidance.

If you have asked a question concerning the approach you should take to a problem you know you will face in the next few months, the buffalo might suggest power and stead-fastness, a 'bullish' approach. This very important sacred and totemic animal also represents the ability and intention to give of oneself fully, whereas a rabbit might suggest a more cautious and gentle approach.

The content of their communication also needs to be borne in mind, as well as the fact that each animal may have personal significance for you beyond their symbolic meaning.

Your purpose on this journey is not to *study* these beings or to experience reality through their eyes – although that may be possible with their co-operation – but to accept them, to interact with them, to learn from them, and to allow them to guide you, as if you were on a journey with a friend. You would not try to analyse or 'see through the eyes' of your friend in order to seek clarification on a certain point he had made; you would simply ask him for more information.

So do not be afraid to ask questions.

You will always understand the answers you get and they will always have meaning. They may not come in the form you expect, however, and they may not even be the answers you expect, since you are now in touch with entities that have a life of their own and who will offer deep and independent wisdom which is not governed by your rational mind. Indeed, their answers may not even come in the form of words, but in actions, perhaps the giving of a gift, or in sounds or symbols that you will recognize as significant.

One of my journeys to the upper world (a place we will visit later) was taken in order to meet a wise being who could offer me advice on a particular financial issue.

It was my intention at that time to create a shamanic camp in France, based on Earth-honouring principles – which unfortunately takes money as well as will. After a year, I was doing well and had maybe half the money I felt I needed. But, to me, things seemed to be proceeding very slowly – a particular pattern in my life, the experience of things moving too slowly for my personal agenda. I needed to find out how I could make more money more quickly.

I begin my journey by climbing the branches of the tree I use for upper world journeys. At the top of this is the vine-like core of a whirlwind which twists into a powerful grey sky – in many ways like an umbilical cord which connects the worlds – and disappears into a hole in the cloud. I follow the eye of the twister up and through the cloud until I emerge into the landscape familiar to me.

Ahead of me is a garden tended by an old man dressed as a Chinese sage. To my right is a sheltered green landscape which runs down to the sea. To my left is a mountainous and snowy region which is rocky and barren, an arduous if not difficult climb, but also picturesque and pure, unpolluted, and entirely, powerfully natural. I feel that the mountain is my destination on this journey.

I begin climbing, all the time with the feeling that I am looking for someone in particular, though someone I have never met before. I have no idea who I will meet.

After a lengthy climb which takes me high into the mountain, with stirring views of a lush green rainforest far below, I come upon a man sitting alone on the mountainside. This, I feel, is the person I have come here to meet.

The snow has disappeared far below and it is now warm and serene, and the view around and below me is truly beautiful. Sitting on a rocky outcrop, looking out over the fertile jungle landscape far below, is a man dressed in light coloured trousers and shirt, boots and hat. He is the image of a Mexican or Peruvian shaman, as played by a young Hemingway, perhaps, in one of those 1940s black and white adventure films.

He does not acknowledge me, but remains looking out over the landscape. There is a sense of calm preoccupation about him. I ask if I might join him and without looking towards me, he waves me to sit near him on the rock.

I have the impression that he really does not have a great deal of time for me, so I come straight to the point. 'I intend to create a community for healing where I can help others with their spiritual and personal development, but I need money,' I say. 'How do I find this?'

At this point in my shamanic development, I am still expecting easy, straight answers, as if my guides were there simply at my beck and call. And, in fact, the spirits have been kind to me so far. Recognizing my novice status, they have usually supplied the instant answers I was looking for.

This time is different. This time I get a question back in response to my own. Clearly, on this journey, I am going to have to work for the information I want.

'Why do you want this community?' he asks. Again, there is not even a glance in my direction. I now have the distinct feeling that I am dealing with a cantankerous and difficult individual, not unlike Castaneda's description of his mentor, don Juan.

I have come all this way to meet with someone who has heard this naive nonsense many times before, cannot be bothered, does not take me seriously and does not want to be disturbed, it seems. Oh boy.

'So I can help others,' I say, in answer to his question.

'But you can help others every day by your very presence here on the planet,' he says. 'We can all make a difference, every moment of the day by our actions and by our thoughts. It is how we interact with others that matters. We do not need a community for that. We just need to act kindly and authentically towards those we meet.'

He is right, of course. But that isn't the answer I wanted. I persist.

'That is true. And I try to do that. But a community based on natural principles and on connection to the Earth would enable more people to be healed more quickly and create more positive energy for the planet. It is not me who would heal these people. Others would also bring their skills and there is a power and an energy in people acting together as a community, with a single mind and

focus, which is itself a force for transformation.'

He says nothing. I have the feeling that he is weighing these words to assess their validity and the truth behind them. After a little while he nods very slightly. I feel as if I have passed some kind of test. He then motions for me to look towards the sun, which is now hanging in the sky just to his left. He reaches towards it and, turning to face me for the first time, hands me a round glowing disk which might be a piece of the sun itself or a golden coin.

'Take this,' he says and turns away again, suggesting that our meeting is now over. I take it and prepare to walk away.

Then, just as I turn away, he adds one more word which sounds like 'Cuero'. I assume this is a Peruvian or Mexican word of some kind and make a mental note to look it up next day.

I thank my ally for his gift, if not his generous willingness to share his time with me, and leave him to walk back down the mountain and to descend the whirlwind back to ordinary reality.

The next day, I logged onto the web and found a number of sites dedicated to shamanism, with the intention of looking up the mystery word I had heard the night before.

Using the World Wide Web as a method of research now seems very fitting – I could, I suppose, have consulted a dictionary or phoned a reference library. Shamans, however, believe that all things are connected one to another through an intricate field of energy which they describe as a 'web'. It is seen as an energy matrix or, symbolically, a spider's web, so that movement in one area reverberates across the whole.

That same autumn day I had stepped outside and, in the misty dew of morning, noticed what seemed like thousands of spiders' webs caught and revealed in the moisture of the air. How like the web of energy the shaman sees, always there but not always visible. Perhaps we only ever do see it clearly when things become 'misty' for us in life.

I spent a good couple of hours that day searching for the

word 'Cuero'. And found nothing. I tried various other ways in which the word might possibly be spelt. 'Cuerro', 'Cuwero', 'Cairro'. Perhaps I had misheard, I reasoned. I tried 'made up' words which were similar but might sound slightly different. 'Cureo'. 'Curero'. 'Curareo'.

Just as I was about to give up my eye caught a word on a page which, although apparently a long shot, might have had some relevance. The word was Q'ero which, I reasoned, could sound similar to 'Cuero'. So I clicked on it. This is what it said:

> *They have been invisible, partly by choice and partly because of geography; they live at 17,000 feet up in the mist-shrouded mountains of central Peru, where the harshness of their physical existence is inversely proportional to the beauty of their landscape. They are ... the descendants of the Incas, the Children of the Sun; they are the Q'ero Indians, and they have only recently reached down from their self-imposed isolation in the lap of the great apus, the sacred mountains, to share their vision with the West.*

The full text, *Stepping Outside of Time*, by Joan Parisi Wilcox – can be found at *http://www.resonate.org/places/articles/shamans/qero.htm*. It went on to describe the vision of don Antonio Morales, a master shaman of the mysterious Q'ero people who number just 700 and who fled from the Spanish invaders in order to preserve their spiritual knowledge for future generations. They remained hidden from the world until as late as 1949 before making a deliberate and conscious decision to re-emerge from their self-imposed exile in order to spread their vision of a new world order.

'Westerners must undergo a personal awakening and initiate a global journey of transformation,' said the article. 'According to Q'ero prophecy, as this regeneration gets underway, North America will supply the "body" or the physical strength; Europe will supply the "head" or the mental acuity; and South America will supply the heart. The result . . . will be the possibility of an evolutionary leap forward for humankind, of a remaking of ourselves and of the planet.'

The vision I had seen the night before became clearer in the words of this article: my image of the 'perfect Peruvian shaman', who had not been pleased to see me, who had wanted to remain 'invisible'; the mountain I had climbed – 'where the harshness of their physical existence is inversely proportional to the beauty of their landscape'; the article's reference to the Q'ero as 'the Children of the Sun' and my being handed a piece of the sun; my desire to create an Earth-honouring community in the West as a means for personal transformation and the reference by Morales to a need for global transformation only possible through remaking ourselves, an action which must begin in the West.

The message from the being I had sought out, through the parallels with the article I had discovered, seemed an endorsement of my intention. My spirit ally was talking to me even outside of my journey.

The intention of my journey was never directly addressed and I never was given instructions on how to make more money more quickly. The strange thing was, though, that even without these instructions, money started to arrive for me anyway, quickly and effortlessly, within days of this journey. This included a new client, who came to me a month later and totally out of the blue, in the form of a North American company I had had absolutely no previous dealings with and who appointed me to work for them, practically on the spot, for a handsome fee, all of which was completely unexpected and, in ordinary reality, highly unlikely. Why a company in San Francisco would approach me, nearly half a world away in Northampton, England, remains a mystery.

I looked back over the article again. 'North America will supply the "body",' the substance, it said. 'Europe will supply the "head",' the thinking and the direction for this work, and South America – the home of my Peruvian shaman guide – 'will supply the heart.'

When you feel you have completed the journey to your satis-faction or when the call-back signal begins on your drumming tape, it is time to come back.

As soon as you hear the call-back, thank your guides for their help and say goodbye to them, just as you would a friend. Then retrace your steps back through the route you have taken and exit at the point where you entered this world.

The action of retracing your steps has the dual purpose of helping you to revisit and remember the key information you have received, allowing you to relive it in effect, and of grounding you as you return to ordinary reality.

When you are back – and not during the journey itself – is the time for reflecting on the journey you have taken and for analysis of its content and your experience. Gently come back to normal reality and spend a few minutes jotting down the key events and insights you have received.

Don't worry if all your questions weren't answered on a single journey. It can sometimes take several journeys to become clear on some issues. By keeping a journey log, you begin to build a map of yourself as well as the shamanic land-scape. And you can always return there.

KEY POINTS FOR JOURNEYING

- Relax, but do not get *too* comfortable. Use sonic driving to help you focus and enter the shamanic trance state.

- State your intention clearly. If you get 'lost' on the journey, or so interested in what you see that you forget your original purpose, come back to the drums, using their sound to re-focus you. Then restate your intention and continue the journey.

- Remain attentive, respectful and non-judgemental through-out. You are always with friends.

- When it is time to return, retrace your steps and spend some time reacclimatizing yourself. Do not try to move too quickly – you will have shifted a lot of energy and need to readjust before you make any sudden movements.

- It is always useful to make a note of all you have seen and heard, so begin a journey log right now.

INTO THE OTHERWORLD

It is time now for you to experience journeying and to take some specific journeys with the intention of reclaiming power for yourself and, ultimately, creating a better world for all of us.

The journey which follows, and the one immediately after it, are probably the most important you will ever take. As the world of shamanism opens up to you, you will begin to develop new sensitivities, to receive deep wisdom and practical information as well as more spiritual insights, and to do so with increasing ease.

I have met and worked with people who feel they have discovered a new sense of reality and purpose, who have come to better understand the meaning of their lives through their experiences with shamanism, and who have radically changed their future as a result of these. None of them did it without first taking these journeys.

When we enter the otherworld, we step deep into the swirls of the hologram and are offered a glimpse of the divine – the potential for all that is. We see the power of the universe open and accessible to us – and ourselves as channels for the infinite.

'When divine power is put into action by human beings, it becomes magic,' Maya Deren remarks in her classic study of Haitian Vodou.[55] By accessing the hologram with the intention of using its energetic power purposefully, we may produce magic in many different forms. Such as divination, where we journey to the future to examine its secrets; or healing, where we may journey to the past in order to change it.

In both cases, in the language of the scientist, a new

unfolding of the universe is made to take place as the raw data of the cosmos are reassembled in a new, empowering form through the experience of the journeyer. Which is really just the same as saying there is magic in the universe and we are part of it. It is quite possible for us to visit the future and the past and to influence both for the greater good of all.

Another 'unfolding' of this magic, which I find fascinating, is psychic detective work where intuitive journeying skills are used to find practical solutions to real-life investigations which may have remained a mystery for decades. What better proof of the magic of the universe and the effectiveness of shamanic techniques for helping us to access it?

Some people working as psychic detectives are so successful that they are willing to undergo public challenges to prove the value and validity of their skills. Jim Watson, a Los-Angeles-based psychic, was challenged by a Japanese TV channel to fly over Japan in a helicopter until he detected a previously undiscovered dead body on the ground below.

'Up in the helicopter, he directed the pilot to fly over the flanks of Mount Fuji,' reports *Kindred Spirit* magazine, which covered this story.[56] 'As the cameras rolled, he pointed down to the forested slopes below and said that directly beneath him was the body of a young woman. He described the condition of the body, its posture and when the death had occurred, adding that it was a suicide resulting from drinking poison . . . Within 45 minutes the young woman's body was found, in exactly the location, posture and condition Watson had described. A subsequent autopsy confirmed the death was caused by drinking poison.'

There is magic in the universe, all right, and this journey is the first step towards seeing it.

JOURNEY 1: TO EXPLORE THE SHAMANIC LOWER WORLD

On our first voyage to the shamanic lower world, you will find your personal entrance and exit points, get to know the terrain of the world you are travelling in and, perhaps, see some of the occupants of this new landscape.

On this and the journey which follows, do not make contact with any of the beings you may see here – just observe. This may sound strange to you now, but once the journey begins, it will all feel very different. You will not meet any beings who mean you harm or wish to take anything from you. Nonetheless, the shamanic universe is very different from ordinary, linear reality. You will be an intimate part of the holographic swirl, the Infinite Now at the heart of 'alternity', and there are new ways of being to familiarize yourself with, and a lot to learn.

Use the traditional Jivaro trance posture for this journey which was described earlier – one arm over your eyes, the other at your side, as you lie on your back in a quiet, dark room. This will help you to access the otherworld more easily. Ensure that the room you are working in remains dark and that you are undisturbed. If you wish, place dark material, perhaps a scarf, across your eyes to further block out unwanted light.

Take a few moments to relax into the position. Get comfortable. Breathe deeply and forget everything else from the external world. Ensure that you avoid alcohol and any form of mind-altering drug for at least twenty-four hours prior to this journey, and preferably do not eat for four hours before the journey begins.

Phrase your intention – 'I am taking a journey to the shamanic lower world to explore its terrain and to get to know the landmarks which will become familiar to me.' Speak it out loud if you wish to give it added energy.

If you are using a shamanic drumming tape, have it on your chest in a Walkman if possible so you do not have to move again, and press the 'Play' button now. The tape will begin with steady rhythmic drumbeats. At this point ready yourself for the journey ahead and form an image in your mind of the point you will journey from and back to, which is the landmark – cave or tree or waterfall, for example – which you know from ordinary reality.

The entry to the lower world is different for everyone, but I will describe my own to you so you know what to look for and will be able to recognize yours when you find it.

Entering the cave

I stand in a green field, looking at a rocky hillside before me. To my right and slightly in front of me is a grey tree, very old. It has no leaves but is very strong and sturdy, a tree which has seen countless ages and survived with new power and energy. Its multiple branches point upwards to a grey and ominous sky. A twisting wind plays and dances gracefully above the tree, swirling upwards to a deep 'whirlpool' within a layer of white-grey cloud. This tree and the whirlwind above it are my means of entry to the upper world.

Looking ahead to the hillside, I see two caves. Both are entrances to the lower world, each leading to a different destination there. Sometimes I am drawn to one, sometimes another, depending on the nature of my journey.

The drumbeats on your tape will begin to speed up. At this point, your journey begins. Enter the lower world now by your chosen route. Whether this is a cave, tree, well, mine-shaft or hollow in the ground, the one thing all lower world journeys have in common is a sense of descent and an entrance into darkness – even though you will be able to see within it – and it is important that you experience these.

One thing to be aware of in the otherworlds, which was alluded to in our earlier discussion of trance states, is that you will not experience emotion here in the same way you do in normal reality. So while words like 'darkness' and 'descent' may have all sorts of connotations for us, positive or negative, they will not have emotional meaning for you once you are in the journey.

I want to draw your attention to this point in another way now, too.

In later journeys, you may decide to interact with the spirit beings you meet and to accept information from them. You may explore painful life dramas together, or see futures you could not imagine in ordinary reality. My experience is that none of this will have significant emotional content for you while you are jouneying. Just as you are aware of darkness without actually *being* in darkness, so you will sense and understand the nature of this emotion without being overwhelmed by it. This facility enables you to continue your journey with a clear focus and to deal later, in a controlled way, with the emotional issues it raises.

Even clients who become tearful during soul retrieval journeys where they experience unhappy events from earlier in their lives, report a different quality to the emotion they experience – as if they are seeing it from a more objective perspective rather than with deep personal involvement, with a sense of melancholy and yearning sadness rather than intense grief.

However, the human condition is to seek balance and you may experience an equal and opposite reaction once you re-emerge, which may mean a profound emotional release. This emotional and energetic release can be a crucial healing experience in its own right, which enables you to let go of limiting experiences from the past by finally expressing them fully in the present.

Just be aware that any emotional content not experienced in the shamanic state may be released upon your return, so be sure of what you are getting into. You can always decline this offer of healing from the spirits.

Move into your entrance to the lower world when you are ready to do so. You will find yourself in a tunnel of some kind. Often it descends at an angle, sometimes steeply, and may appear ribbed. It may also bend. During a first journey, progress along the tunnel may be slow. This is fine. The objective of this journey is to study the landscape, so a slow movement is recommended. Make a mental note of the things you see here, including any animals or other life forms.

Often I am met by my power animals in the tunnel, and you may be too. For the purposes of this journey, however, just make a note of what you see and do not interact with anyone or anything you meet there. If you are approached at this stage, or later in the journey, be courteous and polite, but simply move away, promising to return later when you are more experienced, if you are inclined to do so. You will be left alone and your wishes honoured.

Sometimes in this tunnel you will find your progress blocked by something, which could be an animal, a stone wall, a feeling that this is 'not right', or some other physical obstacle. You have free will and you can make a decision either to find a way around it or to return to the entrance and try again another time. There is no hurry and no compulsion to continue.

Look now for a source of light coming into the tunnel. This is the light of the otherworld, which enters through a portal which is your gateway to the lower world. Beyond it is a whole new landscape and version of reality.

Again, to give you a flavour of progress so far, let me tell you about my experience of the tunnel.

Moving through the tunnel

The pathway slopes gently beneath me. Even from the entrance I can see an outcrop to my right, partially blocking the tunnel space so it narrows to about half its original width. I move around it and know that I am then in the tunnel 'proper'; the outcrop I have passed is a marker of sorts.

The environment around me is dark. But it is not like an Earthly darkness. I can see here. Wherever I fix my attention is illuminated, as if I can project a beam of light using my eyesight and my will alone.

I am joined by Panther, an animal that I never see on any other journey or in any other environment. He waits for me here and here alone, it seems. This is his domain. He walks with me, gentle yet aloof, until we reach a new tunnel of deeper darkness. I know that a few steps beyond this is a vertical drop, straight down, for hundreds of feet, to another world. I step into the tunnel, prepared to fall.

On my first journey, I was aware of this fall before I took it and concerned at what the outcome might be. It is not in our nature to court the experience of falling, we do not have wings. But now I trust it.

I enter the tunnel and step into the darkness. My descent is slow, like floating, and I am aware of the geology of the rock as I fall. The strata tell me that I am entering a very ancient place.

After some time, I land. There is a natural gateway in the rock to my right. I step through into another cave, where a group of Elders, the ancient and wise spirits of this place, sit in circle around a fire. Beyond them I see the exit to this cave. Bright sunlight dances in waves upon the cave walls, in counterpoint to the darkness within.

I make greetings to the Elders. Sometimes I join their circle if I have a question for them but, in truth, their words are usually ones of encouragement rather than divine wisdom. I am not yet part of their circle. Most times I simply walk past this gathering into the bright light beyond them and into the lower world.

The moment you entered the cave (or your other route to the lower world), the normal rules of physics and biology ceased to have a hold on you.

You could see in the dark. You could talk to other life forms. Here, it is even more so. You can, if you wish, fly like a bird; you will be able to breathe underwater and to swim like a fish. You will understand new languages, communicate without speaking, move faster than light between otherworld locations or occupy two places at once – just like Aspect's subatomic particles and Bohm's fish. You are now connected to and a part of all things and can explore the essence of 'you' as it echoes in form throughout the whole of (self-) creation.

All of this will seem perfectly natural to you, so much so

that, on your return, you may forget that what you have just done is 'not possible' (and yet you did it), so remember to make a mental note of all experiences you have here, especially those which defy 'normal logic'.

Move towards your exit into the lower world. How does it look to you? What form does it take? Is anyone waiting there for you? Who? You may find that they seem somehow familiar; perhaps they remind you of a long-dead relative or maybe you have never met them in ordinary reality, but you seem to know and understand them here. Observe, but do not approach them or engage in conversation. Look around you. What do you see?

Enter into this world. Keep looking, listening, sensing. Be open to new experiences and go with them. Make a note of everything you see and experience. When you return, this will be your familiar territory, the place you come back to.

Exploring the lower world

As I emerge from the dim light of the cave, I find myself on a plateau of rock, a ledge overlooking a beautiful green forest some distance below, which goes on for as far as I can see.

My animal allies wait for me on this plateau, they want to know if they can join me or help in any way. They want to experience my humanness. For me, their help is often invaluable. They know this terrain; they can take me to places faster than I can find them.

For them, it is a chance to interact with a human and to experience life in a different form, one capable of taking part in a reality – the world of human life – that they cannot enter.

I throw myself from the thin ledge I stand upon and, like a bird, take flight into the sky and down into the forest below. The deep drop does not affect me at all. In the other world, I would be dead now. But here, I am not constrained by flesh, by blood, by the demands and limitations of the body. I land unharmed.

I am in a clearing in a wood. In front of me is a statue, long abandoned, of Buddha. He sits cross-legged, a giant artefact from an age of spiritual believers. I know that I can, if I wish, ask questions of him and he will answer truthfully, in terms I can understand, and with just the depth of information that I will be able to assimilate. Nothing will harm me here; I will never be given more than I can cope with, one step at a time, one step at a time.

Behind him is a statue of Kali-Shiva-Shakti, many-armed goddess of death, of transformation, transubstantiation. She will give me a different perspective on the nature of life and reality.

Death is part of life, she says, part of the circle. It is there to set us free, so our energy can return to the cosmos. We are children of the stars.

All around these two is a field of crystals, like a small plantation of light. For centuries, shamans have used the power of crystals to communicate with other worlds and draw energy from them – like the power source to a spiritual crystal set. I asked once if I could take one of these crystals. 'Not yet,' they said. 'Not until you are ready to step into your power.'

Behind me, the forest stretches down to a cliff, beyond which is a shoreline and, beyond that, many islands which I may also explore. In this forest I have met with Fear, not as a disembodied sensation, but as an entity, a being who has taught me much.

Fear, it seems, has our best interests at heart. The sole reason for his encounter with us, for Fear to seek us out, is to show us the magnificence which lies beyond fear, how fear is part of a richer, much bigger picture and how, by moving beyond fear, we can experience a deeper understanding of ourselves and our place in the world. Fear is hurt when we run from him. His intention, after all, is to heal. We must embrace our fears to move beyond them.

To my left is a pool, deep and green and still. It is the Pool of Wounds, where we place our hurt and allow it to sink *beneath the surface of ourselves. But we do not bury it for ever. Our nature is to seek out new experience and to hope. And so we risk being hurt again in order to experience and feel.*

Once I found a stone at the bottom of this pool, a beautiful heart-shaped crystal, which I returned to someone in the other reality. It was an aspect of themselves which they had given away to someone that they loved, they said, someone who had broken their heart. Since then, they had been unable to feel, to embrace love in any of its many forms. With its return, they felt immediately more powerful and in touch with themselves. Fear may be an aspect of Love.

To my right is a more dense, uncharted part of the forest. Once I attended a fire ceremony in this forest and was given gifts, shamanic tools, to help me on future journeys. Later, we will take this journey too, to recover the power objects which are of most use to you in your own life.

You may travel in this new landscape as far and as wide as you wish. Remember its features and get a sense of the areas you would like to return to. These are normally the areas where specific information awaits you and which are calling you back. You can return to them at any time.

When you are ready to do so, or when the call-back signal sounds, retrace your steps to the entrance point to this world, through the tunnel you entered by and back to your starting point. Gently return to ordinary reality and, immediately, while you are still in the vestigial stage of the trance state, record your experiences and sensations in a journey logbook which is specifically for this purpose and which will enable you over the coming months to build a map of the other-world emerging.

JOURNEY 2: INTO THE UPPER WORLD

Prepare for this journey in exactly the same way as the lower world journey we took earlier. Lie down in a darkened room where you can be quiet and undisturbed for 20 minutes or so, have your drum tape ready and, if you wish, a scarf for your eyes.

There is no specific trance posture for general upper world journeys, and most people find that the Jivaro position works just as well.

The upper world is entered by moving upwards from your starting point, so have an image of this clearly in mind as you begin. Some people climb ladders or vines, others mountains. My entrance point is via a tree, which I climb to its highest branches and then leap into a powerful wind which circles above it and carries me up into the clouds.

Again, clearly state your intention – 'I am journeying to the upper world to explore the terrain and to investigate objects and areas of interest and value to me for the future' – and then begin your ascent.

At some point you will come to a division between the worlds, often described as feeling like a 'membrane', which you must pass through. It is important that you experience this or you will not know that you have entered the upper world. To me, the feeling is like passing through a material like rubber, which clings slightly to my body and means that I have to exert some force to get through.

As soon as you are through, look around you and notice what the landscape looks like, where it goes, who is there.

However you experience it – in pictures, sounds, sensations or smells – the upper world will feel different to the one you have just visited. The lower world is somehow more solid, earthier, more 'real', while the upper world is ethereal, less dense, more 'imaginary'.

Communication from others will often come to you as images and feelings, and will happen as fast as you can think it. There is no need for spoken words; conversations, like the inter-actions of Aspect's particles, are carried out faster than the speed of light since we are not actually in dialogue with another at all; we are now once again a part of the great universal pool of wisdom to which we are all naturally connected.

Again, the objective is to observe everything, to get a feel for the place. My own first steps into the upper world are like this . . .

Into the land of spirits

The tree rises before me, old and leafless. Its knowledge and its life are contained within it. It does not need to demonstrate its power to the world with a declaration of leaves.

I climb to its topmost branches and look up, then reach for the tail of the wind above me and am lifted swirling, circling, into the clouds.

At its peak, it vanishes into a deep, black hole in the grey layer of cloud. I am caught in swirling chaos and wrestle with the wind to find a foothold, to be still, to enter through.

I push myself through the veil between the worlds. It holds me momentarily, with a surface tension like the membrane of an egg, or the force which keeps water from spilling from a too-full glass. The passage feels like a rebirth through rubber.

I emerge and it is still. Quiet. Calm. Ahead of me is a garden, tended by a man in a robe. He is at one with his garden, but he welcomes me.

To my right, the garden runs down to a lych gate, through a passage of vines which offer shelter from the sun.

To my left are mountains. They are snow-covered, though there is no cold here. And high, though the climb can be completed in seconds. There is no time here and there is no space.

Behind me is a sea, wide and blue and infinite. I know that there are islands out there which keep other mysteries.

Begin to move around this world and to explore. Note in particular any beings that you see here, who may be guides for you. Do not speak to them now, but make a mental note to come back later when you can introduce yourself to them and ask if they have advice or information for you. Although these beings are more likely to appear in human form, just as they appeared as animals in the lower world, they are essentially the same basic forces and energies of the universe.

In many shamanic cultures, animals are not referred to as 'a bear', 'a wolf' or 'an eagle' but as Bear, Wolf, Eagle, the individual representing the whole species. So it is in this world too. The warrior you see is not just 'a warrior', but the archetypal image of the Hero. The ancient sage you meet is not just one 'wise old man', but *the* Wise Old Man of archetype, the expression of your and everyone's Higher Self.

There are no 'mythical' beings here. Some people see dragons or faeries or angels in the upper world. The form the being takes is an expression of the observer's beliefs, values and understanding, rather than its actual appearance. It is the *energy* behind the form which is real. In the upper world we are in contact with deep forces, expressions of pure energy in their most fundamental, elemental form.

Coming home

At some point during your journey, the tape will signal the call-back to you – a change in drumbeat to a slower, steady pulse, followed by a rapid beating for 30 seconds or so and then a return to a steady pulse to end. At this point, retrace your steps and return to your entrance point to this world, to the tree you climbed or to your other transition point, and end the journey at the entrance where you began.

Again, spend a few moments reflecting on your journey, then write down your impressions in your journey log or paint them or express them in some other way. Make it a tangible way, one you can return to. The journey may not make much sense to you right now and your images may have been fleeting, but over time you will begin to develop a topography and geography of these worlds that is uniquely yours and, strangely – should you decide to share your impressions with other adventurers – very much as others experience it too.

Shamanic practices for power retrieval, healing, for seeing the future and reclaiming our past, often involve the use of a power animal or ally, sometimes referred to as a second soul. If you intend to practise journeying regularly and with serious intent, it is as well to make a journey to recover your power animal as it will offer you guardianship, friendship and access to greater sources than you can have alone. For one thing, your ally knows the terrain much better than you, which means you will be able to move around more quickly and with greater confidence.

The relationship between the shaman and his power animals is crucial to the success of some types of shamanic work. Not only does the power animal offer support and protection to the shaman, it has a wisdom and a depth of intuitive knowledge which can be trusted to add a new dimension to the shaman's work.

This was demonstrated very clearly during what turned out to be a quite harrowing journey for Isobelle during her training in soul retrieval work. This journey was undertaken to carry out psychopomp work, the name given to the shamanic practice of conducting and guiding the souls of the dead into the other world.

Sometimes on its journey beyond life, the human soul may become lost. The person may have died suddenly and not realize they are dead; they may remain attached to life because of 'unfinished business'; or those left behind, the grieving and the bereaved, may hold onto that person's soul through their grief or fear of loss, which prevents both sides from moving on and the dead from achieving peace by entering back into flow, the process of re-becoming. The job of the psychopomp is to offer assistance to the dead – and sometimes to the living, too – in breaking these ties and finding peace, by entering the world of the dead to counsel and comfort the soul concerned and to offer help in entering the new world.

This is not without its risks to the shaman. For one thing, the dead know that you are alive when you walk among them and the frustrated, the angry and the needy, the 'hungry ghosts' who remain attached to life, may resent your presence and try to do you harm, or to possess you in order to experience your life energy.

On top of this, talking to the dead is rather like talking to the bereaved living, so sensitivity and counselling skills are needed in order to avoid further trauma, a task not always easy for the shaman who has seen this many times and understands, in a way the bereaved may not, the processes at work in the universe and the flow of death and re-becoming.

Before Isobelle's journey, she took the sensible precaution of consulting with her allies and assembling a team of power animals who were willing to help her. She felt in particular the need for support from one or more of her more powerful allies, like Jaguar or Wolf, who could offer protection as well as wisdom and strength. So she was a little surprised when Rabbit showed up.

'I just couldn't get rid of him,' she said. 'Whenever I shooed him away, he kept coming back, so eventually I gave up and took him along with me.'

Isobelle entered the otherworld and found herself in a deep wood. Trees are important to the dead and, if a soul is lost, it will often try to find trees, naturally aware that they are the great transformers of all worlds. In ours, they transform our pollution into breathable oxygen. In the spirit worlds, they are transformers of energy. The dead intuitively know that trees are a gateway and a lost soul will often head towards one.

Isobelle waited among the trees, still unsure of the exact nature of her mission, until she was called by the spirit of a young child, aged around four or five.

'She wasn't speaking in English. I felt maybe Polish, but I could somehow understand her,' said Isobelle.

'She was asking for her mother and was scared and anxious. My first thought was that her mother must also be dead and that the two of them had become separated when her mother had passed over into the Land of the Dead. I was about to help the child to pass into this other world so she could be reunited with her mother, but then I became aware that her mother was not dead, as I had thought. She was still living and her child had been waiting in limbo all this time until her mother could join her.'

Isobelle was able to comfort the child sufficiently to find out that, although her mother was not yet dead, her grandmother had passed over and to get her to agree that seeing her grandmother again would be much nicer than hanging round in this draughty old wood. She was then able to help the child move on into the next world.

'Then I became aware of something else. A smell of gas. And as I looked around I saw more children, perhaps fifty or so, all of the same age. I realized that what I was seeing were the souls of children who had been executed in a concentration camp during the war. In some cases, their mothers had outlived them and were still alive, while their children waited here alone, not knowing what to do. They were too young to know.'

This is where Isobelle's power animal was able to conclusively prove that, in every case, our allies know best. Rabbit's insistence in coming along was immediately shown to be exactly the right course of action.

'There were so many children I didn't know what to do at first,' said Isobelle. 'Many were crying, distressed, others were alarmed and anxious. I didn't know where to start. It occurred to me to line them up in some kind of order so I could escort each one in turn, but as I dealt with each child, the rest would be crying and panicking and the line would end up totally disordered. That's when Rabbit stepped in.

'He saw I was finding it tough to deal with the situation and immediately bounded into the group of children. They were delighted to see a rabbit and all gathered round to pet him. It was instantly calmer and less fraught and I was able to get on with my job much more effectively.'

166

With his distraction tactics, Rabbit was able to snatch success from the jaws of chaos and restore a sense of order.

'That was why he had insisted in coming along in the first place, and I was immensely grateful as it turned out,' said Isobelle.

Recovering power

You may have noticed that in the opening to this section I did not talk about making a journey to 'find' your power animal, but to 'recover' it. This was quite deliberate.

Many cultures believe that we are born with at least one spirit protector in the form of a power animal who is our ally and guardian throughout life, and whose role is to protect our soul – or souls, since many societies believe that we are born with a number of souls, not just one.

In Siberia and Mongolia it is believed that all people have at least three souls – the 'Suld', which survives us to reside in nature after death (like the soul-essence of Harry Joy in the Peter Carey novel, *Bliss*, which, upon death, became the sentient rings of age within the trunk of a forest tree); and the 'Ami' and the 'Suns' souls, which reincarnate in different forms.

Some groups, such as the Samoyed, believe there are more – four in women, five in men, two in animals (the Ami and the Suns). All souls reside in the field of energy which envelops the body, but the most important is the Suld – if this one leaves, death will inevitably follow, while the others may leave our bodies for brief periods without harm.

For the Toltecs, that group of Aztec descendants who lived in Central Mexico between the tenth and twelfth centuries AD, everyone was considered to be born with a tonal soul, which provides the energy we need to create the person we will become in life.

To become a 'person of knowledge', however, we must also find our second soul, which may take the form of a power animal or ally. This is our nagual self.

From our perspective outside of Bohm's aquarium, the tonal represents all that we can know, the aspects of our 'normal' existence which have their own solid structure and order, whether these are 'rational' and incorporated into the mainstream linear model, or more 'esoteric'. If it is a world which can be known, understood and spoken of, it exists on the island of the tonal.

The nagual is all that we can never know and which must remain nameless. What we can do is to bring this energy, this second soul, back to ourselves and to feel its power, even though we may never be able to explain it or its presence and effect to others or, indeed, to ourselves. 'For he who has had the experience, no words are necessary,' said the ethnobotanist Richard Alpert, describing his own explorations of this world. 'For he who has not, no words are possible.'

When we meet our allies in the otherworld, they, too, are part of the nagual, the nameless energy of the universe. But when we recover our power by adopting the animal we find there – an expression of this great nagual energy in tangible form – and bring it back to ordinary reality, then we make it part of ourselves. The nagual can then enter the tonal of our lives in ordinary reality to expand our consciousness and offer us a deeper experience of the world.

This is the modern world . . .

In shamanic and many pre-industrial societies, the link with our power animals is respected and treasured as a source of real energetic power, companionship and protection for the soul. But in industrial, scientific, linear societies the link to the nagual through our guardian animal(s) may grow faint as we learn not to acknowledge the spirit world, though it is stronger in children and many are drawn to animals as pets or have imaginary animals to play with. Even the toys we give young children – the bears and rabbits they cuddle, the fish and the frogs that share their bath times – reflect unconsciously the affinity we have with animals when we are young.

The modern world is almost entirely focused on the tonal. We learn from an early age to ignore the dark abyss of the nagual, not to pay attention to things we can't understand, or to mess with powers beyond our comprehension. We learn to appreciate that there is something to be feared from the nagual or a sense of futility about exploring an energy which can never be fully explained, categorized or communicated.

'Modern man has left the realm of the unknown and the mysterious and has settled for the realm of the functional. He has turned his back to the world of the foreboding and the exulting and has welcomed the world of boredom,' said don Juan[57] – the world of Hollywood, Wall Street and Lincoln's Inn.

Life in the modern world has demanded that we give up the sacred and the esoteric, the spiritual and the unconscious in favour of a more deterministic, science- and economics-led worldview, which defines our existence in terms of 'careers' and 'duties', 'obligations', and prescribed beliefs. Unlike the medicine men and tribal holy men who may be revered as powerful beyond measure, our Western religious 'leaders' (if they take their role seriously – or are taken seriously – at all) have handed us a spiritually bankrupt world where we are all drowning in a dark sea of chaos beneath the whim of an abstract and humourless god who has his own, hidden, agenda. Only by prayer and supplication to gods and gurus, politicians and priests, and a cruel cosmic judge and jury can we ever hope to sidestep what we know we have coming to us (and probably fully deserve).

By entering the world of the shaman, however, you reclaim your right and power to define yourself, to access a deeper, freer self, and to embrace the sacred as your god-given right. This is a fundamentally different view of reality and, while it is new, creative and empowering, it is 'unorthodox' and can sometimes be unnerving until you are familiar with this new ground.

That is one of the reasons why it is important to recover your ally, who will give you back your sense of power and lay the ground for you to explore this new world.

As you prepare to take this journey, you will no doubt be wondering what exactly is an ally and what should you look for or expect to find?

The nature of the ally

Shamans can sometimes sound cryptic about this, but they are really expressing the difficulty of accurately describing the exact nature of this entity and finding the words to convey the deeply moving and empowering experience of encountering the vast potential of the hologram, embodied in the form of a single being which offers itself to us as a source of guidance, support and unconditional love.

'The only way to know what an ally is, is by experiencing it,' said don Juan.[58] 'An ally is perceived in many degrees. Each of those perceptions is stored in one's body. The sum of those pieces is the ally . . . The way one understands the ally is a personal matter.'

Those who meet their allies do feel it personally and, for many, it is a very emotional moment and one which is completely relevant and appropriate to their lives. Think back to my soul retrieval client, Fiona, whose ally was a 'small, warm creature'. This entity was in dramatic contrast to the linear hardness of her life and also helped her willingly during her journey when she asked for this support, something she had never before felt able to do. Or Isobelle, who was surprised to find an ally in Rabbit but soon saw how necessary he was for the challenge which then faced her.

Melanie came to see me for healing recently and, during her journey, met a very powerful spirit ally which took the form of Panther. She phoned me a few days later to say that everything had changed for her. During the intervening period she had met her mother, a rather domineering woman, for lunch. Her mother's first words had been 'There's something different about you – is it your hair?' 'No,' said Melanie, 'it's my Panther!'

Melanie had been dreading this meeting as she had always

felt very intimidated by her mother. Now she was able to take her mother's comments lightly and at the end of the lunch, they were both laughing together. 'She looked at me very quizzically as she left,' said Melanie, 'as if she wasn't sure I was the same daughter, and I really felt a new respect growing between us. Something had changed in our relationship.'

Having broken through the barrier of her mother's attitude, based on previous interactions and expectations, Melanie felt better able to make changes in her wider life and was standing up for herself at work against her female boss who, she realized, had always reminded her a little of her mother, and among her friends who, she said, 'never really took me seriously before'. The ripples of her new power were spreading throughout the whole pond.

You will also experience your ally and feel its presence on your journey and then in your life, and will be able to call upon the strength, resourcefulness and other qualities of your power animal in your daily affairs. By modelling your behaviour on that of your power animal – a technique shamans know as shapeshifting – you will be able to act with greater courage, or warmth, or vitality, according to your own needs.

The way in which you encounter your power animal during your journey will be the one most appropriate for you in terms of your own current needs, your personal beliefs, and the culture you belong to.

In the Western world people may see their allies as angels or fabulous creatures – dragons and centaurs, winged horses and unicorns – especially if they are taking an upper world journey, where this mythology is encountered more frequently. In the middle world, they may encounter the essence of a great spiritual leader who may be living – like the Dalai Lama – or dead – like Gandhi. Most often, in the lower world, the ally is experienced as an animal, typically a wild animal such as a lion, a wolf, an eagle, a bear or, indeed, a panther or a rabbit.

They are *wild* animals because they are expressions of power – not because they are in any way dangerous to you (though they can be fierce protectors *of* you). Shamanic tradition maintains that domesticated animals have given away their power and become subservient to humanity and weakened power is not what you want. So, naturally – without your having to 'create' or 'imagine' an appropriate animal – the ally that comes to you will be wild and untamed but very appropriate for *you*. It need not be a 'big' animal, since the *form* the energy takes is not the energy itself. Although many people new to the shamanic journey do tend to be met by Wolf, Eagle, Bear, Tiger or other obviously powerful creatures, in reality an ant is as powerful as an elephant – and, of course, one of the strongest entities we are aware of in the world today – the virus – is also the smallest.

The ally is an *expression* of power and, in reality, has no tangible form, just as electricity has no shape or physical structure, though we would not deny its existence or its power. That is why allies can appear in many different forms, just as the appearance of electricity may be moving pictures on TV, sound waves from a radio or heat from a fire.

Given that your ally is there to help you, however, it will assume a recognizable form so that you are aware of its presence and can make contact. Most will appear in an animal form that has some meaning or emotional value for you. An animal which is your ally will never appear threatening to you and will never harm you. Its job is to protect you, including taking direct physical intervention on your behalf if necessary.

Recovering your ally

To take this journey to recover your power animal, begin in the lower world trance position, taking the time you need to relax and get comfortable. Breathe deeply into your abdomen, become aware of your breath and let it 'breathe you'.

Phrase your intention, saying out loud if you wish, 'I am taking a journey to the shamanic lower world to recover my power animal and to understand how it can help me.' Press the 'Play' button now to activate your drumming tape or, if you have someone drumming for you, ask them to begin by giving a pre-arranged signal, such as lifting a finger.

Move into your entrance to the lower world as before and find yourself in the tunnel now familiar to you, then move towards the lower world and enter it through the same gateway you used on your first journey. The landmarks and features of this landscape are now recognizable to you, and you will often also remember things about this environment which your conscious mind has forgotten since your last journey. Do not be surprised by this. Remain open to receiving a power animal and aware of any that move towards you.

You may see many animals on any of the journeys you undertake, so how do you know that this particular one is your power animal? The important thing is that the animal will present itself to you four times in different aspects or from different angles, just so there is no confusion. At this point, for certainty, you can also ask the animal if it is for you.

My own experience is that you will also intuitively 'know' that you have met your power animal and there will be a sense of bonding between you. Sometimes this bond will tie into early childhood memories – perhaps the animal has the same look about it, a similar personality or shares features with an animal you knew as a child or were attracted to in pictures or zoos.

Some creatures are to be treated with caution. An animal which bares its teeth at you is probably to be avoided. Michael Harner also recommends staying clear of swarming insects and snakes as, traditionally, they are often associated with or allied to illness. Others suggest that spiders are to be avoided as well as fish whose teeth are visible. Again, take this information on board but, ultimately, this is your world, so also be guided by your own sense of what is right.

When you are sure that you have identified the right power animal for you, begin to engage in dialogue with it. In particular, it will need to know about you – who you are, what your intentions are, what you want to achieve in your life and how it can help. Don't worry about using normal language and going through the laborious process of speaking aloud everything you think and feel – you are now a part of the infinite and your power animal will understand you as soon as you give thought to your ideas.

You also need to know something about your power animal. Ask it about its history before this meeting, whether it has helped others before you. Many of my clients, on first meeting their power animal, report that it has previously worked with others – which is perhaps not surprising as a power animal is an archetypal expression of *all* animals within its genus and a gateway to the entire natural world more generally. Because we are now a part of this world, it is entirely likely that this energy source has also been accessed by others before you; indeed, many of the great spiritual and social leaders of our time have spoken freely about their immersion in this pool of wisdom, which they have used to guide their actions in the world.

Ask how your power animal feels it can best help you now, its strengths and its willingness to undertake certain ventures or exercises. What is the *essence* of your power animal and how will you benefit mutually from your association?

Now, call your animal to you and hold it to your chest. It will come willingly. You will now bring it back with you to ordinary reality. Remember, what is real in the otherworld becomes energy when brought back to ordinary reality, so although you are holding a real puma or lynx or buffalo in your arms now, do not expect to come back to consciousness and find a lynx or a snow leopard running round your lounge.

Do not try to bring back more than one animal at a time, even if more than one present themselves to you. Adopt the animal you feel closest to and whose particular energy represents the power you need in your life now.

Holding the animal to you, when the call-back sounds or when you are ready to do so, retrace your steps to the entrance point to this world and go back through the tunnel to your starting point, then come back to ordinary reality.

A power animal recovery is often conducted by a shaman for his client and, once you are comfortable with this practice, you may also wish to journey for someone else to help them recover their ally. In that situation, when you are fully back in ordinary consciousness you should use your mouth to blow the energy of the power animal into your client, at the solar plexus and the fontanelle, in the same way as in soul retrieval. Someone journeying on your behalf will do the same for you.

On this journey, however, you are alone, so you will now perform this operation for yourself. Your intention must be to take the *energy* of this power animal into you, to accept it, so first breathe it into your energy body *with intention*, while visualizing the power as it enters you. Spend a few moments in silence, appreciating this new energy and feeling any changes in your body. Then, as an additional measure, breathe out into your cupped hands and hold them against you, with one hand at your solar plexus and the other at your fontanelle. Visualize the energy which flows across them, coursing through your body which now acts as a bridge between your hands. Hold this position for a count of four relaxed deep breaths in and out.

Spend a few moments reflecting on this journey and, as before, write down or paint your impressions.

It is an excellent idea to begin collecting images and artefacts of your power animal now that it is part of you, so you have a visible reminder and something tangible to focus upon. You may also find that these things start coming into your life or are given to you anyway. When I first brought back Wolf, I was given all sorts of pictures of wolves within weeks, and this is continuing. A friend recently returned from Canada and brought back a statue of a wolf for me, without having any idea that this is one of my animal allies.

Find out more about your power animal too. Read a few books on it, its habits and symbolism. After all, you're going to be spending a lot of time together from now on.

Feeling powerful

Many people feel different, more energetic and balanced almost immediately after they have recovered their power animal and, like Melanie and Fiona, experience its presence *practically* in their lives. Enjoy this sensation of your ally working for you in this way, your power flowing freely once again, but also remember that this is a partnership, a *two-way* process.

A power animal agrees to enter your energy body not only to help you, although that is a primary function, but because it also wishes to experience reality in material form. This is a quid pro quo arrangement. By making regular contact with it, you are allowing your ally access to your reality too and enabling it to learn more about you and your world so it can be of even more appropriate help to you.

Some people 'dance' their power animal, which means setting time aside to shapeshift into their animal, to 'become' it and allow it to move through them, using their body to express itself. There is nothing to worry about in this if you choose to try shapeshifting in this way for yourself – you do not *lose* control over yourself during this process; instead, you *relax* control in order to create a deeper bond between you both.

Your power animal can be consulted in order to obtain advice at any time by journeying to the lower world in the normal way and posing your question, or by using the more instant 'check-in' method of Imagework which we will look at in the next chapter.

Your ally will also communicate with you pro-actively from time to time. The shamanic 'Big Dream' is a case in point.

Shamans make a distinction between normal and 'Big' dreams, the latter being extremely vivid and often recurring. For shamans, these are not ordinary dreams or 'symbolic' messages, but direct communications from your power animal of a real future event which will take place. They should therefore be taken seriously and acted upon immediately.

If you have a 'Big Dream' that you are in an accident, for example, this is not a time for analysis or dream interpretations, but for immediate action in ordinary reality. In this case, you would act out the details of the dream exactly, to the point of the accident, including the event itself, in a safe, calm and controlled manner. In this way, you disperse the energy of the event before it takes place, a little like a vaccination, or the homoeopathic practice of deliberately ingesting a tiny quantity of the substance which is causing the disorder, so the body can build an immunity to it.

Serge King makes a similar observation from the shamanic traditions of Hawaii, when he talks about re-enacting an event from ordinary reality in order to change its negative effect for a more positive outcome.[59] Should you accidentally cut yourself, using King's method you would replay the event, drawing the knife across the wound again – but safely and above the wound itself so that it does not touch you – in order to recreate the event with a different result, where the skin is not cut. In this way, you change the energetic effect of the event and therefore also change things in ordinary reality.

In King's experience, wounds heal faster and less painfully when this is done as the flow of energy to the event itself is altered. A friend of mine who stayed with me recently to help with a workshop I was running, actually did cut herself while chopping vegetables in the kitchen one day. She used King's technique, running the knife across her hand four times above the wound before showing me that the blood flow had been entirely stopped. In the morning, there was no visible wound at all.

When your ally brings you news of future troubles through the agency of the 'Big' dream, use this technique to disempower the coming event. From what I have seen, it works.

Should you ever feel 'dis-spirited' or 'run down', this can be a sign that your ally has left you, as not many power animals will stay with you for ever. Like all of us, they need to move on from time to time. At this point, you will need to take another journey to find and recover your original power animal or to find another to replace it as the events of your life also change.

JOURNEY 4: RECOVERING POWER OBJECTS FROM THE UPPER WORLD

Your power animal is not the only ally you have in the other-world. You also have access to tools, items, objects and symbols which can help you.

If you have health problems, for example, imagine how helpful it could be to have the wisdom of the world's greatest doctor on your side. If you need to get directly to a goal in the otherworld, imagine how useful it would be to have an accurate map or a device which allows you to travel quickly from one point to another, like an instant transporter. What these translate to in ordinary reality are devices which allow you to cut right to the heart of the issue no matter what confronts you, and to find the most appropriate and effective problem-solving solution without any distraction or detours. Or, to put it another way, these objects are symbolic representations of your inner power and allow you to have faith in your own abilities by focusing your power in specific areas.

Your subconscious mind and your allies both naturally know the areas where you need most support and will ensure you find the tools most useful to you. Since these are the tools of most help to you right now, by their very nature they also provide insights into your current life needs.

Sheila was given a shield, for example, which she was told could be used to deflect negative energies. As well as being a useful tool in its own right, the appearance of such a shield provided an insight for Sheila into the way her own life was operating, which she would not otherwise have been aware of at a conscious level.

Sheila is a social worker and exposed to a lot of negative

forces in her job. She also works long hours, which leads to some difficulties with her partner. A shield is exactly what she does need, in fact, in order to protect herself from the negativity she encounters each day. The appearance of the shield brought this information to the fore and allowed Sheila to realize the effect that these pressures were having on her. She was then able to make *conscious* decisions about her future.

In one of my own journeys to recover power objects, I was shown to the following items:

- **A globe** – This is both a map in case I am ever lost, and a transporter of sorts. Made of silver, it is round like an orange, and segmented in the same way. I can look at the surface of the globe to see where I am and locate where I need to go and then lift out the appropriate segment, which has the effect of instantly taking me to that place, even if I don't consciously know the way.

- **A tattoo** – This is a tattoo of the sun which was drawn onto my chest during the journey. It is a powerhouse of energy for me which I can call upon as I need during difficult journeys. I can also donate its energy to those I meet while journeying. I have done so for clients during soul retrievals, for example, and in psychopomp work, where lost souls have used it as a boost to help them move through the barrier between life and death and on into the process.

- **A medicine bag** – To carry new items and knowledge found on exploratory journeys.

- **A mask** – This is a great gift. Each of us in life and our interactions with others plays various roles. By wearing this mask, I am able to become an instant expert in whatever subject I need to know about at that time. Sometimes, depending on the journey, I need to be the world's greatest healer, or negotiator, or diplomat or mountain climber. I simply wear the mask and I have the appropriate skills.

- **A spirit-dagger** – To help me cut through resistance and opposition, most frequently in the form of fears or self-limitations which act as blocks to a person undergoing soul retrieval, which I often see as strands of energy connecting my client with another person, event or situation, long past its usefulness for them. At these times, I use this dagger to cut right through these ties. Since I have now made a *physical* representation of this power object, I sometimes also give it to my clients to hold and to use during their own healing journeys.

Dianne used the spirit-dagger in exactly this way during a journey to free herself from the bonds of an old, abusive relationship. Having started the journey, she immediately encountered resistance, and began coughing and labouring for breath. I stopped the drum and we spoke of her fears. Then, when she was ready to do so, she took the spirit-dagger from me and entered the otherworld again, this time cutting through the ties between herself and the people who were still a source of fear and control.

Dianne attended one of my workshops a few months later. During lunchtime, she had an unexpected physical confrontation with one of these people. Driving away from the centre, she almost collided with a car coming from the opposite direction and, when she looked, saw that it was being driven by one of her old adversaries.

'I didn't feel at all scared though any more,' she said. 'In fact, this time, the person in the other car looked scared when she saw me and drove away quickly after she recognized me.'

Your own power objects will undoubtedly be different from mine and have their own meanings and associations for you.

Retrieving your power objects

This journey can be taken to the lower or upper world, depending on the type of power objects you need right now or deliberately set out in search of. In the lower world you will tend to find 'real', tangible objects which have a solid counterpart in ordinary reality, while in the upper world you are more likely to be given symbols, rituals, energy forms or, perhaps, power songs.

On this journey, we will visit the upper world to ask for an empowerment ritual or symbol.

Lie down and relax in the way you are now used to and phrase your intention – 'I am taking this upper world journey for a ritual or symbol of empowerment and to understand how it can help me in my practical, daily life' – then enter the upper world via the route you now know. This is also an excellent opportunity for you to make contact again with your power animal and ask to be shown the way to the items you need to find.

When you identify or are shown items or symbols which are for you, embrace them without question and keep them with you. If you should be shown a ritual, ensure that you fully understand all of the instructions before you return. Thank your power animals and allies for helping you to find these things.

When it is time, retrace your steps to ordinary reality and as you reflect on this journey and record your impressions, also make a note of what these power objects mean to you and how you might use them now and in future.

If you have been shown a symbol, it is a good idea to make it, paint a picture of it or represent it in some other way, and then to keep it with you. If you are given an object, make every effort to find its counterpart in ordinary reality and, if you cannot, then create it for yourself.

I was once shown a ritual which promised a solution to an ongoing problem I had faced for a few months. The ritual had to be performed at the time of the next full moon and in very specific circumstances. Inevitably, I put off doing it and, three months later, the ritual had still not been performed and my problem was, if anything, worse. So, finally, moaning and cursing on the night of the next full moon, I carried a bowl of water out into the garden, blessed it in the way I had been shown and completed the ceremony as per my instructions – all without really putting much effort into what I saw as a bit of a chore.

My lack of effort didn't seem to matter, however. The next day my problem was resolved completely and I just wished I'd completed the ritual three months earlier when spirit had asked me to.

FACT, FAITH OR FICTION?

It can sometimes take a while to trust the spirits of the other-world, to believe that they are real, that our experiences are valid, and that returned energy is flowing within us. Even accomplished journeyers can sometimes have doubts. Many times, I have asked my spirits for proof of the reality of their existence and of the otherworld, appealing to them to show me tangible, incontrovertible evidence.

After doing so on one occasion I was, a few days later, taught a Song for Reclaiming Power during an otherworld journey. Many people are taught quite beautiful songs of healing and power by spirit. Mine, however, somewhat disappointingly, featured a monotonous repetition of the word 'Weya'.

Often these songs are in spirit language rather than recognizable words from ordinary reality – as this one seemed to be – so if I write it down for you now it looks quite meaningless:

> *Weya, Weya, Weya*
> *Weya, Weya, Weya.*
> *Wey-A-Hey-O*
> *A-Wey-A-Hey-O*
> *Weya, Weya, Weya*
> *Weya, Weya, Weya.*

A few nights after I received this song, I attended a lecture at Alternatives in London, given by Jonathan Horwitz of the Scandinavian Center for Shamanic Studies. Part of his presentation was about spirit songs and we all sang two or three of the songs he had been taught by his own spirits. As I was leaving, I picked up a copy of one of Jonathan's articles where he described attending the Pomo Acorn Festival, a traditional ceremony in California.[60]

During the proceedings at the festival, they began a dance and Jonathan was taught a new spirit song, a power song. 'It was very peaceful,' he said, 'yet something was happening, something unseen . . . *Weya,* power, was filling the room.'

My power song – comprised of a single 'meaningless repetitive' word – Weya – turns out to be *the* word for power!

One other thing. The spirit animal that guided me on the journey to recover this Power Song was Wolf. *Wa Ya*, I subsequently discovered, is Cherokee for Wolf.

I had asked the spirits for proof, for a 'power song' – and they gave me exactly that!

Mambo Racine, who taught me her ways of Vodou and oversaw my initiation into the priesthood of Haitian Vodou, has many stories to tell of spirits entering her life, which, for her, more than prove their existence. One of my favourites takes place on the day after she had made a sacred feast for the ancestors. In Haiti, the spirits are fed regularly as a matter of respect and, as part of the energetic exchange between us all, to ensure that we give back to them some of the gifts they willingly bring into our lives. In this ritual, plates of food are left out for the spirits, and each plate has a candle on its centre so that the rising heat of the flame can carry the energy of the food to the ancestors.

Having offered the feast in the ritual space of her altar, Mambo Racine retired to bed. 'In the morning,' she said, 'I noticed that every candle was burned to absolute nothingness – not a drip of wax or a fragment of wick remained in any of the food dishes. "Gosh", I thought, "those ancestors must really have been hungry." '

As I said, in Vodou, the relationship with spirit is based on exchange so, later that day, Mambo Racine began to wonder how many spirits had enjoyed the feast she offered and which of her ancestors would now be available to help her in her own life.

'It was a beautiful spring day and I was walking alone on a country road,' she said. Just then, 'a yellow Volkswagen Beetle came along and honked its horn. I thought that the person must be lost and wanting directions but as I looked, there was no driver in the car. Instinctively, I noted the licence plate. It was 125 LOA.'

The spirits, in Vodou, are known as the *loa*. 125 of them, it seems, were now on her side.

Another of her stories, which she tells with great humour, suggests that not only do the spirits exist, they have quite a different personality from the human being they are called upon to interact with. If the spirits did not exist as quite separate entities from ourselves, but were just an expression of our own inner mind, we might expect their personalities to reflect our own, their likes and dislikes to be similar to ours. But, according to Mambo Racine, this is certainly not the case.

In shamanism, we journey to meet our spirits in their world; in Vodou, we call the spirits into ours and they meet us here by taking possession of the person who has asked for their help and who now becomes the 'horse' which they 'ride' during the possession trance.

'I have a Native American personal *loa*, the spirit of a woman who was responsible for a good deal of land situated around Mount Toby in central Massachusetts,' says Mambo Racine. 'One day, in downtown Port-au-Prince, I found a pair of beautiful *tcha-tchas* (maracas) decorated with faces – eyes, nose, mouth, very realistic, and in the preferred colours of this *loa*. I brought them for her, took them home, and cleaned them.'

Mambo Racine then invited her Native American spirit to possess her so that the gift she had bought for this *loa* could be presented to her. Since Mambo Racine's body was occupied by the spirit at the time, she asked a friend to hand the *tcha-tchas* to the *loa* which was now in control of her mind and body.

'When the possession was over, I asked my friend, "so was La Reinne Indienne happy with her present?"

'My friend just laughed. "La Reinne," she reported, "said 'Those things are hideously ugly and I forbid my horse to keep them in the house'." ' Certainly, the tastes of this particular spirit were very different from the Mambo's own.

Perhaps these stories do not offer you the degree of evidence that *you* require, and I can only advise that you must seek your own proof. It is my experience that spirits do not mind working with us on this from time to time – though they will not want to be constantly questioned and challenged.

I offer the following anecdotal evidence which may also help you decide whether the experience of the spirit world is a real one. The first is a story from my own life.

I am at a workshop in shamanic healing and soul retrieval, working with a new partner for the first time. I know hardly anything about her and she knows little about me. Our teacher has been explicit in his instructions not to talk to each other before this exercise, simply to take a journey for our partner to recover soul parts that they have lost and to bring them back to that person. Only then are we allowed to discuss what they mean – if anything – to the person we are working with.

My partner is taking this journey for me. She will enter the shamanic otherworld and find a part of me which has splintered off. She will then bring it back so that I can re-integrate it and become more whole. The drumming begins and she enters the shamanic world. She will be gone about 20 minutes. My instructions are to do nothing. So, for 20 minutes, I lie next to her and allow my mind to drift.

About 15 minutes into the journey, I am in fantasy land, drifting in daydreams, when I catch myself doing it and decide that I must come back to a shamanic state of consciousness, that, even though I do not have to do any-

thing as part of this journey, it is good practice for me to maintain a sense of shamanic awareness.

As I do so, I become aware of something, some blurred image or energy shooting into my area of vision from the left. I focus on it to see what it is.

When I look down, there, lying on my chest is a small baby with dark hair, wrapped tightly in a blanket or shawl, staring up at me.

I glance at my partner. She is kneeling now; she has a soul part for me. I have no idea what. She blows the soul part into my heart and then into the top of my head, at the fontanelle. Then we lie together, holding each other until the drumming ends.

A murmur, the sounds of laughter, some tears, excited discussion, fill the room as we exchange our experiences and discuss the implications of what we have learned.

'I saw you as a baby struggling to be born,' says my partner. 'I was trying to help you to live, but then I got completely lost and I couldn't decide if I was just imagining things. So I asked for help from the spirits and a man appeared – I want to say your father but I don't know if he is still alive – and he handed me a baby. That's what I blew into you.'

The baby she described was dark-haired, wrapped tightly in what she called 'swaddling clothes' so that its movement was restricted, exactly as I had seen it before it was blown into me.

Of all the images she could have chosen, of all the periods of my life she could have entered, all the thousands of 20-minute episodes that have passed in my life, she had 'happened' to choose the same image I had seen even before it was blown into me.

And what she could never have known, because we had not discussed it, is that when I was born, the umbilical cord was wrapped tightly around my neck and for 20 minutes I was close to death – a traumatic event indeed.

Nor could she have known that my father never wanted a

child before I was born. Indeed, my mother and father had been close to separation so my mother had engineered a pregnancy to make my father stay. This was never a big secret in my family. I seem to remember hearing this story from the moment I was old enough to understand what it meant.

My father had stayed, reluctantly, and our relationship had never been truly nurturing, based more on mutual acceptance than on love. And I remembered truly terrible times of familial war from my 16th birthday onwards, a time of conflict we had never truly recovered from. So, for my father to 'rescue' me, to enable my birth, had profound implications for my feelings of acceptance and being wanted in the world.

My father died sixteen years to the day of this workshop.

Other people who are used to journeying report similar experiences which provide proof for them of the existence of this other world. Patricia, a shamanic practitioner from Louisiana, tells of an experience from her childhood which finally helped her come to terms with the strange synchronicities which seemed constantly to be calling her:

I had begun to question my experiences and my sanity. I was seriously considering going to a psychiatrist and telling him everything. I was really confused and thought that I had to be just having bad dreams or bad food . . . something of that nature. It wasn't real, couldn't be real.

On Thursday, I just snapped under the pressure and told the universe out loud that I didn't know where the line was any more between reality and dreams, and if they wanted me to continue, I had to have some proof that it wasn't all just a really screwed up painful dream. I demanded something I could hold in my hands and KNOW without a shadow of a doubt that what they were teaching me was real and not just a figment of my imagination.

I had had dreams of a now-destroyed staff that my uncle had carved. Friday went by and nothing. I went to my hometown on Saturday and ended up at my ex-stepdad's

*house, not knowing why. We sat and we talked and some-
thing tapped me on the shoulder and said 'Go to the toy shed
... your proof is waiting.' I walked outside and had a look
around in the shed and there was the staff my uncle had
carved for me when I was seven years old, right where I left
it in the dream.*

*What was stranger was that it was intact. It had broken in
my brother's hands when he tried to claim it was his and take
it from me shortly after my uncle died, and my mother had
taken it to the dump and put it through the shredder. But it
was intact, you couldn't see the break marks or scars or anything. It was perfect. That's good enough proof for me.*

Sometimes I wonder if the spirits doubt our existence as
much as we sometimes doubt theirs.

'DARE TO TAKE A CHANCE'

Dr Alberto Villoldo is an accomplished psychologist and an
authority on Latin American shamanic practices, who has
written extensively about the extraordinary phenomena he
has personally witnessed. He, too, has had his moments of
doubt.

Villoldo is the author of *Dance of the Four Winds: A
Shaman's Journey into the Amazon*, director of the Four
Winds Foundation for shamanism in California, and an
adjunct professor in the Department of Interdisciplinary
Studies at San Francisco State University.

In conversation with clinical psychologist, Dr Jeffrey
Mishlove, on the excellent American television series,
Thinking Allowed, Villoldo agreed that 'as one gets into the
depths of shamanism, you are dealing with something which
is virtually incomprehensible from our normal Western
worldview – one needs to enter not only another reality, but
another mythology.'[61]

'What took me to shamanism,' said Villoldo, 'was the

study of the human brain. No matter how you slice or dice the human brain or put it under the microscope, you cannot find "mind". It's impossible to find it . . . that's what took me to the Amazon and the jungles of South America . . . to work with men and women who had mastered the techniques for working with mind to its fullest, and healing and achieving extraordinary capabilities, and phenomena that to us are considered impossible.'

When we explore the achievements and traditions of shamanism, he says, we must avoid looking at them 'through the lenses of our culture'. Instead, we must 'step into a reality where anything is possible and everything is possible'.

The first step is to escape the 'cultural trance' we have been educated into, which limits the capabilities of the mind and disconnects us from true power, for 'you cannot become a caretaker of the Earth until you are able to muster personal power . . . until you can do that everything else is theory'.

By recovering and exercising this power, the shamanic practitioner is capable of events which, says Mishlove, 'border on, or might be considered, miraculous'.

And, indeed, Villoldo has been in many 'miraculous' situations where, naturally enough, he has asked himself the same question as us – are these things 'real' or are they 'imaginary'? He tells of an experience outside Machu Picchu which finally answered this question for him.

There's a death stone outside the city, shaped like a canoe, pointing to the west, that the shamans would come and lie on, and would actually separate their physical bodies from their energy bodies. I always thought this was a very nice myth . . . something to tell my children.

I lay down on the stone and this old, old medicine man I was with looked at me and he said, 'Alberto, belief is not something that is based on proof, like your sciences. It is something that you invest. However much of yourself you invest in the ceremony is what you're going to receive. Don't be an observer; participate. Dare to take a chance.'

I said, 'OK, I'll give it a shot.' I lay down on the stone, and he began to put his hands over each of my chakras, the seven energy centres in my body, and to chant into them, and then took both of his hands over my body and just made this throwing motion. I didn't feel anything.

At a certain point I feel that he's done. I get up, and walk back to take my place in the circle with the other people there, and I see that everybody in the circle is still looking at the stone, so I turn around and I look back, and there's my physical body lying there, and there's this medicine man turned towards me and he's saying, 'Come on back here; get back in there . . .'

And that was how the experience manifested for me – not this archetypal mythical journey but what, from my own cultural perspective, was a separation of my energy essence from this material covering.

If you really experience disengaging from the physical and being conscious in that state, then everything else is just information, it's not knowledge.

SHAMANIC CONSCIOUSNESS AND PLANETARY EVOLUTION

Intention and integrity are crucial when we journey, as we discussed earlier. It is a point which Villoldo echoes.

'Working with this type of energy might be like working with electricity. It's indifferent to our sense of ethics.' The energy a shaman uses to cure a person's illness is the same energy which can be used to kill him, just as electricity can be used to light and heat a village in the depths of winter, or to power an electric chair. It is the shaman's *intention* in using this power – for good or ill – which is important.

Hence the need, when we journey, to be highly focused on our goal and our intent. Intention – Attention – Acceptance – Reflection.

By learning the techniques of journeying, we become part

of a very special destiny, a noble tradition spanning thousands of years and a power for the creation of a new evolutionary future. Indeed, shamanic consciousness, according to Villoldo, *is* the future for the evolution of humanity.

Shamans have developed techniques for not only looking through this crack between the worlds, looking at the mechanisms of destiny, but in the process of looking at them – as quantum physics tells us – they actually begin to influence them. They begin to influence the course of destiny.

And today, we're in extraordinary need of visionaries, individuals who can envision a possible future – not the probable future of pollution and nuclear holocaust, but what's possible for us . . . we have created a world that is no longer enchanted. I think that one of the tasks that we have today is to re-enchant the world.

The human brain has evolved to a place where we no longer need to be adrift in the sea of superstition that our ancestors were . . . we're now in the position to recognize the magic of the planet that we live in, and of our own lives.

All it takes to make a difference is to risk believing, to *just suppose* that it *could* be possible – and to act *as if* it is. To dare to take a chance.

If we do so, the universe itself responds.

EXPLORATIONS – DEVELOPING INTENTION AND AWARENESS

1. The walk of *intention*
The power of intention for the shamanic journey – its focus and purpose and the will to see it through – is vital to success. Every shamanic tradition stresses this above almost everything else.

There are many walks of *attention* in shamanism (largely these come from the modern Toltec tradition and stem from the work of Castaneda – see *The Teachings of Don Carlos*, by Victor Sanchez, for example).[62] There are no walks of *intention* – and yet, this is the key thing to perfect.

The following exercise addresses this. It is quite a wide-ranging exercise and can be used in many ways. Firstly, it is an adjunct, in ordinary reality, to the journeying exercise we have undertaken, where we located a power object in the otherworld. Secondly, a stone is suggested as one of the power objects we look for in this exercise, so this approach can be used when you search for a rock for the divination work referred to in the last chapter. Thirdly, what follows *is* a walk of attention – but, more importantly, it is also an exercise in *intention*. How you choose to do the exercise – in which of the four ways I have suggested it might be used – is also, of course, an exercise in itself in your use of intention since you must remain entirely focused on this single purpose and not mentally skip between all four.

The Walk of Intention is one of my daughter's favourite exercises – she uses it sometimes to find our car when I forget where I have parked it!

Since all things are alive, all things equal and all things connected, it is quite possible to find allies in all realities – ordinary reality as well as the otherworld. The key thing is your intention to do so.

Find a place in the countryside where you are comfortable to begin and allow yourself to enter a light trance state (it is fine to use your drumming tape, but remain standing as you do so), then open your eyes – slightly, rather than fully, so your gaze is somewhat blurred.

State your intention clearly three or four times: 'To find a power object and ally in ordinary reality, willing to support me in my shamanic work.' Raise your arms to shoulder level, bent at the elbow with palms facing forward. Keep your eyes slightly open.

Begin to walk, focusing on the sensation of energy in your hands, which may feel like heat or tingling. Let yourself be guided left or right according to the sensation in each hand. When you feel it is right to do so, stop and look around, letting your eyes 'float' unfocused across the landscape immediately before you. You are intending to be 'drawn' to (rather than actively searching for) an object of some kind, which may be a stone, a feather, a piece of wood, or some other object which now presents itself and is meaningful to you. When you find it, ask its permission and, if it is OK to do so, pick it up and take it back with you.

'The Q'ero teach that there are two realities – the panya and the yoqe,' says Q'ero shaman-priest, Americo Yabar. 'Panya is everything you might associate with the ordinary world, the surface reality we call the physical. Yoqe is all that we associate with the non-ordinary world, what some call the "invisible reality". Yoqe connects us with the mystery, the enigma of the unfolding of the unknown energies which are present in all beings, in all things, people, animals, plants, the dirt under our feet, the stones.'

The access to yoqe or, for that matter, to panya, is through intention.

If you wish to, repeat this exercise – with all due precautions to ensure personal safety – in the town or city, again with the intention of finding a helpful power object or ally. What do you notice about the different energies of the country and the city?

Each power object you find is a battery of energetic potentials connected with the place in which you find it. What energetic difference do you notice between the stones and other objects you find in the town and in the countryside?

2. Zanshin – uncommon awareness

Attention within the shamanic journey is also important so that the full detail of the intense information which floods and can overwhelm the mind is not missed. We are not used to paying attention at closely focused levels since we have been educated to operate within the trance state of normal, habitual acceptance of social reality.

We can train the mind to pay greater attention to the things we most want and need to be aware of. The Ninja, the spiritual warriors of Japan, train their children from their earliest years in the Ways of the Warrior and have many exercises and games for teaching greater awareness, *zanshin*. Here is one such exercise adapted for the modern world.

The next time you are walking down a normal city street, be aware of the sounds around and behind you. Listen, for example, for the sound of footsteps behind you. How close is the person behind? Do their footsteps tell you it is a man or a woman? What shoes are they wearing? And, from knowing this, what else are they wearing to match this footwear? What else can you 'imagine' or sense about this person? Who are they? What do they do? What do they believe?

Now turn around and check your observations. Through exercises like this, begin to be aware of your surroundings and your subtle interactions with others and transfer this awareness to your journeying and your observations of the otherworld.

3. A 'not-doing' for intention and awareness

'Not-doing', in the Toltec tradition, is a way of re-assembling the world in a different way from our normal, habitual way of seeing it. This helps to break the pattern of habit which can, in fact, cause us not to *notice* but, in fact, to *miss* much of what is presented to us.

Strictly speaking, the not-doing of something is not about doing its 'opposite'. The 'not-doing' of seeing a black square on a white page is not trying to see a white square on black paper, for example, or, for that matter, to see a black *circle* instead of a black *square*, since the not-doing of black is not white, but 'not-black' and the not-doing of a square is not a circle, but a 'not-square'. By the same token, the not-doing of sweet is not sour, but 'not-sweet'. This is a fine distinction and we won't worry ourselves too much about it here. Suffice to say that not-doing can be a helpful exercise for developing awareness and, because of the mental discipline involved in holding a new view of reality, it also works to strengthen the intention.

Begin by gazing steadily at the spaces between things – the gap between the books on the shelf rather than the books themselves, the 'cut-out' in the sky represented by a tower block, rather than the high-rise itself, and, classically, the shadows between the leaves of a plant rather than the leaves, so that you use the darkness to assemble a plant of shadows.

Allow your eyes to rest gently on whatever object you are not-doing, using your intention to hold this new assemblage of reality for as long as possible. You may find you achieve a somewhat meditative state while doing this exercise (so don't do it while driving or operating machinery, for example), but do try to remain focused as an act of intention.

If you do slip into a meditation as you do this exercise, note which 'reality' you come back to when you realize and pull yourself out of the trance. When you find you can come back to a 'not-doing' reality or to habitual social reality according to your own will, you will be on the way to powerful intention.

4. Shapeshifting 1 – Working with your power animal
Enter a light trance state and consult with your power animal for this exercise. Ask it for a full description of itself – how it moves, sounds, smells, feels, its qualities,

the essence of itself. You may be surprised.

What we habitually 'see' as a tiger, a bird, a dolphin, etc., is often just a composite of fleeting sensations and images that we take in without really noticing. Bird = Beak + Wings + Flight + Nest + Feathers + Tail, etc. Rarely will we actually truly see what a *bird* looks like, let alone *this specific bird*. Rather, we see a 'sky-thing' comprised of a combination of bird-like qualities.

I learned during art classes with life models that the human body, with all its angles and dimensions and shapes and lengths and contrasts of light and dark and texture and substance and form, is nothing at all like the image of a person we might draw from memory. In fact, I was so used to drawing 'image-people' that when I began to work with life models, real people seemed to be put together all wrong!

So, really get to know your power animal and then begin to mimic its obvious characteristics and looks, gradually working down through the levels until you can associate with it and act in accordance with its essence and energies. Then you will fully understand this animal and be able to shapeshift into the basic nature of your power animal whenever you need its strength, its cunning or the many other qualities it offers you.

You might then want to expand your practice to work with other animal essences. It is very helpful in many circumstances to be aware of and be able to use these essences – to become Tiger when faced with an aggressor, or Bird when you need quickly to take flight, for example.

Which qualities do you most need in your life right now, and which animals will give you these?

5. Shapeshifting 2 – Walking in power
In this chapter, you have explored another reality, met with your power animals, reclaimed power objects of value to you now – and gone a long way to recovering

personal power and expanding your repertoire of emotional skills. For 'power' does not just mean 'force' or imply 'control over' another person. It may instead mean the power to achieve warmth, to appear vulnerable, to allow other people to get closer to this new, empowered you. Now it is time to 'dare to take a chance' and to explore your power in all of these aspects.

Spend a single day at first, then perhaps a week, and then maybe longer, acting *as if* you truly are this new, powerful, you. Call it 'play-acting' if you wish, although actually it is shapeshifting.

It is sometimes helpful to begin this process when you are away from normal surroundings and the people you know – on holiday, perhaps – where you will automatically be more open and relaxed, acting 'out of character' and unimpeded by reminders from others of who you 'really' are. This will give your body time to absorb the memories of its new way of being and behaving. The acid test, however, is when you can continue to 'act' *as if* during your 'normal life' and usual interactions with others.

Note how the experience feels – to your body and also to your mind; the two sensations may be very different – and begin a lifestyle inventory of how this new person, this new you, thinks and acts and behaves in the world, much as method actors will do for a part they are rehearsing and a character they are about to play. What habits, interests, dreams and ambitions does this person have? How do they act and behave in certain situations? What motivates them?

Make two lists, side by side on a single sheet of paper, headed 'you' and 'not-you' (or 'old you' and 'new/empowered you'), which includes all your behaviours in all situations and circumstances which are normal in your life (you may need a separate sheet for each area of self or interaction with others) and how 'not-you' would react in the same circumstances. This will, of course, require a fairly detailed review of your day-to-day behaviour, interactions, reactions and associations.

List headings may include 'Career', 'Relationship to money', 'Relationships with friends', 'Lovers', 'Spiritual life', and so on. The list below this should include all typical thoughts, feelings, behaviours and spiritual orientations towards each of these categories and the situations that arise from them.

When this list is complete, review both sides of the sheet and decide if you would like to adopt any of the characteristics of 'not-you', your empowered self. If so, begin to move into them gradually by behaving in ordinary reality *as if* you were this person in this situation. Continue to compare both sides of the list and review the impact of any changes you make – which will, of course, have knock-on effects for other areas of your life since every human being is a holistic system and part of a wider connection to others.

It is quite possible to become 'someone else' and to act always from a position of power if we so wish.

5

THE WAY OF THE *URBAN* SHAMAN:
WHERE MIND AND SPIRIT MEET

*Profound but contradictory ideas may exist side by
side . . . Each tells us something important about
where we stand in the universe.*
– Neil Postman

*There are trees, I forget the name of them, that cover acres of
land, like any English forest or everglade. But they keep a
secret. When researchers came to study them, they found one
root system, not several different ones as you would expect.
In fact, they were not looking at a forest of trees, but at one
giant plant.*

*Above the gound, in the visible world, they are separate
trees sharing a common landscape. Below the soil, in the
deep structure of the invisible landscape, they are intimately
connected. They are one.*

*Just as human beings, so very different in so many ways,
are deeply connected at levels we are just beginning to understand. What is the nature of this connection, and how did it
come to be?*

*I have been part of a shamanic group which has journeyed
together to explore the destiny of human souls, to experience
what happens to us after death and to see the fabric that
binds us all – and I know the answer to this question.*

Mysterious things will happen on this journey. There are twenty of us in the group. All of us will hear singing and the sound of pipes although in 'reality' there will be no singing and no pipes will be played.

All of us, independently, will experience the same things on this journey, and many of us will use the same images to describe what we see. My own experience, in many ways, sums up the experience of us all . . .

I reach the upper world and meet my guide. I ask about the nature of reality, of the universe, the reason for our being here, the intention of the soul.

'There is a drifting energy in the universe and it is all equally conscious,' he says. 'You are that drifting energy and you may explore reality from wherever the drifting energy that is you lands. Wherever that is, is entirely accidental, like pollen caught in a breeze and scattered randomly.

'Millions of bits of you will land in millions of different locations. You have no control over that. But you can choose to experience reality, to "turn yourself on" at any one of those locations. You have chosen to "turn on" in this location, in this human form, at this time, because that is the one that holds most interest for you right now. You can never be more than one life form at a time so you must choose carefully which bit of the drifting energy you will give your attention to and experience fully.

'To experience reality, you must create it by imposing your own meaning on it. Meaning is the glue for your experiences. The imposed meaning is the experience.

'You are here to explore the destiny of souls – but there is no such thing as "destiny". The word implies an order and an end. There isn't one. There is no such thing as "soul". If you name it, you create it. What you call soul is merely energy, drifting energy.

'Bite into the apple,' he says. 'What do you see?'

I move into the lower world, a more concrete, experiential realm, and meet with one of my allies.

'Soul is only consciousness,' he says. 'All things just are.

It's no big deal, just energy, endlessly circling.'

I ask to experience being this energy, outside of human form, beyond life, beyond death, pure 'soul'. Immediately, I am split into millions of specks of light, each one conscious, which spray like shot from a gun, away from the Earth and out into the deep, vast, blackness of space.

As I travel, I find I can play with this energy. All of the parts of me, separating out at fantastic speed, with the explosive force of the first Big Bang, are accessible to my will. I can become any one of them and focus my attention there, so that I see the entire universe from a million different perspectives. I can experience reality, a different reality, from any perspective I choose. Each one has its own meaning, though there is no sense of attachment to that meaning. I haven't yet decided which of these forms I want to be and without placing my attention there, there is no emotional attachment.

There is something vast here, coming towards me. From my perspective, it is like a giant eagle. In human terms, I know it would be bigger than the planet we occupy. But now I cannot tell whether I am tiny, subatomic, and it seems huge by comparison, or whether it really is the colossal size it appears to be.

Either way, I am just a speck, smaller than the tiniest mote of dust. I enter through the eye of the eagle. It doesn't even notice.

I pass through its body and find myself in a dark landscape. There is a huge whirlpool in front of me, like a giant waterfall, but circular, and all the energy of the universe is roaring and bubbling into it.

I dive into it and am swept down – and into the strangest contrast I could imagine.

A white room, through which runs a conveyor belt, lined by white-suited people who are cheering and clapping. I am on this conveyor belt, which takes me through a doorway into a viewing room where they are showing a movie of endless lives, my lives. Each one lasts a second, a flicker on the screen. Bavaria, 1850. America, 1955. England, 1600. Each one blending and merging with the next. Goodbyes, hellos, laughter, pain, endless me's, endless experience.

Then I am back in the lower world, whole again.

'Life is such a small thing, almost insignificant,' says my ally. 'With death you are merely set free. Death releases your energy to allow you to Become once again.

'Energy takes the shape of whatever it inheres in. If you choose to be human, you will take human form. You could take any form and the energy would mould to it to allow you to experience the reality you become.

'Then, when you die, the energy will exit from your mouth to seek a new experience and will drift off to become . . . whatever you choose. Energy doesn't want or need, it just is.'

I ask about reincarnation and about karma. Are we here to learn, then, is that it, and do our achievements in this life have an impact on the next?

'Not at all,' he says. 'There is no good, no evil. Our energy simply takes on shape and form in this life and through this, we apply meaning to the world. We may describe our experiences as "good" or "bad" in order to give them meaning, but it is all just the flow of energy.

'But the experiences we have in this life do create beliefs about the next and this guides our intention and helps us to decide what shape to give our energy when we return. We maintain our perspective until we change it. That is all.

'What draws us back is interest. It is less boring to Be. The universe is nothing. It is meaning-less, point-less, empty-ness. What gives it a point and fills it with meaning is simply the meaning we give it. In order to give meaning, we must have form, we must be outside of the void itself and look into it from the perspective of our experience. Then we can project meaning onto it.

'Our way back is through intention – we must intend to Be. The engine for our return is will, and the fuel of the will is emotion. We are attracted to strong emotion. Love, anger, regret, compassion, it is all the same.

'We die and drift away from human form when we lose interest, when we no longer believe in ourselves. Then we become something else. Endless experience. Life experiencing itself.'

The group is quiet when we return. We need a break before we can talk about this.

'I became a mist, like lots of small particles. Above me, an eagle was flying. I was absorbed into it,' says one participant.

'I fell into a white hole, like a waterfall with energy flowing into it,' says another. 'There are more stages beyond this life that I could choose to go through.'

'I ended up at a waterfall, but it was a complete circle,' says another.

Someone else is crying softly. 'There is nothing there,' she says. 'It is totally boring. I always expected the afterlife to be beautiful, full of angels and love, understanding and peace – and there was nothing. The space of nothing is all there is. The ultimate was nothing.'

Experience is what draws us here. Experience and the need to connect with others, a connection which may be 'good' or 'bad', 'positive' or 'negative', as long as it is an emotional one. Beyond this life is the holographic plate, full of meaningless swirls of light and dark. Our lives and our choices give meaning to the pattern, illuminating it in the light of experience. Rebirth fills the emptiness, the nothing, the lack of emotion and disconnection from others. It is more interesting to embrace life and to Be – right here, right now. To Be Here Now.

The shaman who is guiding this journey merely nods. He has heard these stories many times before. It is the experience of many others who have taken this journey.

'It's like this,' he says. 'Once – although it wasn't "once", of course, it was rather "No-Time-At-All" and "No-Place-Whatsoever", there was a sentient being. And after several millennia of nothing going on, this being, this "nothing" became totally bored, so it split itself into two "somethings", equal and opposite forces. Yin and yang, male and female, sweet and sour.

'They had to be equal and opposite Somethings because Nothing can only result from the coming together of equally balanced positive energy. One plus minus-One equals zero, Nothing.

'And, of course, that is why we are attracted to each other – because we are the opposite of each other and we are aware that, by coming together we create wholeness again. But it is the wholeness – the hole-ness – of Nothing. Which is why we cannot ever truly meet and enfold each other. If we did, we would be cancelled out and become Nothing again. We search for god, but we are already the complete expression of god, we have only to look back at ourselves.

'And so we have war and we have love, and they are the same. They are both an expression of the deeper connection we have with each other.

'And so this being got to experience Something and was less bored because something was going on at last, in time and in space, rather than infinite void and nothingness.

'And YOU are what is going on. You are the experience that the nothingness was seeing. You are the means by which it experiences. You are the Something.'

I am reminded of an ancient Egyptian legend which tells how the universe was created by Osiris Khepera from the vast dark emptiness of the void through the speaking aloud of his own name. And in that moment, Something was created from the womb of nothingness by the act of its name being spoken aloud.

Experience is infinite. And we can choose what we want to experience – love or hate, war or peace, as caretakers of the Earth or her destroyers.

We are all connected. We are all one. And we have a choice, a blank canvas and a full palette. It is entirely up to us whether we create colour in our lives.

It is another beautiful day on the Greek island of Skyros, where the mountains around and behind us sweep down to a wild rocky shoreline and gentle bay, and low clouds paint the sky in intermittent splashes. It is the sort of day where sea-spray freshness hangs heavy and the air is painted turquoise by ozone.

But few, if any of us, are aware of it. We are looking at the woman on her knees in front of us in the middle of this circle we occupy, me, her, and 50 other people. Her name is Carrie. And she's screaming.

I only met Carrie a few days ago – as we all did – and now she's kneeling in front of us, beating the ground and screaming through an exorcism of the pain she has carried with her for many years.

She has an image of herself as a lion which has been turned to stone by an evil magician, a once powerful, wild, and regal creature, which had had all of its free will removed. Now she wants it back. And she is willing to fight for it.

Her screams of rage and pain are deafening but the woman sitting next to her, holding her, has her own head inches from this woman whose voice is unearthly, like nothing I have ever heard before. She doesn't even flinch.

And just when we think that Carrie must be all screamed out, the woman sitting with her says, 'I think there's more in there, isn't there? I think you can scream louder, get it all out . . .'

Carrie is in control, at no point is she going to lose it, but even she may be surprised at what happens next, by the new round of screams that convulse from her, and at the force of the energy released.

At one point, very briefly, she looks towards the mountains that surround us in this circle, she nods, smiles ever so slightly, then continues to scream and scream and scream.

And then suddenly she's calm.

The woman with her – whose name is Dina Glouberman – hugs her and Carrie sits up. She looks changed, radiant almost.

The next day Carrie comes back into the group and she's smiling.

'I found my lion,' she says. We know she means this

symbolically, that she is back in touch with what it means to be a grounded, powerful woman.

'No, I *really* found it,' she says. 'Yesterday, I took a walk into the mountains. I remembered looking over there during the group and it was there, the image of a lion on the rock in the side of the mountain, exactly in the shape I saw myself, and exactly where I knew it would be. I left flowers for it.'

Carrie had found her power again, the strength, the pride and regality of the lion, and she could honour it and leave the image of the stone lion, her petrified self, behind as a monument to her past. It stands there even today, in the mountains on Skyros island, just where she saw it. Carrie could move again – and she was moving on.

PERSONAL REALITIES BEGIN RIGHT HERE

Before anything can be created it must first be imagined. Images are reality before it becomes visible to others. 'Imagination is the beginning of creation,' said George Bernard Shaw. 'You imagine what you desire; you Will what you imagine; and at last you create what you Will.'

Because of this, images – our own and those of others – have a power which can be used to remodel – re-vision – our lives, to solve problems, to deal with issues which are unresolved and perhaps not even a conscious part of our lives; they have been absorbed within our personal mythology and become part of our dream of life to such an extent that they have become intrinsic to us and we are not even aware that we are repeating old and negative patterns.

When this personal image is understood as a metaphor for our lives, it becomes a powerful description of where we are at, both mentally and spiritually. The journey to reclaim our power and our personal truth then becomes one of unravelling the metaphor. To be turned to stone by an 'evil magician' is a powerful metaphor for an unhappy relationship where one partner, unintentionally perhaps, has used his greater – 'magical' – power to subdue the other, to turn her to stone, unable to move, powerless to use her strength, or even to escape.

Once she was able to connect with this new information about herself, Carrie could deal with the issues it raised in a way most appropriate to her for exorcizing and cleansing herself. For Carrie, that meant a walk into the mountains to meet physically with her lion self and to celebrate it. For you or I, it might have meant a completely different form of releasing ritual.

The search for personal meaning must come first from within ourselves. Even if we could find an objective reality 'out there', it would still be the *meaning* we attach to it – the feelings we have about the circumstances and events we are part of – that would be most significant in our understanding of this reality. As Carrie's story demonstrates, *the* truth is our *own* truth.

We have Imagework and its pioneer, Dr Dina Glouberman and her book, *Life Choices, Life Changes*, to thank for giving us a framework for working with our images in order to uncover this inner truth, this inner reality. Dr Glouberman was for many years a Western psychotherapist and teacher and also set up two holistic centres on the Greek island of Skyros. A profound and shamanic experience had galvanized her, some years before, into expanding her use of images, not only for personal discovery, inner guidance and healing, but for exploring the other dimensions of the spirit world. Her technique is a powerful one, cathartic even, but the idea behind it is exquisitely simple.

Show two people a random shape in an inkblot and one may see a bright shining sun, while the other sees a black hole. Who is right? The answer, paradoxically, is neither – and both. There is no 'truth' in an inkblot and, as every first year psychology student knows, what is actually revealed is more about our personal worldview than the ink on the page.

As Carrie shows us, it is possible to see our own inner

experiences – *our* construction of the reality around us – in terms of a potent and pervading image that becomes a metaphor for that experience. Dealing with the issues revealed by that image becomes a mythical saga, an heroic adventure, which will literally enable us to change our minds and, as a consequence, to change the shape of our worlds.

When Carrie saw herself as a lion which had been turned to stone, the image had meaning for her in the same way as an inkblot would also take on a unique form as an expression of her worldview. If that inkblot, or her image of herself, did not have personal validity, *ipso facto*, she would have chosen – or been chosen by – a different image of herself.

But *unlike* the inkblot, the image we have of ourselves has an internal force which belongs personally and uniquely to us. It has an intensity and a charge which can never be present when we project our world into the random shape of an inkblot or, for that matter, onto the group structure of a political party or a work environment or a religious assembly, or any group whose rules and ideologies we may choose to subscribe to in order to help us to define ourselves.

Of course, it doesn't matter if the lion that Carrie saw in the mountainside was 'really' there – or if you or I would have seen it. We might not have agreed with her either if she had described what she had seen in an inkblot on a page. But we would not question that she *had* seen it. For Carrie, the lion on the mountainside was real and purposeful in helping her to let go of a part of herself which was no longer serving her.

THE IMAGE *IS* THE REALITY

The image we have of ourselves and our circumstances is the key to our experience and understanding of the universe, and of ourselves within it – whether we see it as something to be feared and enjoyed, an adventure, or a daily grind. In fact, it *is* our selves and our situation.

Studies of human performance tell us of the many positive effects of working deliberately and consciously with our images in order to generate new outcomes for ourselves, and underline the fact that a real, material impact is created in the world when we do so.

Charles Garfield spoke of peak performers who 'develop powerful mental images of the behaviour that will lead to the desired results. They see in their mind's eye the results they want and the actions leading to it,' while Stephen Devore 'noticed an almost universal trait among Super Achievers and it was what I call sensory goal vision. These people knew what they wanted out of life and they could sense it multi-dimensionally before they ever had it. They could not only see it but also taste it, smell it, and imagine the sounds and emotions associated with it. They pre-lived it before they had it. And the sharp, sensory vision became a powerful driving force in their lives.'

We use the energy created by our images most effectively when we begin to build a new picture of ourselves in the world and, by better understanding ourselves, automatically come to understand others in their interactions with us. In this way, the whole world begins to change as those we meet are also changed through their connection to us – and we begin to unravel the deep structure and meaning of the entire universe. In short, once we understand something, we can change it, and ourselves, for the better.

Imagework is a simple approach which gives us this initial understanding of ourselves and leads potentially to this powerful chain reaction, by showing us a way to harness the images which pass through our minds almost constantly but which are rarely focused upon or directed with intention to give us the information we most need about ourselves. Instead, they are left to drift, unquestioned and unused, as fantasies and daydreams, when actually they are deep re-flections of our inner selves, messages from the core of our being, and often also from the transpersonal space around us.

In the city environment, the traditional ways of the shaman

are not always conducive to train timetable, business meetings and 'power lunching', but Imagework can be used effectively in any situation as a form of 'instant journey', and a way of 'checking-in' with our true selves, to discover what it really is that we want in our lives and to guide the array of choices facing us every minute of the day. Because there is less set-up and ceremony associated with Imagework, it is very conducive to urban shamanizing and accommodates our modern city lifestyle where there is little time available for the sacred.

WHAT THE CATERPILLAR CALLS DEATH – THE BIRTH OF IMAGEWORK

Imagework, as pioneered by Dr Glouberman, is firmly rooted in the Western psychotherapeutic tradition and, in particular, owes much to neurolinguistic programming, Silva Mind Control, and Gestalt, as well as the spiritual insights of Findhorn's David Spangler. Its origin, however, is also steeped in urban shamanic vision.

'There are no mistakes, no coincidences, all events are blessings given to us to learn from,' said Elizabeth Kübler-Ross, the Swiss-American psychiatrist who pioneered the concept of thanatology, the study of death and dying – a statement which sums up what Dr Glouberman calls 'one of the defining moments' in her life which 'shaped my understanding of the other dimension and led me to use Imagework as a more conscious way of exploring it.' The following description, from the unpublished manuscript of Dr Glouberman's second book, *The Healing Imagination*, captures the essence of shamanic 'seeing'. She is at a lecture by Elizabeth Kübler-Ross, who is talking about children in the Nazi concentration camps. At some level, they knew they were going to die, and they would draw pictures of butterflies on their walls, an archetypal symbol of freedom and liberation from pain. 'And how did the children know that death is a butterfly?' Dr Kübler-Ross asks.

At that moment a column of energy rises up my spine and bursts into my brain ... I move around in a dreamlike altered state, tuned into love, wisdom, and the other dimension ... The spirits are whispering to me constantly ... Ordinary scenes looked mysterious and otherworldly, as if I was witnessing a historic moment set in the larger frame of lifetimes. The women standing in the bus queue chatting could almost be speaking in tongues. Extraordinary coincidences seem normal ... What I sense now is that the meaning of life is embodied in a process that stretches across lifetimes. Understanding one lifetime is like selecting a random section of a curve on a graph and trying to make sense of it. It is too short a perspective.

I make predictions about the future, some of which turn out to be incredibly and strangely accurate ... The one book that I had brought back from my last visit to the States was William James's book The Varieties of Religious Experience. *When I picked it up to take it with me, I didn't really know why. Since then, there had been a fire in the basement of my old house which had destroyed all my other books.*

What I read [in James's book] basically reassured me that the experiences I was having were normal, fit into a pattern, and might be letting me know something real, even though it was not the reality that most people were aware of most of the time ... The kind of people that did tend to have mystical experiences and glimpses into this other reality rather than conventional religious experiences were the sort that had one foot in this world and one foot somewhere else.

The concept of having one foot in the 'real' world and one in the spirit world is extremely shamanic, of course. The writer, Mircea Eliade describes the shaman as a walker between worlds, in exactly these terms.[63] The shaman's challenge is to harness this power, to integrate it and to use it positively for personal power and wider good.

THE IMAGE IN ANCIENT AND MODERN WORLDS

Using images to explore our inner world is as natural as using words to explore, explain and describe the social world. Words are the way of the social world, enabling us to think logically and analytically and to exchange our ideas with others, while images are a personal and intuitive way of communicating with the whole of ourselves.

We may never be consciously aware of the personal symbols we are using to describe ourselves and name our experiences in the world – as we saw with Carrie, who was a very strong woman who would never *consciously* have connected with a view of herself as in any way stuck or disempowered, but who, nonetheless, at a deeply unconscious level *imagined* herself as an animal turned to stone.

These personal symbols, as Dr Glouberman points out, 'structure our thoughts, feelings, attitudes and action', and continue to have a major impact on our lives, the world around us, the choices we make for ourselves and others, and the actions we take in life, even if we are never knowingly aware of them. By choosing to use our images in a fully conscious and constructive way, we gain access to more choice and greater personal freedom. Life becomes richer, more meaningful and more expansive.

Using images in this way is an ancient and universal tradition and a capability innate in all of us. Philosophers and scientists, old and new, have attested to the power of the image. 'It is impossible even to think without a mental image,' said Aristotle; 'Imagination,' said Einstein, 'is more important than knowledge.' James Watson who, with Francis Crick, discovered the physical structure of DNA, tells in his book *The Double Helix* how 'a non-trivial idea' 'emerged' one day – 'came to me' – as he was drawing, lost in an image of something else.[64]

In ancient Egypt and Greece, healers would ask their patients to visualize good health in order to overcome disease, or to imagine healing delivered to them by their gods. What was important, in both cases, was an act of *faith* that it was possible to be well, and the expression of this faith was an image.

Imagery is also what babies and young children first use to make sense of the world. Words come much later than communication, and when we do learn to speak, our brains are reshaped in order to accommodate our emerging vocabulary, and we lose some of our intuitive ability as a consequence. In so doing, we also lose something of ourselves. Maxwell Cade's biofeedback research suggests that 'the ability to think in sensory images instead of words is an absolutely essential first step toward the mastery of higher states of consciousness,'[65] which is really just saying that, in order to develop more fully as human beings, to use the powers inherent within all of us, and to find a way back to the sensory fullness of childhood, we must first develop our imaging abilities.

THE NATURE OF IMAGES

Images are unique statements of personal experience in the moment – far from the abstract and immutable social constructs that we habitually live by and have come to understand that we cannot change. Because they speak to all parts of us and, indeed, *are* an integral part of us, they allow us to live through any experience, past, present or future, as if it was happening right here, right now and, while they do not prescribe an outcome, they will often suggest a way forward to the resolution of a problem.

The psychoanalyst, Carl Jung, encouraged his patients to use their images in just this way, as a route into their unconscious, and spent many years himself, some in the winter wilderness of Bolligen, delving into his own deep unknown. His descriptions of the unconscious world he found there are so similar to the otherworlds of the shamans that some of Jung's own followers now describe him as a 'neo-shaman'. It is a position Jung never dared to claim for himself, although he does tell us that many of his ideas came to him in visionary states, particularly as he strengthened his relationship with his 'spirit' guides, whom he would meet in image-journeys taken to dark caves, the depths of ancient wells, subterranean waterways, and other shamanic land-scapes. One of Jung's guides, Philemon, was undoubtedly a vital ally for him, and of the journeys he took in general, Jung would later say, in his autobiography, that 'the years when I was pursuing my inner images were the most important in my life. In them, everything essential was decided.'[66]

For Jung, the unconscious was a world in itself, with its own evolutionary history, meaning and potential, stretching right back to the dawn of the human species, a history shared by all people regardless of race, culture or individual experience. As part of the Infinite Now, the world of the unconscious is also linked to the future of all mankind and can be entered at any point to create new outcomes from the potential it contains. The psychic energy of our species, too, is holographic.

As well as a personal unconscious, there was, for Jung, a 'collective unconscious', very much like the shaman, don Juan's 'tonal of the times', which contained a vast kingdom of archetypal symbols – such as the universal (Earth) Mother, (Sky) Father, God, Devil (Pan, God of Nature), and the Hero who journeys between them. These archetypes reveal themselves in 'images' – in dreams, visions, and the myths and fairy tales of all cultures. And, just as with shamanism, mythological stories and common images occur across many remote cultures which have had little or no contact with one another – the Sky Father and Earth Mother are classic examples – and all cultures have their own concept of what is good, evil and taboo, however these are defined by particular cultures at particular times in their history. Archetypally, they are represented in the collective unconscious in the image of 'the Hero', 'the Lover', 'the Teacher', 'the Devil', 'the Rock Star', 'the Crone', 'the Drug Addict', 'the Mobster', 'the Child Abuser', imaginary composites we can all more or less agree upon and take a moral stance for or against. It is the *social reality* – or our conception of it – which counts, although the 'actual' reality may be different (no parent of a teenage child, for example, is really likely to see their child in the collective image of the Drug Abuser, even though she knows that her child has smoked pot, but the image will remain).

We even see the effect of the collective unconscious in the *Zeitgeist* of mainstream culture – it is rare that a single new film will appear on a particular theme, for example. Typically two or three, conceived, written, directed and released independently from one another, will come out at the same time. Just think of the films that were big at the box office in recent years. *Deep Impact*, for example – a film about 'a giant asteroid heading towards Earth which will create an Extinction Level Event unless mankind works together to find a solution'. And *Armageddon* – a film about 'a giant asteroid heading towards Earth which will create an Extinction Level Event unless mankind works together to find a solution . . .' – both of which were released in 1998.

Even given Hollywood's naturally incestuous cash-in disposition, there is a coincidence at play here, one which sums up the preoccupations, the *Zeitgeist*, the collective unconscious, the tonal of the times.

Jung theorized that the same archetypes exist in every culture and in every period of history. As well as a personal unconscious, people are part of a single universal unconscious which contains the whole library of myths of our entire species. As aspects of the hologram, we gain access to our own inner worlds and, potentially, to the archetypes which connect us all, when we allow them to enter our consciousness as images. Not only do these powerful internal worlds offer us profound wisdom, but we may also enter the universal and take ownership of knowledge spanning the history and the future of all mankind.

ENTERING THE OTHERWORLD THROUGH IMAGES

Everyone can do Imagework. If you relax and close your eyes right now and think of a specific situation you have been in, an image of that situation will come to mind, which could present itself in the form of a feeling, a smell, a sense or a picture of the scene. It may not be the exact replica of the scene itself – this is unlikely – but it will be an accurate re-flection, however presented, of how you feel about and experience that situation – like Carrie and her expression of herself as a stone lion in a relationship she is powerless to escape from.

For example, if you think about your job, you may not see yourself in the office shuffling paper and dealing with staff problems, which might be the literal view you have of your work and the tasks your day is filled with. Instead, you might see an image of a monkey house at a zoo or a picnic by a river in summer. Normally, you might be surprised or even irritated at these 'intrusive' images which are 'preventing' you from thinking about your work. But if you pause for a moment and allow the impression to remain with you instead of pushing it away, you will see that each of these images gives you very different information immediately about how you feel at the moment.

In any film, the director has chosen the look and feel of each scene. The people in the background are not there by accident, they are actors paid to be there because they are necessary to the plot and the rest of the film would not work without them. The fact that this scene takes place at a diner and not the Ritz is not a fluke, it is the result of a carefully written script and days of painstaking location scouting to find just the right diner for this scene. The actors, the setting and the action taking place is all there purposefully.

In daily life, your unconscious is the director and the images it gives you in response to your questions are equally purposeful and have just as much meaning to the film – which is your life as a whole.

In different life circumstances, Carrie might have seen herself as a beautifully painted butterfly or a crystal. Or a flower. Or a lake. But she saw herself as a lion turned to stone. The image that came into her mind, by which she was able to summarize her feelings at this moment, was a reflection of her current life situation. It had meaning and relevance for her; she could identify with it. And because she had experienced it, it was real.

Everyone is capable of getting an image in this way, about ourselves or another, although this may not necessarily be visual. Research suggests that only about 15 per cent of us actually see visual images. Another 15 per cent hear words and meaningful sounds during our image journeys, while most of us fall somewhere between the two. But everyone is capable of some form of image awareness, whether it is through sight, sound, smell, touch, a feeling, an intuition or a sense – and even if you get no image at all to begin with, that in itself may be useful information. What is this nothing? What was your question – is it in any way meaningful that 'nothing' comes to you in response to this question? How does the nothing feel about this? These are all questions you can ask of the image itself if confronted with a wall of darkness, for even the dark is an image which has form and information for you.

Here is a short exercise you can use to explore how you prefer to receive your own images (bearing in mind that, in answer to some questions, and at other times, other senses may tend to dominate).

Imagine . . .

You are standing in an orchard where limes grow on the trees	*Where are you?* *What is this orchard like?*
You pull one of the limes from a tree to use in a drink. You are thirsty. It is a warm day	*Does the lime resist your pull?* *How thirsty are you?* *How warm is it?*
You walk back to your kitchen, feeling the texture of the lime in your hand and thinking of the drink you will prepare	*What is the walk like?* *What does the lime feel like in your hand?* *How heavy is it?*
You place the lime on a chopping board in your kitchen and cut into it. The knife makes a sawing sound as you cut through the skin and the lime is so ripe that juice spurts from it	*Can you hear the knife as it is cutting?* *Do you feel the tension of the skin and the lime juice on your hand?*
You make your drink and add the slices of lime to it, each slice chinking against the ice cubes you have added to your glass. Condensation forms on the glass, making it slippy in your hands. You pause before you take the first sip to suck the sour lime juice from your fingers	*Do you hear the chink of the ice?* *Can you feel the glass in your hand?* *What does the lime juice taste like?*
You take a long drink from the glass. It is cool and refeshing in contrast to the heat of the day	*Can you taste it?* *Do you feel refreshed?* *Can you feel the heat of the sun on your skin?*
It has been a long but successful and rewarding day, and now it is time for you to relax and enjoy the evening, as the sun begins to set	*Do you feel as if you have enjoyed the day?* *Are you relaxed?* *What does the sun look like as it sets?*

Chances are that not only did you experience that image through at least one of your senses, but you also added more information – the look of the kitchen, the colour of the lime, the type of glass, and so on. This is perfectly natural. Your unconscious is providing you with new information which, even in this seemingly unimportant example, may be useful to you. What does it mean to you, for example, that your kitchen was large and expansive and painted blue, rather than small and untidy and white (like mine!), that you found yourself in an Eastern palace surrounded by servants, rather than a French peasant's cottage surrounded by chickens or, indeed, anywhere else in the world?

The Imagework process is in some ways similar to the journey of exploration taken by the shaman, as you may have recognized from working through this example. The key difference between the two is that the shaman's journey takes place in the otherworld of the nagual, whereas the Imagework journey takes place in the known world of the tonal – even though we are working with the unconscious mind, it is still *mind*, a landscape which can be known.

Because of this, the experience of these two states is different. The shamanic journey tends to be more motive and fluid, an actual journey from a point of entry into the otherworld, through the gathering of information, to the return to an exit point to carry this information back to ordinary reality. The images the shaman encounters *en route* have an objective reality quite apart from himself; his interaction with spirit allies such as power animals is democratic, respectful, egalitarian and friendly, as it would be if he was interacting with a human companion of equal status on a real journey of discovery.

In journeying, we go out into the otherworld as adventurers. With Imagework, we bring the experience back into ourselves and use the power of our conscious and unconscious minds to unlock the deeper secrets of the information we receive. Our images are aspects and reflections of ourselves and can be studied for information as much as interacted with. To get a feel for the difference between the two, compare the following account of the Imagework experience with the shamanic journeys you have taken.

Karl is using Imagework to consult with his inner child – the person he used to be, full of innocence, hope and dreams, the person he put away as he grew up and became socialized into the adult world.

Today, in his mid-thirties, Karl is a successful businessman with the 'right' car, the 'right' flat, the 'right' girlfriend – who also often feels lost and alone. Consciously, he explains this as the result of a house move his parents made when he was much younger, which took him away from his friends just at the age when he had started to become more social and in-dependent in the world. The place they moved to was rural and isolated and he never again had the same opportunity to adventure out into the world. In fact, the closest child of his own age now lived some ten miles away and Karl was entirely dependent on his parents for transportation and support if he was to have any social life at all.

He has lived for thirty years with his frustration at having his independence snatched away from him just when he was beginning to find it and has built a safe, predictable world for himself as a wall against unforeseen change.

He begins the Imagework journey.

I close my eyes and am aware of a happy five-year-old boy in shorts and a T-shirt. It is a summer day and he is playing in the back garden of the house his family lived in then, just after they moved from the city.

In his hand he holds a model car, an Aston Martin. He is James Bond today.

It is fascinating that I can clearly see many of the details that I have now forgotten about that house – the size and shape of the garden, the colour of the paintwork, the flowers that grow there. There are apple trees here. I had for-gotten that.

The five-year-old is alone. He is happy but there is a stoic air about him. He is lonely but he is resigned to that. He is making the best of things.

I am not at all surprised at this since I have always known I had a lonely childhood. My sister is eight years older than me, my father works away much of the time and there are few other children of my age nearby. I am left to my own devices for much of the time and used to finding my own amusement. 'Just play quietly by yourself,' my mother tells me.

I am a little confused by this picture of the five-year-old, though. I have always 'known' that I was a lonely child, rejected by my parents, forced to move away from other children and leaving behind all the people I knew and the security I had. I guess I always felt resentment over that. I was not even consulted.

But I can't see that in this little boy. He may be lonely, but he is also genuinely happy, not resentful. What's going on?

I become my five-year-old self, step into the image of the little boy in order to feel and experience his emotions and to see the world through his eyes. What I realize is that this little boy really is happy and, what's more, he's not actually lonely – he's bored. And there's a big difference. He wants company because he wants stimulaton. He's not resentful of the situation he is now in, he just wants his mind to be occupied.

I realize then that I've been conned – by myself. I've spent the last thirty years caught up in this personal myth of a sad, isolated, powerless childhood and have lived my life as if the myth were reality. But the five-year-old doesn't feel that way – he's not feeling 'sad' or 'isolated' or 'powerless' – he doesn't even have the mental understanding to know what these words mean – he's just 'bored'.

I see I have some decisions to make now. I have been living 'his' life, as if certain aspects of it were true, as if it has always been my destiny to be isolated and powerless. But maybe these things were never true. I have constructed an elaborate reality to make sense of life events from my childhood and, in a way, to make up for lost time. But maybe my past is not as real as I have assumed.

The key thing I now see is that I have led my life defending this five-year-old on the assumption that he needed this protection. That's why I've engineered my own life in this way, with the barrier of social status around me to protect us both.

But this five-year-old is tough. He doesn't need protection – because he isn't powerless and he isn't a victim.

Leaving aside the content of this exercise, you can see that, although you move between the image (in this case, the child) and yourself (the adult), it is you who control the process. It is less of an interaction, with all participants playing an equal part, and more of a guided exploration into the meaning of a single image. You are the film director controlling the action.

The shamanic journey is different in that no single image is studied in depth and the action is not controlled in this way. It is the autonomously unfolding story which is itself important.

It is also possible to examine the image from all sides, from above and below, and from all aspects and angles, like a film director panning in and out, changing the camera angles and slowing down or speeding up the action, to reveal information from a new perspective and to deliver new insights. When information is given to us about our lives in this way, we can actively question the basis of our assumptions about our past and create a new truth for ourselves to move forward from, which may also include redefining the past so we can recover a new sense of the present and the potential for a completely different kind of future.

Images are a repository for our inner truth and they can help us to question the mythological models we are using in our lives, revealing a different truth which we could not consciously have considered; it simply would not have occurred to us.

EXPLORING THE INFINITE THROUGH A MEETING WITH YOUR TRUE SELF

My experience is that journeying to the future to meet our true selves – the people we would truly like to be (as we will shortly do) – and to understand how our lives *will* turn out if we remain true to our vision, can be one of the most powerful exercises we undertake for self-transformation, whether we use the classic shamanic journey to visit a potential future within Lilly's 'alternity' of infinite possibilities, or use Imagework to achieve the same sense of understanding.

Since, in the world of the shaman and the physicist, all things are connected and take place right now, our actions in this moment shape our futures by creating a probable path for us to follow from one of a million different potentials which are also all open to us. It is quite possible for us to journey to the future to meet with the people we will become if we follow our paths of this moment – or, indeed, journey to the past and change it.

We can also use Imagework to consult with our true self by finding out what our real purpose is and what we truly aspire to as a reflection of this. To do so, firstly we ask for an image of ourselves to emerge as the person we are destined to become if we continue on our present path. From this perspective, we can then look back over the decades of our life, first from the position of someone who has lived authentically and tried to remain true to their ideals, to their spiritual and life objectives; and then from the perspective of someone who has taken a more conventional and easy route without remaining true to these ideals. The contrast, returning to the opening section of this book, is between someone who has given up on the search for personal meaning and someone who has continued as a seeker and been able to discover an authentic sense of truth for themselves.

How each picture looks to us, the key images revealed, the age at which we appear in each image, what each feels like for us, are all insights into what it is that drives us, what our higher, spiritual self yearns for, and what we can do to make our lives more purposeful and real. Almost universally, the picture is brighter when we have been true to ourselves rather than compromising our ideals.

When I was guided through this journey by Dr Glouberman, my image of my true self was of being part of a holistic community based on natural, simple living, with others invited to join and contribute as they wished. I was in a loving environment, with a supportive partner and many children around me. I felt satisfied and complete in my old age, as if my life had meaning and purpose and I was happy to greet Death knowing that I had made a contribution to the world. The key thing was *contribution*. In the vision of my authentic self, I had given something back to the world, not just taken from Her.

The image of my inauthentic self was quite a contrast – the vision of an 80-year-old, taking more self-development courses and still looking for answers, still *taking* from others. As I stood waiting to enter my latest class, a bolt of lightning came down from the sky and pierced my chest, killing me outright. In a symbolic way, at the age of 80, I guess I did finally achieve 'enlightenment', but it felt like it had been a hard, lonely slog to get there and then it was, literally, all over in a flash. Sometimes, I realized, we need simply to commit to a worldview and live it rather than constantly seeking evidence and sifting through the minutiae of possible truth.

I knew which of these two images I preferred, but wasn't sure how to get there. Dr Glouberman's advice was to use *hindsight* rather than *foresight*: to imagine my life in the future from the perspective of my true self and then look back, over all the years up until this point, so I could *know from the past* rather than *search the future*. 'See the events of your life as if you have already lived them,' she said, 'and not as a mystery which still lies before you. It's always much harder to look forward from the present and try to see how to reach a destination because there are always many options you'll meet and forks in the road along the way. Instead, ask your true self what you *did* to get there. The options you *took*, the decisions you *made* and the paths *you've already walked*. You already know the answers. The trick is to see them clearly and for that it's easier to look backwards than forwards.'

When I did so, I saw that I must make a definite break with my present life in order to create a new dream that I could grow into. I became a traveller, a wanderer among ancient civilizations and the wise and simple people of the world. It was an interesting image as I had been told many years before this by a wise woman I had met in Ireland that I would learn most in my life from 'experience' and from 'simple people'.

As I travelled the seeker's path, I reflected on the route I had taken and the people I had met and was able to assimilate their wisdom into my life *in that moment* and then to make decisions for the future based on information from a new personal history I had lived through. The effects of some of those decisions are still manifesting in my life right now.

MEETING YOUR TRUE SELF

Before you try this exercise for yourself, I recommend that you review the following pages, which outline the procedure for Imagework.

When you have done so, find a quiet space where you will not be disturbed for half an hour. Then close your eyes, relax and be open to whatever images come up for you.

Ask your unconscious for an image of yourself at 80, 90, or whatever age seems most comfortable to you – the age in your life where you are aware that no further choices are possible and you can reflect on the life you have lived, knowing that this is all for you, no further actions or possibilities of action remain. You will be sum-

ming up your existence and your achievements in the image which follows.

First, ask for an image of yourself at this age from the perspective of the you that has not lived to the fullest of your potential, the you who has given up the quest of the Hero and not followed your dream. Again, intention is paramount, so phrase your words carefully, perhaps along these lines: 'Show me an image of myself and my life at 80, if I have not lived to the fullest of my potential.'

How does it look? How does it feel to be 80 and to know that you have not achieved all you could have been? Perhaps you are content with this image and think you have done the best you could. Or perhaps you feel you could have done more, even one small thing, and your life would have turned out very differently.

In either case, you need to find out how you have arrived at this place. In your life outside of the image there are still many choices to make, many paths to walk. You need the advice of the older, wiser you to show you which of these paths you have walked so that your life turned out this way.

So ask. Ask to see the significant turning points in your life and the choices that were open to you. Ask which you took, and why.

In the imageworld we can explore these, re-running the history we have yet to come, to see our lives as our personal scripts might lead us to live them, and to make decisions now about how we will react to those choices when they come upon us in real life.

Now, ask to visit your future self at the same age, this time as the you who has lived authentically.

You may be struck by the contrast and ask yourself where this incredible difference in perspective came from. The answer is that it came from you and the choices you have made based on how you have decided to live your life: as a seeker who genuinely wanted to find a personal truth for authentic living, a real 'design for life', or as *someone who gave up and opted in to the consensus reality we have all agreed to live by.*

Ask yourself how you arrived at this place. What were the choices you made and the repercussions they had for your life history? Was there ever a time when you were not like this and, if so, what did you do to change things?

Sometimes you may get stuck between the two images. A choice from one 'reality' may seem extremely enticing, even though you are not sure whether it will ultimately bring you joy or unhappiness.

For clarity in situations like this, Imagework offers us two secret weapons. One of these is a magic wand that you simply wave over the situation and ask to be shown the best possible outcome. Where would you really like to be? What would really make you happy?

Allow the image to change as you wave the wand over it and accept that the new reality you see is the best of all worlds for you at this time, according to the deepest source of wisdom within you. What you later decide to do with this information, of course, remains entirely up to you.

The second tool of the Imageworker is the personification of the universal wisdom which flows through all of us, in the form of the Wise and Loving Being who, like the ally of the shaman, is a source of infinite knowledge, compassion and love for you, and is there to support you, when asked to do so, in any and all of the situations you meet.

No 'truth' is ever absolute; it is always personal, referential and based more on 'fitness for purpose in the present moment' than an immutable reality fixed for ever. In some Imagework exercises you may therefore come to realize that two different, equally profound and attractive – and mutually contradictory – ideas both seem to have a valid point to make for you. This is not so surprising since, in the words of scientist, Niels Bohr, when we enter the holographic world, 'the opposite of a profound truth may well be another profound truth'. How can you find a satisfactory resolution, an authentic solution to the different aspects of this single issue, and what is the best possible outcome for all concerned?

This is the perfect time to use the power of the Wise and Loving Being. To do so, ask for an image to emerge of a cosmic entity, ultimately loving and infinitely powerful and resourceful, who cares deeply about you and can arbitrate expertly in this situation where you feel lost between choices. His is the power, like the shamanic ally, to offer a wider view, to calmly present the other side of an argument and to explore new possibilities from a third-person perspective on events.

Merge with the image you have created of this Wise and Loving Being and look at these two choices now open to you. How do you feel about them now that the wisdom of the universe is available to you and you are full of love for the human who stands before you and who does not have this knowledge? What advice can you give your human self for the best possible solution? You may be surprised at just how objective, sympathetic and helpful you can be to yourself when you are a Wise and Loving Being.

Working with the inner child, as we will do later, and journeying to the true self are, perhaps, two of the most important aspects of Imagework. The former teaches you about who you have become and why, the latter about who you still can be and how. 'It is as if with imagery we can open a window into a dimension which does not respect the boundaries of past, present and future, nor the boundaries between people, and we can connect directly with experiences that are not part of our personal history or, indeed, that have not yet happened,' writes Dr Glouberman.[67]

We are part of the hologram and all that it contains for us and our place in the world, and everyone naturally has the ability to connect with this otherworld since we are all a part of it. It is a capability which we are encouraged to lose quite quickly in Western society, however. We are taught to replace our natural use of images with another form of communication – words.

THE WORLD AWAITING CHILDHOOD'S END

The Jesuits have an expression, 'Give me the child till the age of seven and I will give you the man.' Childhood is where most of our formative experiences lie; it is the world many of us are still unconsciously living. And yet words, actually quite limiting as a method for sharing ideas and getting our meaning across in any case, are our bluntest tools for entering the world of childhood, and many of us have forgotten our earliest experiences simply because they are beyond words: the sensory world of the child is too big for them.

As young children, we know more than adults, we are at home to the spirits, and their communications come naturally to us through images, not words. No wonder we find it difficult to shoehorn our reality into the narrow expression of the spoken word because, as children, we do not experience the world as a description, we *live* it, with no differentiation between ourselves and any other thing or time or place.

We have no conception of time – whatever happens takes place now and lasts for ever. An hour takes an age or flies by in a second depending on our experience of it, whether we find it enjoyable, boring or painful. Linear time does not exist at all: it is a concept which we come to learn and a myth which we, as adults, come to accept.

And there is no conception of space. The child's world is entirely personal, with no objective world 'out there', where others might have a perspective different from ours. All things are connected.

There is no time and there is no space.

As Piaget showed, when a young child's ball rolls out of sight, he does not bother to look for it because it simply does not exist any more. There is no external world where it could be which is beyond his vision or experience.

'Our lives then were totally active, committed and involved at every moment. We did not separate ourselves from anything else; we were the world and the world was us . . . and our first symbols were images, active images of relationships rather than objects; of rattling rather than of a rattle, of mothering rather than of a mother out there.'[68]

As we grew, we learned how we 'should' approach 'reality' and to understand that we had an existence separate from everything else, and a past, present and future which existed outside of us, in incremental bits of reality called 'time'. This is extremely useful information. To know that we are separate from the car coming towards us is to be able to get out of the way and so avoid pain. To know about time is to be able to learn from past experience and to make plans for the theatre on Saturday.

'To perceive a world of hard objects that had either a positive or negative value must have been utterly necessary for our ancestors' survival,' said don Juan. But 'after ages of perceiving in such a manner, we are now forced to believe that the world is made up of objects.

'It is unquestionably a world of objects. To prove it, all we have to do is bump into something. We are not arguing that. I am saying that this is first a world of energy, then it's a world of objects. Everything is energy. The whole universe is energy.'[69]

By absorbing the social dream and adopting words as our way of interacting with others, and with time as our reference point, and 'hard objects' as our reality, we gain much that is useful. But we do so at the loss of something equally valuable – our access to greater power and creativity and to a sense of deep connection between us all.

Learning that we are separate in the world means that we are unique and powerful individuals – potentially. But also that we are alienated from the experience of others, unable to truly connect at the most intimate level with another, and never again able to be the centre of our own universe of images and experience. We become just one small part of a world which is ambivalent, indifferent, and sometimes even hostile to us. Or, at least, that may be the illusion we have come to accept.

'There is only one wound of the spiritual body, and that is the illusion of separation,' said Dick Olney.[70]

'At the heart of alienation is the feeling of unconnectedness and separateness. The need to connect with others is what separates you from others, because to say "I need to connect" is to say, "I am separate". There is no need to connect with me because you are me.

'For us to be separated physically, there would have to be a thin film of nothing between us, but there is no such separation. We are a physical continuum.' We are one. Part of the same organism, intimately connected in holographic space-time.

A lot of the work of shamanic healing is about tackling the problems of alienation, dispelling the myth of separation, and reintegrating parts of ourselves or others which have simply splintered away through the effects of life on soul and the illusion of aloneness, part of which arises from our earliest experience of replacing images with words.

THE CONSTRUCTION OF A MYTH IN WORDS

Thinking in words means we can communicate with the social world, the verbal self taking on the role of code-breaker in order to make sense of the world for us. The problem is that the verbal self can be a misguided fantasist at times, applying definitive meaning to events even when it doesn't really know what it is doing.

Dr Glouberman gives the example of research carried out with a man referred to as 'PS', who had a split brain, a severed connection between his left (verbal) brain hemisphere and his right (non-verbal, image-led) hemisphere so that one side of himself literally did not know what the other was doing.

You might expect this to cause a few problems – the left hand not knowing what the right hand was doing – so that the interpretation of reality – what is real – could become problematic, for example. Far from it: PS simply made up his reality from the information he had available at the time.

In one experiment, researchers flashed a picture of a chicken claw into the visual field of his left hemisphere and a snow scene into his right. They then asked him to point to a picture, in each case, which most closely corresponded to what he had seen.

He chose a chicken with his right hand – quite correctly since the right hand is connected to the left hemisphere of the brain, which had seen the chicken claw. He chose a shovel with his left hand, again correctly, since this corresponds with the image of the snow scene shown to his right brain.

He was then asked to make sense of both items together, the relationship between chicken claw and snow scene, so now he had to consider both pictures together.

Since his response was in words, it was controlled by the left hemisphere whose job it is to make sense of the available information.

His explanation was that he had seen a chicken claw, so he had picked a chicken and he had picked the shovel (not because of the snow scene, but) because 'you have to clean out a chicken shed with a shovel'.

This explanation is perfectly valid as one version of reality, but it is not the version which most accurately fits the facts. His left brain was creating a reality based on disconnected evidence. We all do something similar every day of our lives. There is little in the world that is clear-cut and unambiguous so the left (verbal) brain simply makes up a story for us based on the information at its disposal. This is how personal mythology begins.

And the stories we create have a profound existential impact for us since they dictate what is real for us in our lives, including our personal history till now and the interpretation of events we have lived through. Only by dispelling these myths – what shamans call 'erasing personal history' – seeing them as just one of many possible truths, and then accepting the ultimate wisdom of our true selves (sometimes despite the 'evidence' of the world) can we ever fully heal ourselves and move on from the limitations we have come to accept for and about ourselves.

In order to 'decondition' ourselves, said Dick Olney, it is not even necessary for us to uncover our childhood memories; what is important is that we 'become free of them. It is not necessary to remember the event. What is necessary is to reclaim what was lost.'[71]

He offers a simple three-part model for doing so:

1.   childhood experience
2.   self-image that arose
3.   unfulfilling behaviour

'Do not make the mistake of blaming 3 on 1,' he says. 'The real work is depotentiating 2. A traumatic example of this is a woman who has been molested as a child and who, because of what she experienced then, carries the self-image of help-lessness that has a pervasive influence on her life. Regaining her sense of power, rather than remembering the molestation, is what will free her.'

Similarly, writes Dr Glouberman,

Through the years, we have created deep programmes or patterns or models that tell us what the world is like, what we are like, and how to relate to and operate in the world. These programmes are by now usually habitual or unconscious, even if they were once consciously chosen.

Before we decide to make changes in our lives, we need to understand and respect our present self. This means finding out about all the programmes that we are now unconscious of.[72]

The first step in accessing these inner programmes through Imagework or the shamanic journey is to be open and receptive to the images which are given to us by our unconscious or our allies.

To do this, we simply ask. And then we listen, treating the image seriously and with respect. While using these techniques can be fun, it is not a game; they will provide us with vital information, but we have to meet our images and experiences at least halfway by accepting the meaning behind them. This does not imply that we must rush out immediately and drastically change our lives, but nor should we ignore the message we are being given. Journeying and Imagework will give us greater choice, but with every choice comes responsibility.

IMAGEWORK IN ACTION – USING THE TECHNIQUE

The basic structure for Imagework is very simple. The description which follows is my own adaptation of Dr Glouberman's technique based on her workshops, on personal communication and on the steps she outlines in her book, *Life Choices, Life Changes*, which provides much fuller information on the background to Imagework and the use of the method.

GIVE YOURSELF TIME AND SPACE

Make sure, first of all, that you have a clear space and time set aside for yourself to undertake an Imagework journey. You don't need long – 20–30 minutes is the average length of an image-journey, and once you become practised in the technique, you can dip into an image very rapidly, as a quick check on a decision you are about to make at work, for example. But to start with, it is good to set aside the time to get to know yourself, so you can keep your focus and your intention pure.

Everyone naturally uses images all the time, although we are not always conscious of them. All you are doing here is asking that your images become more apparent to you.

Don't try to force an image, though, or you will become tense and your mind will pull you away again. It may take a while for anything to come up. Instead you may just see blackness at first. This is quite natural. Do not give up; instead, step into the blackness itself. You will often find that it is multi-layered, never entirely dark, but with images and associations behind and within it.

Once you have made a connection with an image, no matter how it comes, as a feeling, a smell, a remembered sound or a picture, you can explore it more fully.

Imagework can be used for more 'esoteric' questions and for practical information on everyday life. Whether you want to find out more about your inner child and the events of your past, or your future self, or to ask a practical question about your work life or relationships, always enter the imageworld with a specific question in mind – for example, 'Show me an image of a person with my name in forty years' time' or 'What is the outcome of my accepting the promotion I have been offered at work?' – rather than just 'drifting' in the journey.

Open-ended questions – 'What should I do about . . . ?' rather than 'Should I do this . . . ?' which requires a 'yes' or 'no' response – provide a richer soil in which images can grow.

EMBRACE THE FIRST IMAGE WHICH COMES TO YOU

If you are like the rest of us, you will not always immediately understand and sometimes will not even like the images that come to you.

Keith's image of himself was of a lone tree standing in rocky soil just outside a lush forest. He wasn't immediately attracted to the image as his own view of himself was as a vivacious and outgoing person – the life and soul of the party – and this seemed a lonely, isolated image.

Exploring it further, however, he was able to discover deep and valuable truths about himself and his early childhood relationships which had left him with a residual feeling of aloneness. Once he understood this, he was able to work with these feelings to a positive outcome. He was also able eventually to embrace the positive attributes of the image itself: standing outside of the group also implies a pioneering, creative and innovative spirit, which Keith certainly is.

Emily, in a journey to say goodbye to someone important in her life, saw that person as a skeleton standing alone in a desert landscape, which was, at first, quite a distressing image. When she herself became the skeleton, however, she realized how liberating it was not to have a body and to feel the cool breeze blowing through her. The real meaning of the image, she discovered, was about freedom and the liberation of spirit and not, as she first thought, about isolation and death.

Margaret had an image of her inner self as a huge black spider, which was quite disturbing for some people in the workshop group. To Margaret, however, it was a very positive image. She recalled that her grandmother had always told her 'It is very lucky to have a spider in the house.'

The thing to remember is that all images come to you as friends. They come *from* you, the deep you, and they are there as helpers and advisers *to* you. Sometimes there are certain things about ourselves which only our friends can tell us.

WORK WITH THE IMAGE YOU GET

Once you get an image, guide your interaction with it so that, in a sense, you become two people. When you are 'in' the image, you are the person, the object or the entity the image represents. Step into it, feel like it, 'see' the world through its eyes. You are free at all times and at any point to step out of the image you have created so that you can examine it from new perspectives, bringing your own interpretation to its meaning.

As the observer who interacts with it, you can walk around the image, see it from all sides, including top and bottom, and examine all aspects of it for new information. Try looking at the image from a distance and in a wider context as well as close-up. This often reveals new information. You can then 'become' the image itself to examine the world and think in the way of the image being; to see how it feels to be a skeleton or a tree or a spider, and how the world looks from here.

In a session to explore his life in the present and the near future, Daniel saw himself as the image of a white bird flying down a beautiful valley, following the course of a wide blue river into the setting sun. As the bird, he was enjoying the scenery around him and the ability to explore the beauty of his surroundings and the freedom that his wings gave him. There was just one thing that troubled him. He seemed to be alone and he felt that he would like someone in his life, a partner with whom to share the adventure.

So, while he was enjoying his solitary flight along the river valley, he was a little disappointed that he was taking this journey alone. But was he alone? There *did* seem to be a sense of uncertainty about it . . .

I pull myself back from the image to take a wider view of the scene and the solitary bird in its surroundings. As I do so, I see that I do, indeed, have a partner with me, another bird, a beautiful female, flying alongside but slightly behind me, never quite catching up. I join the second bird to see why she is not flying with me.

I know that some cultures believe in the supremacy of the male and make their partners walk a few paces behind them. I would hate to find out that I wanted anything similar. My parents, also, were from a generation where the man made most of the decisions and the woman was happy for him to do so – they called it 'chivalry' – but I am not happy with this possibility either. The world has moved on since my parents' generation.

So what is going on here? Consciously, I have no desire for a partner who follows me. I want a mate who is strong, independent and who wants to fly alongside me.

So I am very relieved when I ask the second bird why she is flying behind me and she answers, simply: 'Because you're going too fast.' This is an explanation I haven't even considered with my more intellectual theorizing!

The message is that there will be partners in my life who want to be with me but I am moving ahead with my life too quickly for them to quite catch me and until I slow down, they will be unable to be fully part of the journey with me.

This is a valuable lesson and I can already see the parallels with my own life. People are always telling me to slow down and stop taking on so much. Previous partners have told me they are never quite sure where they are with me because I get involved in so many new things and move my attention so quickly between the different subjects that attract me. A girl-friend had joked one summer, when I had enrolled for a number of courses and workshops, that I would leave the house to go to my reiki group, get to the end of the road and have enlisted on a scuba diving course instead.

I enter the image of the me-bird and explain to him that he has a beautiful partner who wants to be with him, but that he is going too fast for her to do so. What is he – am I – going to do about that?

As the bird I slow down to allow my mate to join me and we are both then able to fly on together, wingtip to wingtip, into a shared sunset.

When you work with images in this way, you are working closely with the unconscious, which is deeper and wiser than the layers of rationalization and intellectualization that we often smother it with. The insights of the unconscious are usually subtler, more straightforward and more illuminating than our rational thought.

Colours may be important, for example, and have their own significance for you. Red may mean danger in the outer world, but to you it may hold a very different meaning. For example, it may be associated with a particular parent because they often wore that colour, or with a pleasant memory from childhood because you had a favourite toy in that colour.

The sounds you hear may resonate with impressions or experiences from childhood or from other places.

Jokes and puns can feature heavily too – the unconscious and the spirits both have a sense of humour.

Christopher saw himself as a cartoon Thor, for example, a three-foot God of Thunder, running round in circles, banging his hammer noisily all around himself, but to no real purpose.

In reality, having just finished university, he had no clear idea of where he wanted to go and what to do next and, while he threw himself vigorously into a number of new projects, his life still lacked direction and he was frustrated at himself for this. His image paralleled his life.

I pointed out to Christopher that 'thaw' also means 'to melt, to go with the flow' and to allow himself to blend with his surroundings so that a natural direction, a 'water course' of action, emerges.

Nothing that comes up is irrelevant or accidental, it all has meaning, and it is a meaning which you have created, so it is vitally important to you.

RECORDING THE FACTS

When you return from the Imagework journey – which you do quite easily by simply inviting yourself to return to reality in a calm and rested way and opening your eyes again – it is a good idea to take a few minutes to note down your memories and impressions in a journal, or to draw them, creating a visual impression of your insights. Others have created poetry or songs, dances or sculptures from their experiences, or, like Carrie, acted out the image they have created, and then found a closing ritual to release it.

A journal often proves an invaluable reference source over time and will provide new information and insights for you as your experience of Imagework increases.

For instance, Daniel's image of the flight of the birds down the valley was the middle journey in a series of three which were linked by a common motif. This only became obvious to him when he looked back at the journal entries he had made at the time. In the first session (to explore his image of himself) he saw himself as an honesty plant on a hillside into which had fallen a white feather. Honesty – the search for truth – and the feather – for Daniel, a symbol of peace – were both images he could relate to. Peace held by honesty, a search for meaning realized.

The second session – to explore his life journey – was the flight of the birds. White feathers featured strongly again.

In the third session – which took him right back to the moment *before* his birth to look at his intentions in being born – Daniel saw himself as an angel-like being with white wings outstretched, whose purpose was to heal and to help those in need. There was a sense of peace and of faith, acceptance and trust which connected with his very first image of the honesty plant, and a sense of purpose and intention which linked with the (almost too) purposeful flight forward of the white bird in the second image journey.

Daniel had gained useful knowledge and insights from each session independently, but it was only when he saw the three as a continuum linked by a common motif that new and even deeper meanings became apparent.

KEY POINTS FOR IMAGEWORKING

- Welcome the first image that comes, whether it is desirable to you or not. Every image is useful and, indeed, the less you like it, the more helpful it often turns out to be. If you get a number of fleeting images, choose the one which seems most powerful to you – this may not necessarily be the nicest, or most comfortable image to you.

- To guide the Imagework, it is necessary to stay in touch with the reality of the image, while also giving the procedure structure and direction. This is a lot easier than it sounds once you realize that with Imagework you *can* be in two places at once.

- Study the image, from above, below, from all sides, and within the context of its environment.

- Ask questions, but remember, images are pre-verbal communication forms. They are the language of the child. Sophisticated language will not be understood, is too open to interpretation and will destroy the feeling behind the exercise and hamper your natural intuition by creating intellectualization and distance. Dr Glouberman offers useful advice when she suggests that we 'speak in words a five-year-old would understand, and as if the image were here in the room with us, not a distant object to be studied. Respond to it sensitively, as you would a friend.'

- Become the image. Step into it and experience what it is like to be you in that form. What do you see, hear, smell, feel, sense, experience? Who are you with or are you alone? What is the best and worst part about being you? Allow the image being to answer, and accept its answers, even if they do not immediately make sense to your more rational self.

- Now step back and look at the whole scene. What is going on here? How do the different image beings interrelate?

- Become the whole environment. How do you feel about the image being and the relationships it has created around it? What would be good for it? What do you think it should do next from your wider vantage point outside of the aquarium?

- Become the image being again and get a sense of your history. Has it always been this way for you? If not, when and why did things change? And in what way?

- As the image being, consider your future. What possibilities are open to you? What can you create? What is the best way for you to go? What will be the impact of this? What is the best possible outcome for you?

- Wave a magic wand over the scene. If you could wish for anything, any change to this picture, what would it be? And what would its effect be for you and others?

- What steps could you take to make this future a reality for you? What steps *did* you take?

- As yourself, tell the image being what you have learned and ask if it is ready to commit to the changes you would like to make. Will it (your unconscious) support you (your conscious self)?

- Become the image being again and plan the changes you are going to make. Be aware of all the implications of change for both of you. If the image being is not ready for change, do not force it; repeat the exercise later and see if it is now ready to move on. If it is now prepared for change and so are you, agree on the steps you will take.

- Appreciate and reflect on the information you have been given and thank your unconscious self for the images it has sent you.

- Gently come back to full awareness and paint or draw your image or make a note of the information you now have at your disposal. Over time, a map will emerge not only of your unconscious but of your life and your reality.

- Even though the exercise is concluded, it may not be entirely finished so be aware over the next few days of any new information that begins to emerge – in the form of dreams or daydreams, insights, synchronicities or intuitions. The unconscious will continue to work gently on the problems you present to it and it is important to remain open to the fresh information it sends you.

IMAGEWORK IN ACTION

IMAGEWORK 1: *WHO AM I?*
THE IMAGE AS A METAPHOR FOR YOUR LIFE

*Every person, all the events in your life are there
because you have drawn them there.
What you choose to do with them is up to you.*

– Richard Bach

If you relax and ask for an image to emerge right now of who you are, how you see yourself, how your life is going for you and what the future is likely to hold, you will receive an image and it will have meaning for you. Imagework is as simple as that.

Exactly what this image will be is as individual as you are, and as different, personal, unique and meaningful. We have looked at some of the images experienced by others – a stone lion, a lone tree, an honesty plant, a Thunder God, a bird. There is a qualitative difference between the image of a bird and a tree which is representative of that person's life. In each case, the question was the same and in each case the answer was different, personal, unique and meaningful.

MEETING YOURSELF

The first step always is to phrase the question. '*Who am I and what do I need to know at this point in my life?*' is a good starting point. From here, you can ask questions about specific issues or concerns.

As the image becomes clearer to you and takes on more definite form, begin to notice details and characteristics about it – its colour, its sound, smell, the way it moves and the space it occupies in its environment – as well as what it is.

Try not to analyse too much at this stage or to get too involved with the image being. Some images defy all known laws of physics or biology and you may not even know what this image is. That is fine. Images are allowed to defy the laws we have to operate by. Simply ask it what it is and it will tell you.

Get to know it from as many different perspectives as possible. Then step into the image you have created and experience the world from its perspective. If you are a tree, how does it feel to be rooted in the earth? What does the wind feel like in your leaves? How does it sound? How do you experience sunlight or rain? As food? What does it taste like?

Having taken on the persona of the new image, the tree image, ask questions, such as: what is it like to be you? Do you ever wish you could move? How deep are your roots? Where are you? What is going on around you? How do you feel? Do you feel safe and secure or uncomfortable, threatened? Ask any others that occur to you – remembering always that at this point these are questions *to the tree being*, not to your rational mind.

As you enter the image, you are more fully operating from the imaginative brain, rather than your conscious, rational mind. You are not drawing any conclusions or parallels with your own life. Ask questions *to* the image being and answer *as* the image being or you may find yourself slipping into premature analysis.

There is a definite 'flow' to Imagework. Your rational mind is dominant as you phrase your initial question, then as you enter the image you begin to get more in touch with the emotional brain where feelings, memories and insights will begin to emerge. You then re-engage the practical brain as you come out of the image state and analyse the information you have received. By understanding the history of this image, you can get a feel for major life events which have brought it (you) to this point and see where decisions were made which have affected you in the present and will continue to do so in the future until the situation is changed in some way.

For this reason, it is helpful to be as precise as possible about when things changed for the image being. Knowing that an event of three months ago was the vital point of change and not (as you had always thought) an event which took place in childhood really is useful information.

In a similar way, you can ask the image being what its future holds and so get a feel for the possibilities that are open to you. Possible questions include 'What needs to happen for you to move forward/be happier/get past this, etc.?' or 'What's stopping you from making this move?', 'How would it be if you did X, Y or Z?' or 'It's now a year into the future and you *have* moved forward positively and achieved real results. What did you do?' You can keep asking 'What's next' questions until you are sure that you have exhausted all possibilities.

Sometimes, if we are truly afraid to see ourselves as we are, or to move forward in our lives because of the possible repercussions if we do, our unconscious will naturally protect us by not allowing us an image of ourselves or of a possible future if we do move on. In this case, thank your unconscious for its concern and reassure it that you really do want to know. Tell it that you understand that *it* doesn't want to do this but ask it just to imagine how it would be *if it did* move forward. Since this does not actually commit the image being to moving forward, it is often more willing to entertain the idea of a new future and reveal this to you.

Now tune back into your original image to reflect on this information. What does the future look like to you now that you have seen it?

Emerge from the image journey and spend a few moments considering the experience you have just had. How does the image reflect your life? What feelings does it raise for you?

Do you connect with the period in the image being's history when the key change took place to make it what it is now? Is there a correspondence with actual events in your own life (there usually is)?

Does the situation of the image being seem in any way similar to your own (were you a big fish in a small pond, or a small fish in a big pond? If you were a tree, how did you feel about being rooted – secure or stuck?). Where, in your own life, do *you* feel like this?

What did the image being have to say about how you could move forward? How do *you* feel about this? How do you feel about the future if you make the changes recommended to you?

Look forward from this point as specifically as possible. If you actually put these changes into place, how would your new life be? How would the new you feel about getting out of bed in the morning? How would you dress? What would work be like? Would you still be doing the same job as you do now? What would your home be like and who would you share it with?

Some counsellors use this approach by asking for an image in their own minds of the person they are counselling and their life situation. They then pass on the image to their client and ask whether it means anything to them. 'In my experience,' says Dr Glouberman, 'the image has an immediate and powerful significance to the other person in 99 out of 100 cases and often represents the turning point of the counselling session.'[73]

IMAGEWORK 2: *HOW DID I GET HERE?*
MEETING THE CHILD WITHIN YOU

The truth you seek has no past or future.
It is, and that's all it needs to be

– Richard Bach

In the linear universe things move forward in time, and forward only. While we accept that the actions we take today may change the outcome of tomorrow, it seems a strange idea that our actions today could actually change our past. But in the holographic universe, nothing is more natural.

John Perkins writes in the introduction to this book of a healing by the Amazon shaman, Daniel Wachapa, where a young woman's hearing was fully restored. How did the shaman accomplish this when the best that modern medicine could provide was a hearing aid to treat the *symptoms* and not the *cause* of this illness? By helping her, through the shamanic journey, to go back 'to that time when things were being said that were too painful for her to hear' and empowering her to break through the energetic barrier to sound that she had created in her own defence at that time.

In this journey we, too, will revisit our past – taking with us the greater power and understanding that comes with adulthood – to see how these problems look to us now, and to use our adult power to readdress them *in the moment* of their occurrence.

THE PRESENT IS THE PAST AGAIN – SOMETIMES

We communicate with our past through memory, which is fallible and can also be selective about the events it chooses to call important.

We make sense of our life in the present by reference to these events of the past, perhaps of childhood – like Karl who saw his family's move from the city as the most important shaping factor in his life since then. But, as Karl discovered, the reverse is also true – we experience the present in a particular way *because* we have chosen to define the events of our childhood in that way.

Some people find it hard to trust others, for example, because they felt rejected or abandoned as a child, and this can badly affect their present relationships. But the reverse may also be true – they do not trust others and explain this by reference to childhood abandonment. This can become a feedback loop which will lead to a pattern of abandonment and lack of trust as people in this situation become more and more cautious of involvement with others because they then make themselves vulnerable again to hurt. Their partners, meanwhile, feel as if something is missing from the relationship – which it is: trust and true connection – and may actually leave them because of this, which reinforces their feelings of abandonment and hurt.

The only way to resolve this is by breaking the original pattern and redefining the myth, since 'memories are not simply an objective record of the past. Like any historical record, they are part of a particular approach to history . . . If we want to change our personal mythology, we need to go back into the old records and find new ways to make sense of them.'[74]

By doing so, we can redefine our past, bring new understanding to the present, and create a new foundation for our future.

BEFRIENDING THE CHILD TO YOURSELF

Allow an image to emerge of a child you once were at a key point in your life. If you wish to examine a particular life event from your childhood, you can be quite specific about what this child looks like, how old she is, and so on. Otherwise, simply allow an image to emerge of the child you used to be and notice what age you are. Your unconscious will be advising you of an event of significance which took place at this age and which still has an impact on your life. The image you get could be a memory of yourself, an image from a photograph or a 'sense' of yourself at that age. Notice how the child looks, what she is wearing, how old she is.

Tell the child what you see and how you feel about her, and ask any questions that seem important to you – 'How do you feel about [person/event] . . . your relationship with . . . the fact that . . .', whatever needs to be asked.

Then become the child.

How do *you* feel about this adult, knowing that she is the future you? What does the world look like through *your* eyes? What is important to *you*? What is good and not so good? What would *you* like to change?

Talk to the adult, recognizing that she cares about you and that you can be completely honest with her. Is there anything you would like to ask the adult about her world?

Continue this dialogue, exchanging roles when you need to in order to ask and answer appropriate questions. Sense how the adult may be able to help the child, and vice versa, with the qualities that you both have. If you feel that the child is going through a difficult time, be prepared, if you wish, to step into her world and to help her.

Susan's image of herself at the age of eight is of a small, timid girl who is now being beaten by her father for some minor transgression. The beating is quite out of proportion to any 'wrong' the child has done. He is in a rage and has lost control of himself. Susan is cowering in front of him and crying, but he will not stop hitting her.

Adult Susan is furious at the image and steps into the child's world as her adult self. She shoves her father away and hugs eight-year-old Susan to her to protect and comfort her.

When she is calmer and the eight-year-old is less distraught, adult Susan is able to intervene between the parent and the child, explaining to her father the psychological and physical damage he is causing to his daughter by acting in this way. She is able to offer protection, support and healing to eight-year-old Susan and to let her see that not all adults are bad. Together, they help her father to see that Susan has needs and rights and that she is an intelligent, lovable girl who deserves better than this. The past has been changed.

Notice the environment of the child and the important people in her world. How does she relate to them and they to her? How does she feel about the world she is in? Get a feel for the situation as the adult you, able to understand the complexities of relationships and situations which are beyond the capabilities of a child. How does this environment look and feel to you? What about the behaviour of the people here – as an adult, with your wider experience of life, do you feel the same way about their behaviour as a child would?

Become the child again and let her memories come through, revisiting other, earlier times from the life you both share. Have things always been this way? What changed? When? How? Why? How did the child feel at those moments?

If you need to, relive each scene again as your adult self and explain to the child sensitively and honestly what is happening, in a way that the child can relate to.

We adults can do incredible damage very easily to a child, even with well-meaning intent, sometimes even by 'protecting' them from the 'harmful' truth or giving them only the information *we* feel they can cope with.

Jane has spent her whole life never quite being able to disconnect from the brother she was close to as a child. She has always felt his presence and used him as a reference for many of the decisions she has made in her life (*'What would Simon feel in this situation? What would he do? How would he act?'*). She feels that half the time he is speaking for her and she never quite answers for herself or is in full control of her own life.

Simon died when they were both very small and Jane's parents, thinking they were protecting her from harm, never explained to her what had happened. Simon just didn't come home one day and, even though she is now aware of the truth, she was never given the chance to say goodbye. To her, Simon was not really dead, he was simply 'not there'.

Using Imagework to meet with her brother again, Jane was able to reassure herself that he was OK, to get a sense of his new existence, and to ask the questions of him that she has never felt able to ask her parents about his death. Finally, she was able to say goodbye to the brother she had loved, to wish him well and to begin to fully embrace her own life.

If there is anything the child would like to change, which makes sense to you, remember you have the resources of the magic wand and the Wise and Loving Being we referred to earlier which can help to make this happen for both of you by suggesting a new way forward. What would you like to change? What would happen if you did? How do you feel about this?

Go forward into the future as the child. What are things like when *no* change is made? Do you notice any recurring patterns or situations? What does this mean to you? What happens if things *do* change? What does the future look like then?

Decide together, if appropriate, that you will make these changes. Look forward into possible futures where the same situations may arise. How will you behave differently this time?

Once you have fully rehearsed your future actions and responses together and agreed that you will create a different future, make a pact to use the resources you both have to make this better future for you both.

Thank your child for her honesty and for what you have been able to learn from her. Appreciate the child for her strength, for surviving, and for giving life to the adult you.

I was reminded of the importance of this appreciation recently, when I tuned into an image of myself at the age of 10. I had never much liked myself at 10. I seemed to have few friends. I did not enjoy, and was not particularly good at, school. I seemed to be stuck and powerless to change my world, even though I knew I was not enjoying my life. Why was I so weak and stupid at that age? Look at all I have achieved since then. Why couldn't I have been smarter, stronger, more resourceful then, instead of having to struggle for the next several years to get this far? If only I had been tougher, who knows what I would have achieved by now. All my younger self had done was hold me back.

And then it occurred to me – just who did I think *had* got me this far? Not the adult me since the adult me did not even exist then. I am the adult me now precisely *because* that 10-year-old boy had the strength, the energy, the brains and the will to change his life *for me* and to create the things in my life which I now enjoy.

Once I realized this, all the criticisms I had of this child vanished and the journey turned into a celebration of his strength and the struggles and sacrifices he had made for me.

The exercise also helped me to better appreciate the feelings of my own flesh and blood children. They cannot see into their future any more than I could at the age of 10. They long to be grown-up, so things will be better for them and they will have more control over their own lives, as if being grown-up is a magical formula. What they do not see is that it is *they* who already have the power. They have the strength *now* to create the adults they *will* be. Following this exercise, I was able to celebrate with my children the uniqueness and specialness of each of them and the unlimited power within both of them.

Questions I have asked of my inner children – and sometimes of my real children – range from the sublime to the extremely mundane. Here are a few which you may like to use.

QUESTIONS FOR SELF AND OTHERS

What is your earliest memory?

What do you remember from before you were born?

Am I a good friend to you?

How loved do you feel? By me? By others?

What do you think your mummy and daddy were like before you were born?
How do you think things changed when you came along?

What is the bravest thing you've ever done?

Are you happy?

What was the saddest day of your life?

When were you most scared?

What do you really feel inside when someone does something to hurt you?
How does it make you feel about the world?

What would you like me to ask you? And what would you like to ask me?

Who would you most like to be?

Do you think there's a perfect soulmate – a 'special someone' – waiting for you?

If you were to die tomorrow, how would you like to be remembered?

What do you wish for most?

What do you wish you'd done that you haven't done yet?

What do you think it's like to be a parent?

What does it mean to be honest?

What is a good daddy/mummy like?

What would you like to change about me?

What's the best thing I've ever done for you? And the worst thing I've ever done to you?

When you look at photographs of yourself as a baby, what do you see?

Tell me the biggest secret about you . . . ?

What do you think you'll be like ten years from now?

*Have you ever really wanted something
but felt unable to ask?*

Why do grown-ups make war?

*If you could change one thing about the world,
what would it be?*

Why do some people have more things than others?

Is it better to be free or to be safe, secure?

What's more important – being rich or being happy?

Why do you cry? What makes you laugh?

*When grown-ups make decisions for you, do you think
they're always right?*

Do you think I'm proud of you?

*What would you like your life to be like
when you're my age?*

Do grown-ups play enough?

Is there enough magic in the world?

It is also important to appreciate yourself as an adult for taking the time to check in with your child and to really listen to what they have to tell you.

When you have opened your eyes and returned to awareness, drawn or written down your experiences and feelings, remember also to stay alert to other sensations and recollections over the next few days, and to make contact again with your child from time to time. Your child is now alive within you and to ignore her would be like ignoring your own children – ultimately you will lose them.

Revisiting past wounds in order to heal them is not the

same as going through them again as you did when you were a child. As an adult, you have the benefit of knowing what happened so you are prepared for it. It is also more distant in time, and you now have an adult perspective on things too. The adult you has more power than you did as a child when this event took place and can step into the image at any time to protect and support the child who is going through this for you, to negotiate with others and finally, if necessary, to intervene directly on behalf of the child. You also have a magic wand you can use at any time to change what is happening and to alter the outcome positively, as well as the assistance of a Wise and Loving Being who will gladly intervene to offer protection to you both.

If, at any point, you need to pull back from painful memories, you are perfectly free and able to do so. It is possible to gain a sense of emotional distance by introducing a 'distancing element' into the image drama – seeing yourself as the audience in a personal cinema, for example, where the image you are watching is just another version of reality and one where the ending can be changed through the re-editing which you, as director, are about to carry out.

If you need to withdraw from the image completely, give yourself full permission to do so. Speak to the child first to explain that you are leaving for a little while but are most definitely not abandoning her. Say your goodbyes and re-assure her that you will be back.

Let the information you have learned settle within you for a few days, paying close attention to any new memories, feelings or insights which arise, and try again when you are ready to re-enter this point in your life. There is never any hurry, never any pressure. Your life is not an exam and it is certainly no race.

IMAGEWORK 3: *WHERE AM I GOING?*
VISITING A POSSIBLE FUTURE

*Don't turn away from possible futures before you're
certain you don't have anything to learn from them.
You're always free to change your mind and choose a
different future, or a different past.*

– Richard Bach

Imagine how useful it would be to have an insight into your
future and how things might turn out for you before you
make an important life decision. Everyone can be wise *after*
the event, but to be wise *before* the event is a real art.

People bring all sorts of questions to this Imagework
exercise. Career concerns ('Should I take the new job I have
been offered?'), relationships ('How will things turn out if I
decide to move in with my boyfriend?'), financial decisions
('What is the outcome of my deciding to buy this new car?')
or general questions about the future ('What does life hold
for me if I continue on this path?') are just a few of them.

There is no time constraint to this journey – 30 minutes
into the future to check the outcome of a decision you are
about to make, or thirty years to see how your life will turn
out if you continue along your current path: both are equally
valid and effective. In this exercise we will visit a possible
future to see where our current lifepath will take us and to
decide from there if – and how – we would like to change it.

MEETING YOUR FUTURE SELF

To take this journey, relax and allow an image to come to you
of a road, which you are now walking along, and which
represents your life at this moment. What does it look like?
What do *you* look like? Who else is there with you and how
do they relate to you, or are you alone? What is your

environment like? And, perhaps most importantly, how do you feel on this road?

Get a sense of your destination. Where are you going, and why? What do you hope to do or find there? And, if you find it, how will you feel then? What will change for you?

At some point along this road, you will reach a place where the road divides and find a signpost which points in different directions. How many roads are there? What do the names on the signpost suggest about where these roads lead? From where you stand, what does each road look like? Do you have a sense that whatever you are looking for is at the end of this road?

Choose the road that seems most appealing to you from where you now stand. Does it change in any way now you are travelling along it? Is the going easy or hard?

Step into the future on this path – five, ten, fifteen, twenty years from now. How does it feel at each point and what is going on around you?

Float above the scene so you can see yourself on the road in the context of the whole environment. How do things look now? What part do you play in the full scene?

Become the whole environment. How do you feel about this person who occupies your space? What would you like to say to them about the road they are on?

Return to the crossroads and try each of the roads in turn. Ask yourself the same questions and notice how each path is different for you. Commit to one of these roads – just for today – as the future you will now explore in full.

See yourself at the end of the road you have chosen, at the end of your life. There will be no more travelling. Invite an image of a person with your name who has arrived safely at the end of this lifepath. How old is this person? How does it feel to be you?

What are your feelings and recollections about the path you have walked? Where were the ups and downs? Was the going easy or tough? At what age did you meet the highs and the lows, and how did you respond to them? What was the outcome? What adventures did you have along the way?

All things considered, was this a good road for you? If you could have your time again (which you can), would you take this road again or another?

Imagine yourself as truly content, having reached the end of this particular road. What are the most important things you did to achieve this?

THE ROAD NOT TAKEN

Linda sees herself as an old lady, pushing a trolley round a supermarket, trying to scrape together enough money for her shopping. Just to add to her woes, one of the wheels on her trolley is loose and she has to struggle with it in order not to keep going round in circles. She is cold and alone and the store is crowded and uninviting. She is disappointed because the path she chose to follow had seemed so appealing and was such an easy road to travel. Why did things turn out like this?

Then she sees that the outcome of her life is precisely *because* she took the easy road.

She'd had some important and tough decisions to take in her life – she wanted to change careers, to retrain, and to put more effort into her relationships which she never seemed to have time for. Travelling the easy route allowed her to avoid these decisions and, while this was comforting in the short term, she can see now that avoiding these choices was ultimately unfulfilling for her.

She returns to the crossroads and marks the signpost 'Unsatisfied' as a reminder that this road is not the one for her. The next road she sees looks a lot harder to travel. It rises steeply and the landscape looks bleak and unwelcoming from where she stands. Nonetheless, she starts to walk and soon the slope of the road evens out. She begins to enter country-side. Birds sing, the sun is shining here.

She becomes the 'older Linda', the person who has already walked this path. She sees that it was hard at first but eventually – and actually quite quickly – got her to where she really wanted to be and she was then able to enjoy her life in the knowledge that she had more fully achieved her potential.

A few months after this journey, Linda did, in fact, sign up for a retraining course and had plans to change her career. Her current job is demanding and, when I last saw her, she was finding it hard to get the time off work she needed for her retraining. But she was committed to doing so and, despite the difficulties, seemed happy and fulfilled in herself.

As the older you, you are able to look back at life from the vantage point of a wiser, more realized and more self-assured person who has overcome the obstacles and challenges they were faced with. From here, you can see your younger self just starting out on their road and can offer advice and support to them, to this person who has made this effort for you, as part of your becoming this older and wiser self.

From the perspective of the older, wiser you, get a feel for your life, having taken this road. What have you accomplished and how did you do it? How do you feel about yourself, about how life has treated you? How did you take care of yourself along the way – and what can you learn from this *right* now?

You can enter the future by many other routes besides the road into the future:

- Climb into a time machine or a transporter which will take you to a specific date in your future history.
- Enter a cave where you will meet and dialogue with the older, wiser you and ask her to tell you about the road she took and the choices she made and how they turned out.
- Make a date with Destiny to consult with Her on your future.
- Step into the vortex of the hologram and emerge in a new time and space.
- Enter a cinema where they are playing the re-run of your life and you can stop the film at any time and re-edit it. How will you change the ending or make that slow part in the middle a little more exciting?

If any of this feels difficult or strange, that is perfectly natural. The trick is to keep practising. Trust your intuition and your feelings on this. If it works for you, that is all you really need to know. If you experience it, it is real.

EXPLORATIONS: EMBRACING YOUR IMAGES

1. Dreaming awake
Begin practising Imagework gently by paying more conscious attention to your day dreams and reveries during the day. As soon as you 'catch yourself' daydreaming, don't shake yourself out of it, take yourself *into* it. Ask yourself why these *particular* images are entering your mind at this time. What events are taking place around you or happening to – or within – you to make these specific images come to mind? Track back: what were you thinking or what was said to you immediately before you entered this image state? What is the connection between this image and what took place just before it?

2. Tuning in
Work with a partner to practise tuning in to them, their feelings and their thoughts through images. Sit quietly together and ask your allies for an image which represents your friend and their life at this time. When an image presents itself to you, share it with your partner, without making any value judgements or offering any kind of analysis. Simply state the facts: 'When I tune in to you, I get the image of a . . . [whatever] Does this mean anything to you?' Notice how this image corresponds with their situation, thoughts and feelings.

3. Self-reflections in Light and Dark mirrors
This technique is a variation on the European tradition of scrying, where the future is revealed in the play of light and the energy of fire. A similar exercise is also undertaken as

part of the initiation rite of the Dagara, where the candidate is expected to stare patiently at a living thing, such as a tree, until its purpose and its spirit-essence can be clearly 'seen'.

In this urban shamanic form, first set up a lit candle in front of a mirror in a darkened room. Allow your eyes to drift out of focus, looking through the candle into the image of yourself in the mirror. Feel relaxed – not as if you are looking *for* something but *into* something.

In the first part of this exercise, the Dark Mirror, allow to be reflected back to yourself an image only of those aspects of yourself which are currently 'true' in the world – how you present yourself, how others see you in the many roles that you play, the aspects of you that are projected out, *into* the world, beyond your physical, material self. Get a sense of the overall feeling and sensation of what it means to be you. Spend about 30 minutes with this and make a note of all that comes to mind, the images that present themselves to you, the associations you make.

Allow yourself a break of at least 30 minutes or, better still, attempt the second part of this exercise – the Light Mirror – on a different day. In this exercise, allow to be reflected back an image of yourself as seen from the domain of potential, seeing only the light essence of yourself, the power that you hold, all worldly problems, issues and concerns aside – the boundless you that connects *inwardly* with the essence of all things. This is the you that came into the world. Knowing this, again make a note of all images, impressions and sensations that present themselves to you.

You can work more fully with any of these aspects of self by using Imagework to explore each set of images fully, or by journeying to the core essence of each expression of you.

In the Dark Mirror exercise, you are reflecting back the socialized self, with all the gloss of the culture and society you now belong to and the roles that you play within it.

With the Light Mirror, you are reflecting back the energetic essence of yourself from the time before this learning.

Your two impressions are likely to be very different. Seeing this, what is your *quintessential self* and what does this tell you about who and what you truly are and your potential in this universe?

6

ENERGETIC TRANSFORMATION: SHAPESHIFTING FOR PERSONAL AND GLOBAL CHANGE

When one person has a thought it is a real thing, with a pattern of electro-chemical energy that can be measured. Every time the pattern is activated in that one mind, it becomes stronger. This pattern can be shared with another mind, and when two people think the same thought, it becomes stronger still, perhaps more than twice as strong. When millions of minds think the same thought, it may have a permanent place in the collective unconscious.
At no time in human history has there been more change. It has thrown the collective unconscious into flux, and global communications are expanding the ideas it contains and creating new ones. So which ideas will be strong when the dust settles?
The ones that are clearly stated and strongly expressed in symbolic form – the ones that connect with people's experiences and are compatible with what they feel to be true, the ones that work in their lives . . .

– Robert M. Underwood, M.Ed.,
teacher and Western shamanic practitioner

Where two energy fields meet, there is always power. Where the sea meets the shore, the breeze is stronger, the sea air fresher and cleansing. Where the sun meets the Earth, there is warmth. Sometimes, we can even see the power. The thin line which separates the sky from the tops of mountains on a hazy day is where the upper world begins for the shamans.

Every living thing has a heart. The land is no different, and every land has an energy centre which ensures the flow of life throughout it. The Black Hills of Dakota are the sacred energy field of the Lakota, the prayer-grounds of their nation, and the 'heart of all there is'. The land transforms this energy and lets it flow.

When satellites recently photographed these hills from above, scientists were able to see what the shamans of the Lakota have always known. From above, the Black Hills are exactly the shape of the human heart, with all of its chambers, veins and ventricles.

The Lakota had no satellites or aeroplanes. How could they have known what these hills might look like from the skies?

The answer is that the Elders did not need planes or satellites because they were one with the land, they understood it and were part of it. It was their own heart they were sensing. All the land is sacred.

And yet.

The Amazon is the world's largest rainforest, the lungs and the breath of our planet. The forests clean our air, absorb our greenhouse gases and give us back pure oxygen. It is the work of a friend who loves us or a parent caring for his child. Every one of us produces more than 400 pounds of CO_2 each year, simply by breathing. The forests take this give-away and their gift to us, in turn, is the stuff of life. Purely and simply: without the rainforests, we die.

We know this. Yet the deforestation of the Amazon increased by 30 per cent in 1998, despite all the measures to curb it. More than 6,500 square miles of forest – an area more than half the size of Belgium – was destroyed. There is *nothing surprising in this. In the last twenty years or so, more than 200,000 square miles of rainforest have gone – about 13 per cent of the entire Amazon region.*

And even that may not be the whole story since the satellites which monitor this can only see large areas of deforestation and will miss areas of cumulative, incremental damage of 14 acres or less. There could be hundreds of 14-acre patches criss-crossing the rainforests right now, like a patchwork quilt of greed, which we are not even aware of.

Only 22 per cent of the world's old growth forests, our planet's greatest allies for transforming energy and pollution, currently remain intact.

And without trees, we die. It's a very simple equation. But we don't seem to get it.

NASA scientists tell us that the planet is now off the scale of normal climatic variability. There is no longer any doubt about global warming. It is happening. The question is what we choose to do about it.

The answer is, not very much, it seems. Unless the giant energy companies are prepared to shapeshift their own dream, our life among the stars will be a short one, for fossil fuel emissions are one of the main problems facing us as a race. It will be a dishonourable death, an exit with a whimper, where we all go gently into that dark night. Today, the oil and gas industry spends more than $150 billion a year on new 'exploration' and almost none on the development of renewable energy sources, while the majority of us allow it, through fatigue, ennui, a sense of powerlessness about it all.

The land will not sustain us for much longer when its own existence is threatened in this way. The Earth will go on living either with or without us – just as we will tolerate another creature, an ant or a spider, walking on us until its presence becomes bothersome. We do not tolerate it with compassion but with indifference. Then we remove it and think no more about it. The Earth is a living being and Her reaction will be the same.

If all of human life is snuffed out tomorrow, we should not fool ourselves that the universe will care or even notice. It will be just one less beacon in a universe of light. A pity, maybe. But for the universe, not the end of the world.

All the land is sacred. And yet, we do not see it.

We each of us have the power to change things for the better. That is the essence of shapeshifting.

All thought and all matter is essentially a configuration of energy. We have seen in the work of the scientists and the shamans that our ideas are what give structure to the world and determine how we experience ourselves in that world. The tallest skyscraper begins with an idea, takes form as an architectural blueprint which is the material expression of that idea, and is realized as a tower block that embraces the arc of the sky. And so it is with all things – a painting of the Birth of Venus or the conception of a child begins first with an idea and then with our focus of energy in the direction of that idea in order to make it real.

As the scientist, Carl Sagan remarked: 'By changing our perspective, we can figure out how worlds work . . . understanding where we live is an essential precondition for improving the neighbourhood.'[75]

We change our perspective every time we journey, and we then have the power to transform this energy, to reshape and re-vision it and to create a different outcome. When we bring this energy back with us into ordinary reality, via the creative nerve centre of our minds, we give ourselves the power to shape and change ideas, to produce new and tangible effects in our bodies, and to improve our lives, our society and our world. We can achieve all of this very simply – by moving energy from one place to another. By deciding that one way is not working for us, and directing our attention and our intention towards another solution. All we have to do is change our minds.

'The universe is made up of energy fields which defy description . . . [our] *will* is not only responsible for our awareness, but also for everything in the universe,' said don

Juan.[76] By changing the configuration of energy we are using to empower ourselves (or otherwise), and anchoring it in a new form, we also change ourselves and our lives.

And a little energy can go a very long way. Amy, in a journeying workshop, relates a true story which comes originally from Dr Caroline Myss, a pioneer in the field of energy medicine and human consciousness.[77]

She tells of a car accident where the driver, Maggie, is so badly hurt that her soul literally takes flight, leaving her body to float above it and the wreck of the car she is in. All the time, she is fully conscious of events around her, the other cars on the road, the onlookers, and those who rush to help her.

Then she becomes aware of something else: a beam of light coming from the driver of the fifth car behind her in the queue of traffic now forming. The light enters the wreck of her own car and then her body, slumped unconscious in her seat.

Then all is dark and silent.

Maggie wakes some time later in hospital and, when she is fully recovered, remembers the sensation of floating above her body and the strange beam of light she had seen. She finds that she can remember the number plate of the car behind her, the one the light had come from. That is the first curious thing – only if her consciousness, her soul, had truly left her body could she even have seen this number plate. It seems that there *is* something within us, some form of energy, which is not pure matter but which is conscious.

Now she has the number of the car, she is able to find the driver and calls on her one day. After introducing herself, she relates the sensation of floating above her body and seeing the light which had entered it from the person she is now with.

'Do you have any idea what that light was?' she asks.

'Oh yes,' says the other driver. 'At that point, I was praying for you.'

A little energy goes a long way. In this case, the energy of one simple prayer helped save a life.

What Amy is relating here is a story of soul loss as a result of severe trauma and the retrieval of this energy by someone untrained in shamanic healing but who earnestly cared about the suffering of another human being. Compassion, intention and the focus of the will – the essence of prayer – has a real and tangible effect on the universe itself.

I was privileged recently to meet a very wise and beautiful shamaness who had lived for many years among the Hopi Indians of America. She told of the power of the blessing rituals she had witnessed among these people, where the shaman's prayers for another were able to bring peace and healing. Relating this to modern scientific practice in the West, she remarked that Kirlian photography has been used to capture on film the essences – what we call the auras – of a number of living things. In one experiment scientists had photographed food, which was then blessed, using words of love to imbue the food with the qualities of love itself. When it was re-photographed, rays of pure light were clearly visible emanating from the food. The power of the blessing it had received was *scientifically* evident.

My friend Vee, a shamanic counsellor trained by Sandra Ingerman, one of the world's leading Western experts in soul retrieval, told me a similar story recently. During her healings, Sandra keeps water next to her and her client. This water has been analysed by scientists, who have found that the quality of the water is actually changed, made purer and more wholesome as a result of the healing work itself. Our *intention* to heal has a tangible effect on living matter.

A few months ago, I attended a workshop in London with a very powerful and charismatic shaman from Finland, Christiana Harle-Silvennoinen, who has worked extensively with the shamans of Tuva, on the Russian–Mongolian border.

The Tuvans use a ritual of blessing in their healing work, to give energy and power to a person or an endeavour or situation, by journeying to the spirit world and allowing a spirit song to come through them which they sing to their client as they work with them to heal them. Christiana allowed us all an opportunity to try this for ourselves. I worked with Eve, who had asked for a blessing for her own healing work with individuals and groups.

I stood before her as she knelt on the ground and, as Christiana began to drum, I entered the trance that takes me to the otherworld. Suddenly, Eve was no longer a person kneeling before me, but an energy form covered by what seemed to be a dark pyramid of cloth-like material. Holding the rattles I would use this for work, I began at the base of the pyramid to lift the material from her, using the energy of sound.

As it was removed, I saw Eve as a bundle of light fibres, each one luminescent and pulsing with the colours of the rainbow. Some of these fibres had been drawn outwards, as if by static, when the cover of the pyramid was removed, and were now floating in the air around her. I rattled around Eve's body, massaging and stroking these fibres back into the light bundle that she had become, then worked upwards, smoothing and shaping it and, at the top, casting off any dark patches, which I intuitively *knew* to be unhelpful energies.

As I was working, I became aware of the most beautiful music filling the room and listened closely to see where it was coming from. I was surprised to discover that it was the sound of my own voice I was hearing. But I was not singing – in fact, my lips were hardly moving at all – I was *being sung* by spirit. The words were in a language I did not recognize – but I knew what they meant and so I translated for Eve:

> 'There are oceans between us, still we are one.
> The child in you, the ancient in you knows
> That Spirit walks with you.
> We all are one.'

When the song ended and the drum was silent, I reported my journey to Eve and gave her the words of her song. There were tears in her eyes as she took them from me. Her fears were lifted and she felt lighter, cleansed. She knew she was special in the eyes of Spirit. And *she felt blessed.*

Christiana told us that in Tuva there is no distinction between a blessing and a curse: it is the same energy which is used and both have an effect on the body. It is the intention – to harm or to heal – which is important. It is the same in Haitian Vodou – and, I suspect, the world over. In Vodou, the Mambo or Houngan may use their connection to spirit and to the energy of the universe to bring good fortune and bless-ings to a client or to assist that client in an act of revenge upon another. The same energy is used; the difference is in the direction it is given.

We all have access to these powers and we all have a choice in how we use them. It is our intention which counts above all else.

Thermodynamics tells us that energy cannot be created or destroyed; it can only change its form. This is the Law of Conservation of Energy. We work with this law whenever we enter the shamanic otherworld to retrieve a power animal or object, return a soul to another, offer a blessing, or consult with our inner child or future self. We move energy from one state to another so that effective changes can take place at a physical, spiritual, mental or emotional level.

When energy blocks are removed, physically, we have access to powers which are the basis for the 'miracle' cures of shamanism as well as the scientifically endorsed success of visualization with cancer patients. For the shaman, there is no such thing as 'illness'; it is merely energy in an in-appropriate place or form – not good, not bad, just inappropriate to our needs. The 'illness' is cured by removing the energy block, or 'spirit intrusion' as traditional shamans would say.

When energy changes form, we feel spiritually uplifted, at one with ourselves and others, a part of the whole once again. Mentally, we unleash new capabilities for progress by revealing powers perhaps we never even knew we had, and by working through our old fears and the beliefs which are no longer serving us. Emotionally, we touch parts of ourselves which have been hidden for too long so we can bring these back into ourselves.

When energy is changed within us, we have the power to change the universe.

TRANSFORMING ENERGY

The basis of the shaman's power for energetic transformation is the removal of energy blocks, firstly by understanding where, why, when, how, and sometimes as a result of whose actions, the natural flow of energy came to stagnate at this point. From there, he can release this energy back into the whole body, using ritual and affirmation as concrete, three-dimensional representations of the energy we now have available to us and our intentions for its beneficial use.

Before we can make effective use of our energies, we need first to understand where we are in our lives, where our energies are flowing freely or trapped within us, and then to redirect and rechannel them to where we want to be.

If we imagine our energy, our vitality, our ability to act, as water flowing through a tap, we may find that the flow is sometimes not as strong, not as energetic as we wish. We may suppose that this must be due to a blockage of some kind in the water pipe, which is not letting enough water through, but we have no way of knowing this unless we are willing to roll our sleeves up and take a good look at our plumbing. The alternative is simply to remain ignorant and put up with the problem – which may be fine until we desperately need to drink. Then we either get the problem fixed or die of thirst.

Perhaps the flow would have been sufficient if we had not removed, or even noticed, the blockage. But, still, the tap is more effective now it is clear.

Or perhaps the situation would have progressively deteriorated until the water trapped in the pipeline froze one winter. Then the tap would not function at all and, even worse, the growing pressure of the expanding ice might easily have caused the whole system to blow.

This is the problem with blockages. You just never know.

To resolve the problem, we must identify where the blockage has occurred and then take action to remove it. This done, the water will flow again through our system as it was designed to.

Energetic transformation is a way of locating the blockage and dealing with it, to relieve the immediate problems and protect our system from future pressure overloads or energetic drought.

THE TRANSFORMATION PROCESS

Energetic transformation is a *process*, an approach, rather than a prescription, and there is plenty of room for individual creativity; indeed, the shamans would say that *the* most important thing is to make it a *personal* process, something you are comfortable with and believe in fully.

The four steps to change are:

1. to find the problem and locate the point of blockage;
2. to gather information on the causes and probable cures;
3. to identify the transformation point – the heart of the issue – and the actions you can take to make a difference – and move beyond it into a new sense of self;
4. to emerge into a more positive and energetic future.

1. LOCATING THE BLOCKAGE

In shamanic terms, there are many reasons why the natural flow of energy in our bodies might become blocked. Physical accidents, like the one related by Amy, and the emotional and spiritual trauma and shock accompanying it, are obvious examples.

More subtle forms of abuse – deliberate or unintentional –

such as mental cruelty, neglect, assault, the post-traumatic stress and delayed shock typical of soldiers and victims of war, and the self-abuse which comes with addiction and the surrender of our power to another are other examples which, immediately or cumulatively, can be just as devastating. Even the stress and tension, the manipulation and lack of human warmth typical of the twentieth-century workplace, with all of the demands it makes upon us, the artificial environment we occupy there, the jockeying for power, office politics and unnatural competition we agree to get involved with means that some form of energetic power loss is probably the norm and not the exception in the world we have created for ourselves today.

We are perhaps all aware – at least sometimes – of a sense of numbness, separation from the fullness of the world, alienation from ourselves, or maybe just a general and unnamed sense of frustration, sickness, uneasiness or fatigue. All of this is symptomatic of a blockage in our energy system, perhaps one that we have even unconsciously created in order to numb ourselves to this pain.

There is no substitute for working with a shaman-healer in extreme cases of soul loss and when you feel your lack of personal energy and power to be severe. For less extreme cases, there are a number of diagnostic tools you can use to better understand your situation and circumstances. Using these techniques is strong medicine in its own right since, by the very act of doing so, you are already reclaiming power by taking action *yourself* to address *your own* problems rather than automatically passing over the responsibility to another 'expert' or 'authority', like a medical doctor and the pills he prescribes.

Many approaches have proven effective as guides for people looking closely at their lives. Here are three which seem particularly appropriate to me because of their direct shamanic lineage or because of their 'shamanic wisdom' in that they recognize the interconnection of all things – between the world and the will, physical and psychic reality

– rather than just carving our species up into convenient categories according to some arbitrary dream of what makes an 'introvert', an 'extrovert', a 'leader', a 'schizophrenic', etc., as many psychological models are apt to do.

The three tools I suggest are the medicine wheel, a traditional shamanic tool and, in this context at least, a very advanced tool for personal psycho-spiritual exploration; the Life Wheel, a more recent psychological technique, in many ways rooted in the same ancient principles; and Mind Mapping, an approach developed in the 1970s by Tony Buzan,[78] which has now been adapted for use in a variety of life-issue scenarios.

2. GATHERING INFORMATION

Once we have established where the energy blockage originates, journeying and Imagework – exactly as we have practised them in earlier sections – can then be used to examine the issues arising from this exploration of the self, and to point the way towards their resolution.

3. MOVING TO RESOLUTION

In this stage, we use the power of personal rituals to 'anchor' the solution we have discovered through our journeying.

Any ritual takes the form of a meaningful, though often simple – in many ways, the simpler the better – passage from one state of being to another, more empowered state. In all cultures they have looked at, anthropologists have found that rituals follow a typical three-stage process, representing, respectively, *severance* – leaving the old ways and problems behind and allowing the unfulfilling patterns and non-useful parts of ourselves to be cast off; *the threshold experience* – which is a time between worlds as you prepare to give birth to a new expression of yourself; and *integration* – where this new sense of yourself can emerge and become incorporated into your new life.

4. EMERGING

Finally, we make a commitment to the changes we have made and a promise to ourselves to move forward positively into a more fulfilling future. It is like a permission to ourselves to shapeshift our future, or a personal blessing which we give to ourselves, and take as a gift.

Let us now take a look at all of these stages in a little more detail.

LOCATING ENERGETIC BLOCKAGES: THREE HELPFUL TECHNIQUES

THE MEDICINE WHEEL

Many cultures use medicine wheels, the best known of which are probably from the North American and Mayan traditions. The word 'medicine' is synonymous with 'power', so we are essentially describing a wheel of power or energy.

The medicine wheel has been used, over the ages, as a way for humanity to understand the universe and themselves within it. It can be used symbolically, to understand the worldview of a particular society, its political and social systems, the role of the individual as part of this order, or any aspect of the self (such as one single person's development and maturation, or orientation towards 'love' or 'family'). In this way, the medicine wheel is a mirror of the entire cosmos and goes from the macro-level, right down to the thoughts and feelings of a single human being, since both are parts of the whole: the energy of the universe which flows through all things. In what follows, I am not describing any specific medicine wheel tradition, but rather, looking at one aspect of the approach: its ability to help us understand ourselves.

The medicine wheel is arranged somewhat like a compass and, in its most basic form, is divided into four primary areas corresponding to the directions of North, South, East and West. Each direction has different attributes, qualities and insights into the human condition associated with it.

It is circular because the energy of the universe itself flows in a circle, a sacred hoop, and everything in life is circular. '*The Power of the World always works in circles*,' said Black Elk, '*and everything tries to be round*':

> *In the old days when we were a strong and happy people, all our power came to us from the sacred hoop of the nation. The flowering tree was the living centre of the hoop and the circle of the four quarters nourished it. The East gave peace and light, the South gave warmth, the West gave rain, and the North, with its cold and mighty wind, gave strength and endurance.*
>
> *Everything the Power of the World does is done in a circle . . . The life of a man is a circle from childhood to childhood, and so it is in everything where power moves.*[79]

As Black Elk implies when he talks of the qualities of the four directions – the peace and light of the East, and the strength and endurance of the North, for example – each direction or 'segment' of the wheel contains particular guidance as to where we, ourselves, are in life, and has specific information for us on how to understand ourselves and, indeed, to change ourselves if we wish. Wherever we find ourselves on this compass is like a map co-ordinate which reflects our current path and stage in the journey through life. Each of the four directions also has special qualities, animal and mineral and other representatives associated with it, which help us further to understand where we are currently 'at'.

In *Principles of Shamanism*, Leo Rutherford of the Eagle's Wing Centre includes a very helpful diagram of these medicine wheel qualities, based on the Mayan tradition.[80] The following illustration is adapted from his work.

Element **Air**
Kingdom **Animal**
Human aspect **Mind**
Age **Elder**
Positive aspects **Wisdom, balance, harmony**
Negative aspects **Tendency to 'know too much' ('bullshit')**
Manifestation **Knowledge and teaching (philosophy, religion, science, mathematics)**
Heavenly body **Stars**
Season **Winter**
Animal totems **Buffalo, Wolf, Horse**
Colour **White**

The 'Knowing' Place

Element **Earth**
Kingdom **Mineral**
Human aspect **Physical body**
Age **Mature adult**
Positive aspects **Introspection, intuition**
Negative aspects **Inertia**
Manifestation **Security and responsibility (law, insurance, etc.)**
Heavenly body **Earth**
Season **Autumn**
Animal totems **Bear, Owl, Jaguar**
Colour **Black**

The 'Looks Within' Place

POWERS OF THE NORTH
MIND
POWERS OF THE WEST
BODY
WHOLE, BALANCED, INTEGRATED YOU
SPIRIT
POWERS OF THE EAST
EMOTIONS
POWERS OF THE SOUTH

Element **Fire**
Kingdom **Human**
Human aspect **Spirit**
Age **Child**
Positive aspects **Play, pleasure, enlightenment, beauty**
Negative aspects **(Misuse of) power through lack of understanding**
Manifestation **Creativity (art, media, etc.)**
Heavenly body **Sun**
Season **Spring**
Animal totems **Eagle**
Colour **Yellow, gold**

The 'Sees Far' Place

Element **Water**
Kingdom **Plant**
Human aspect **Emotions**
Age **Youth**
Positive aspects **Trust, innocence, adventure, discovery**
Negative aspects **Fear**
Manifestation **Music**
Heavenly body **Moon**
Season **Summer**
Animal totems **Mouse, Coyote, Serpent**
Colour **Red**

The 'Close-to' Place

Adapted from Leo Rutherford's Medicine Wheel

THE MEDICINE WHEEL

We can see, broadly, how this compass works if we consider the life cycle of an average person.

We are born to the powers of the East and bring with us the passion and fire of the child, who is 'un-cultured', free-spirited and creative, totally at one with the world, but who can also be demanding and powerful in her own right.

As we grow to youthfulness in the South, we still carry with us the trust and innocence of the child, but we are also learning that the world is not entirely within our control and that we must find out how to work *with* it, rather than demand *from* it. While we still retain the exuberance of youth, there is also a certain fear of the world 'out there' since we do not yet fully understand its rules, which accounts for many of the problems of adaptation faced by our teenagers, who are exploring new avenues and interests trying to 'find themselves'.

As we enter adulthood in the West, we have overcome many of these early problems and our focus now is on consolidation, of all we have learned, all that we are, and all that we have achieved. This is a time for security-seeking activities, for settling down into a steady career, for marriage and children. The danger now is one of complacency, of settling for what we have rather than seeking more for ourselves in terms of our spiritual and emotional development. This is the time of decision for the seeker – whether to give up on trying to understand the world or whether to quest for knowledge of 'true reality'. For some, of course, this can lead to the so-called 'mid-life crisis', where the person decides that he does want more from life than his dull but steady existence and so changes jobs midstream, develops new interests, or finds a new partner who can better support his emerging self.

As we overcome these hurdles of life, we find wisdom, and so the North is the place where, in our old age, we are content with what we have achieved – whether it met all of our aspirations or not – and can look back on life from the perspective of worldly wisdom, knowing that the way of the world is illusory and our inner peace and sense of what is right is all that matters. This can lead to some very interesting exchanges in our culture, which separates its young from its old, between these two factions. A young person of the South, anxious to get on in his job and willing to do all it takes, may ask his grandfather for advice, for example, only to be told that work is not the most important thing in life, to get out and see something of the world. His Elder is speaking from a place of truth, though the young man is hardly likely to see it!

In more traditional societies, by contrast, the young and the old are in daily contact; the grandparents, indeed, may often raise the child, and so the harmony of perspective between the ages is retained. There is a spiritual dimension to this. Traditional societies recognize that children are born to the world *from* spirit, while the Elders will soon enter the doorway of death to return *to* this realm. The Elders are therefore extremely interested in the state of affairs in this other world beyond our own, since soon they will return there once again and become one with spirit. The children of the tribe have profound wisdom for the Elders in such matters, while the young ones themselves are interested to learn the truths of tribal living, which the Elders can instruct them in from a place of deep wisdom. Because of these complementary concerns and mutual interests, there is little conflict or inter-generational strife in pre-industrial societies, but rather, a deep sense of respect for all of life.

At the centre of the wheel is Great Spirit, Great Mystery, the essence of all things and of unity, integration, holism and balance. It is the still point of the sage who sees all things and can touch all aspects of the wheel but who remains unaffected by the spinning of this universe of changes. The ultimate aim of travelling the medicine wheel, as we all do in life, is to reach this point of harmony so that we can be content with all we have achieved and greet Death with a sense of deep peace and fulfilment. Less prosaically, the point of the medicine wheel is to help you get the most out of life by seeing the bigger picture and freeing yourself from the dictates of the matrix.

We can look at the medicine wheel, therefore, as a record of the things which will concern us at different stages of our lives – our mental, emotional and spiritual stages of development as well as our physical maturation – and draw from it an understanding of the processes we are going through. There is also a sense of comfort to it since it stands as a record of the fact that, no matter what confronts us, we are never alone; many thousands of other people have walked the same path as us and the medicine wheel reflects that by offering a distillation of their experiences of life.

But we can use the medicine wheel *pro-actively* too, since it is possible to draw into our lives the helpful wisdom and approaches of these other directions. In this way the wheel acts as a guide to how we can change ourselves for the better. If we are open to it, it is like having the wisdom of the world's best experts on our side. We can tap into the understanding that comes from age, even if we are physically young ourselves, by drawing the powers of the relevant direction to us as we meditate on any issue.

The people and the wisdom of the Four Directions

Kenneth Meadows, one of the foremost Western experts on the medicine wheel, examines its qualities in some depth in his *Earth Medicine* series.[81]

In the Native American tradition, he tells us, North is associated with wisdom and so, energetically, people of the North may be concerned with deep philosophical and spiritual knowledge and its applications in problem-solving and advancement, or with intellectual and academic pursuits. If you are not a 'thinker', but more of a 'doer' yourself, it might perhaps be helpful on occasion to draw from this pool of knowledge.

Each *aspect* of the whole also has its limitations, of course – like firing on only one cylinder instead of four:

- People of the North are focused on the mind and may be erudite and extremely good at analysis and logic. They may excel at careers in science or policy, for example, but completely overlook the knowledge which comes through the body or emotions, or from spirit. Such people may become powerful and decisive leaders, who can understand a situation quickly and weigh up all the pros and cons. But they may lack the support of those who follow them and be unable to motivate people enough to execute their plans effectively, since they may not have developed the necessary sense of empathy or compassion for others. Instead, they rely too heavily on the cold and emotionless analysis of the 'facts'.

- People of the South may be firing on the single cylinder of their feelings, and be excited and enthralled by emotional exchanges and the adventure of living. They may be drawn to music or other creative pursuits which capture the energy and vitality they feel but, unable to temper this attraction with the rational guidance of the North or self-analysis of the West, they may go too far and become thrill-seekers, or burnouts and end up ultimately unfulfilled with their path. Experience suggests that those who are obsessed with pushing back the boundaries of experience in this way are often motivated by fear, most frequently of death – by throwing themselves into life, they are able to forget or ignore their mortality. This can be a cross to bear for people of the South which the allies of the North and the East in particular can help them overcome. The former brings with it the wisdom of the Elders who are at peace with their lives and at one with the notion of death, while the East brings with it the certainty of recreation and the renewal of life.

- People of the West are concerned with matters of soul-searching and introspection, of what is right and wrong for themselves and for others. They may find employment as lawyers, civil servants or government officers, jobs where an understanding of moral principles is required, along with their interpretation and introduction to society as matters of process and procedure. Too much analysis can, however, lead to inertia and lack of action, of course, which is where the sense of creativity and playfulness of the East can be helpful in order to counteract this tendency. Behind over-analysis and matters of procedure and law can also lie a need for security, to be part of some vast, accepted system, rather than putting ourselves forward and recognizing our own needs and rights as individuals – which is, perhaps, our stereotype of 'faceless bureaucrats' and grey 'men from the ministry'. In order to ensure that we make the most of *our* lives, the 'pleasure principles' of the East and the exuberance of the South can provide a useful counterbalance.

People of the East, meanwhile, are in tune with their playful and creative energies and may find happiness in work which enables these qualities to shine. They may be so involved with this process of creativity, however, that in seeing the big picture, they lose sight of the immediate details. Thus, the 'go-getter' journalist or the paparazzo may be so intent on getting his story that he is simply unaware of the intrusions he makes into the lives of others and the effect that this may have on them. A useful balance for such tendencies may be the intuition and empathy which the West can bring, the emotional understanding of the South, or the refined wisdom of the North.

To approach life from any one direction is both to give ourselves immense strength in that particular aspect of the whole – and to artificially limit ourselves so we are cut off from our full power.

Uniquely, the medicine wheel offers us all the chance to cultivate and include in our lives the qualities associated with all four directions. This opportunity leads us to the still point of harmony and balance at the centre of this circle, with all aspects of self fully developed and integrated.

In order to make such cultivation easier, let us look at the particular qualities of these directions, according to Meadows, and see how we can use them in our lives.

Qualities of the Four Directions

• **East – Fire – Birth:** East is represented by yellow and by the totem animal of Eagle, a bird which symbolizes the power of 'illumination', the ability to see clearly from on high and from afar. Since the medicine wheel begins in the East, this is also the direction of birth and the creativity, intuition, and capacity for learning which comes with it. It is the direction in which we seek new knowledge, enthusiasm, life force, and to be reborn with the potential for new growth and experiences. According to Meadows, the attributes of this direction are as follows:

Birth date:	21 March–20 June (Aries, Taurus, Gemini)
Personality:	Determined, resourceful
Feelings:	Tense
Nature:	Industrious
Element:	Fire
Animal:	Eagle
Mineral:	Jasper bloodstone
Plant:	Wild clover
Colour:	Yellow

To draw the magic of this direction into your life, it is helpful to work with bright colours, such as gold, yellow and orange, perhaps choosing clothes of this colour; to carry the appropriate mineral; to find images of eagles that you can display in your home; to keep clover in the house, and so on. The energy of this direction will be drawn to you through your actions, and you will be focused on these powers. And so it is with the other directions, too.

• **South – Water – Childhood:** Represented by the colour red, for the passionate nature of youth. One of the creatures of this direction is Salmon, which is driven by life, and the desire to recreate life, and one which was believed, particularly in the Celtic tradition, to swim the waters of wisdom and insight. The whole focus of this direction is on vitality and a sense of 'power coming into itself'.

Birth date: 21 June–21 September
(Cancer, Leo, Virgo)
Personality: Energetic, confident
Feelings: Passionate
Nature: Demanding
Element: Water
Animal: Salmon
Mineral: Carnelian
Plant: Raspberry
Colour: Red

• **West – Earth – Becoming:** Represented by the colour violet and, in Meadow's interpretation of this medicine wheel, also the home of Snake, a creature which is able to reinvent itself by the shedding of its skin. This is symbolic of the self-questioning which comes from adulthood and, particularly, middle age, where there is often an impetus to find and adopt a new sense of self. In the West, we grow to maturity and find within ourselves the wisdom, compassion, and reconnection with spirit which comes from the experience of life. Its energy is the power of self-reflection – and of seeing ourselves reflected in others and in all that there is.

Birth date: 22 September–21 December
(Libra, Scorpio, Sagittarius)
Personality: Impulsive, ambitious
Feelings: Hidden
Nature: Enquiring
Element: Earth
Animal: Bear
Mineral: Amethyst
Plant: Thistle
Colour: Violet

• **North – Air – The Wisdom of Age:** Represented by silver and white, colours symbolic of the lightness of being, the ability to tread lightly on the Earth, which comes with age and with worldly knowledge. It is also the direction of the sacred White Buffalo of legend, representing abundant riches and the willingness to give fully of itself. Even though North represents old age and the accumulated wisdom of our 'Earth walk', it is also, for Meadows, associated with the totem animal of Otter, a playful, persistent and caring creature which shows that, in old age, we return once again in a sense to childhood. North emphasizes the harmony between all things – young and old, gentleness with power, innocence with wisdom, experience with humility – and empathy for others, the sacrifice of oneself for the good of all.

Birth date:	22 December–20 March (Capricorn, Aquarius, Pisces)
Personality:	Friendly, independent
Feelings:	Detached
Nature:	Humanitarian
Element:	Air
Animal:	Buffalo
Mineral:	Turquoise
Plant:	Fern
Colour:	Silver

Meadows tells us that each of these Four Directions has a particular intention, aspiration and purpose, which we can use as a further clue to our own spiritual identity and, of course, draw from by focusing on the powers of a different direction whose energies we can use to complement our own.

Some of the intentions he identifies are shown in the following table.

Direction	Life intention	Conscious aim	Subconscious desire
East	Possession	Security	Freedom
South	Rulership	Control	Emotional stability
West	Introspection	Satisfaction	Spiritual union
North	Imagination	Knowledge	Wisdom

Direction	Lifepath	Positive traits	Negative traits
East	To find lasting value	Strong-willed, persistent	Possessive, inflexible
South	To find purpose	Generous, creative	Dogmatic, intolerant
West	Sensitivity	Purposeful, imaginative	Secretive, suspicious
North	Creative strength	Inventive, perceptive	Tactless

So, for example, if we are children of the South and the desire for control is too manifest in our lives, we would do well to meditate on our own subconscious need for emotional security, or on the overall purpose of our lifepath, and to reflect on whether control will best serve us in getting where we truly want to be. We might then want to consider drawing the powers of the East or the West into our lives so that we can surrender control for greater freedom, or simply achieve more satisfaction with what we already have.

The wheel as the shield of self

In this way, the medicine wheel can be used as a map of the psyche and the whole self, and is also a guide to where we are putting our energies, the things we are seeking in our lives, and the stage we have reached in our development. It teaches us to be tolerant and compassionate to others, since we will all naturally find ourselves coming to occupy all parts of the wheel as we enter each of our four ages – birth, childhood, maturity and old age – and understand the wisdom which comes from each. Its final teaching is that we can bring those energies which are helpful to us into our lives right now.

By reflecting on the qualities of the Four Directions and on the qualities present in your own life, it is possible to see yourself in relation to the attributes of these directions. You will find that you are naturally 'drawn' to or feel an affinity with one particular direction of the medicine wheel, and recognize yourself in the qualities it represents. In this way, you not only identify your strengths but also the qualities that are currently missing from your life, and you are able to see where these can be found on the wheel.

When I first discovered the teachings of the medicine wheel, many years ago, I decided to create one for myself. This is a useful exercise and one I recommend to you.

I began by creating a circle of rocks in my garden and dividing this into four sections, to represent the Four Directions. I then placed objects and artefacts in each quadrant to represent the qualities inherent in each – a container of water, a red-painted stone, carnelian in the South; an empty bowl to represent air, a white-painted stone, and torquoise in the North, as well as representations of the plant and animal allies found in these directions.

Each day, I would go out into the garden and spend a few quiet moments reflecting on how I felt that day and the qualities I felt I needed to support myself in whatever lay ahead. I would then move the appropriate objects from the other directions into the quadrant where I felt my energies lay that morning. If I had a tough meeting ahead, but I was feeling in a playful mood where I knew my defences were down, I might move some of the items from the North, symbolic of age and wisdom, or from the West, symbolic of security, into the East section of the wheel, the place of childhood and playfulness, where I saw myself.

Each month I would carry out a slightly more detailed 'life review' to see how things were going for me overall, and to make any adjustments I thought necessary. The practice helped me to focus on the issues forthcoming in my life and, like a ship's captain, to take my bearings periodically in order to sail a more certain course.

As I continued with this process, I found that I was able to build a personal map of the Four Directions and of my life, and to use the medicine wheel to assist in my own transformation. I was able to travel the wheel to recover the powers I most needed by surrounding myself with the qualities, attributes and artefacts of the direction most useful to me at that point in my life.

The medicine wheel is a subtle, non-prescriptive, non-judgmental tool for establishing 'where you are at' and where your present energy may be blocked. At the same time it recognizes the power and sanctity of each one of us, the contribution we make to the whole, and our innate ability to create change.

THE LIFE WHEEL – A CIRCLE OF SELF

The life wheel is a psychological tool which works in a similar way to the medicine wheel by helping us to map our worlds according to the qualities we have created in our lives right now. By doing so, we can again see:

- Where we have what we need
- Where we are satisfied with our creations
- Where we are unsatisfied
- Where we now need to focus our attention
- Where there is more work to be done

Creating a life wheel is easy:

- Start by drawing a circle on a blank sheet of paper.
- Now subdivide the circle you have drawn to create three inner rings, representing 'high', 'average' and low satisfaction levels.

- Finally, draw an 'X' across the whole circle to divide it into four discrete areas. In this example, these sections will represent your spiritual, physical, mental and emotional worlds, although they could stand for any aspects of your life you care to examine.

- It is important to remember that you do not have to limit yourself to just four areas; you could choose as many – or as few – as you wish. You might also decide that you want to look at your life in more detail, in which case you may choose to include ten (or more) inner rings to enable you to rank all aspects of your life more precisely than the general scale of 'low', 'average' and 'high' will allow. You can be very creative and have a wide choice over what you include and in what level of detail.

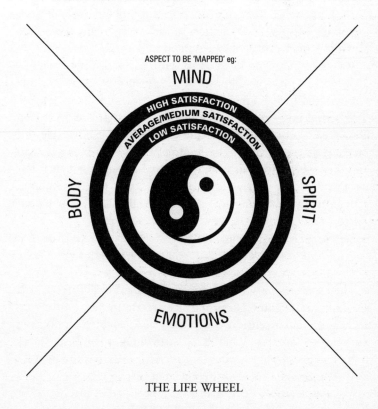

THE LIFE WHEEL

Jack Black of MindStore has pioneered this approach and suggests using the categories of 'family life', 'social life', 'personal development', 'health', 'attitude (to life)', 'career', 'finance', and 'spiritual life'.[82]

But there is no 'right' way of doing this exercise and the categories you choose may be entirely different. Indeed, the act of considering *which* aspects of your life to include can itself be useful since, in doing so, you are looking at your world in its entirety and selecting the most important things for you at this moment.

Debbie and Christine are both married, in their mid-thirties, and working mothers. Yet when Debbie did this exercise, she chose relationships, family, health, children, spiritual and personal development as the areas she wanted to look at, while Christine developed a much simpler wheel, including only work, finances and leisure, which perhaps illustrates how different our personal maps can be.

Whatever map you develop for yourself, it is always a good idea to date the wheel you produce since, like all maps, this one will tend to change over time.

Whether you choose to use three or ten rings, the next step is to give a score to each of the attributes you have selected in terms of your level of satisfaction with it. For example, you may be very happy with your personal development but not with your home life, which you are finding too demanding. Thus, you would put a cross in the 'high' ring for personal development, but in the 'low' ring for family.

When you have done this for all attributes, join up the crosses and you will find that you create a shape within the wheel. This is the shape of your life right now.

The most desirable shape for most people is a circle, which suggests that all things in their life are balanced and flowing and that equal attention is being given to each, with nothing missing or lacking. Even if all attributes have low scores (which suggests that more work is needed 'across the board') at least there is a sense of balance here.

Of course, few people ever do produce a circle. Most

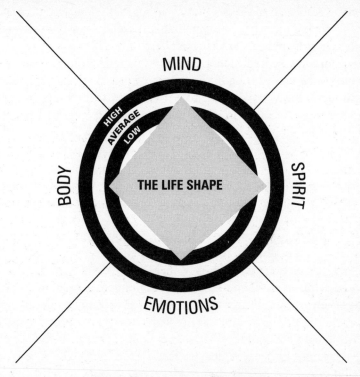

MIND

HIGH
AVERAGE
LOW

BODY

THE LIFE SHAPE

SPIRIT

EMOTIONS

COMPLETED BASIC LIFE WHEEL

shapes are irregular, with high scores in one area and low scores in another.

Spend a few minutes getting to know the shape of your life and see the connections between the scores you have given. For example, does a high score in one area indicate that too much attention is being given to this, or that not enough attention is being directed elsewhere? These are not the same question. The net effect may be the same but the solution will be different according to which answer you give.

Sometimes, a high score in one area does result directly in a low score for another. Debbie had a very high score for 'personal development', an area of her life she was extremely satisfied with, but a low score for 'family'. This was a definite reflection of her life – too many weekends away on courses were resulting in a lack of time for her family and friends and the emergence of fundamental differences in worldview between Debbie and other members of her family.

Christine scored highly on 'work', a reflection of the long hours she was putting in there, but low on 'finances'. She had thought she was working to earn more money but realized after this exercise that, while she was earning more as a result of putting in long hours during the week, she was also spending more to cheer herself up at weekends, so putting in the hours was not only pointless, it was actually self-defeating.What she in fact needed was a new perspective on life, one that would provide her with a more balanced and harmonious existence.

Using the Imagework techniques we have looked at previously, you might like to explore the shape your life wheel has created. See it as a three-dimensional representation, an actual physical thing and begin a dialogue with it. This is an entirely optional stage but sometimes rewarding.

Ask yourself: Is Life happy being this shape? How would it change if it could? What shape would Life like to be?

Become Life. How do you feel about yourself? What has caused you to be this shape? Have you always been this way or when did things change for you? How would you go about altering your shape to a more appealing one? And what would the impact of this be?

In taking this exercise further, you can also, if you wish, overlay your personal life wheel onto the medicine wheel to see where new meaning is revealed. Allow the key attributes of your life to sit within the sectors of the medicine wheel where they seem most appropriately to fit. If you are passionate about your career, for example, and this appears as an area of your life wheel, you may wish to allocate this to the South, the direction of the emotions, to represent your passion. Your health may be a concern for the West, the direction of the physical body. Personal development issues may be allocated to the North, and spiritual life to the East. In this sense, you are using the composite of 'life-medicine wheel' like a mirror to *reflect back* to you the current context of your life.

Or you may wish to *work with* these aspects in a creative way, in which case, you may choose to place them differently. For example, you may wish to understand more about shamanism, so 'spiritual development' may sit most appropriately in the North, the direction of mind and knowledge. Perhaps you wish to discover the essence of what is important to you in work – the real meaning behind the activity you are engaged in – before you change careers, in which case this future-looking activity might best be placed in the East, the direction of insight into spiritual principles.

With the two laid one on the other, you now have new information about the stages of change in your present situation since where you have placed the most important 'aspects of you' also determines where the others lie.

If 'career' is your most pressing concern and you have placed it in the North, the direction of potential for rebirth, this may suggest that it is time for a change of job or of career. Where your other life attributes now sit as a consequence may offer other insights into this. If 'personal development' now sits in the East, suggesting a new focus or beginning, are these two facts related? In other words, do you need to reconsider your career in order to allow more time for yourself and for your *personal* rather than purely *professional* growth?

By referring back once again to the attributes of the Four Directions, you can now see the items which you can beneficially bring into your life to help you to move from one situation to another.

MAPPING THE CONTEXT OF YOUR LIFE

Mind mapping, a concept developed in the 1970s by Tony Buzan, began life as a technique for enhancing creativity and memory, and for understanding the structure and working of the mind. But it is adapted very easily and powerfully to deal with matters of spirituality and personal growth since the world we create in our minds *is* the world we live in and experience. Since we create our own worlds, the map of our mind is the map of our world and can be used to effectively plot both our inner and outer experiences of reality. Thus, the map you create will give you a clear and holistic overview of the issues current in your life right now and show you where you stand on each of these in relation to the pattern as a whole.

For Buzan, the human mind is not an organic machine quietly filing away information in a linear way into neat little compartments corresponding to precise areas of brain matter – which is the perspective of the 'old science'. Instead, said Buzan, it operates by making associations between things, linking them to form new pictures from the material it synthesizes, much like the illumination which arises when the information crossing the hologram of the brain is pulled into form by the interpretative decisions of the observer. The work of the brain is a creative *process* in constant flow rather than a routine *procedure* following a linear plan.

Think of the word 'red' and many associations may come to mind. Red can be an emotional state ('seeing red'), a reference to political affiliation, a sexual description for an area of the city ('red light district'), and many others, depending on your personal history and interests. Red need not only be a colour.

Mind maps allow us to see our own associations clearly and, by implication, the unconscious assumptions we have about the world, our lives, and the personal myths we have come to live by as our adopted realities. Using a mind map you can record these associations visually, to give you the full picture, the complete context of your life in reference to a particular issue. The map becomes a holistic representation of your worldview and a record of your actions and interactions in the world. At the same time, every item on the map is effectively also the centre of a new map.

So, for example, Ken's map places 'work' at the centre of

his life since, to him, his work is the most important, fulfilling part of his world. Everything else stems from this since his family life, his hobbies, his enjoyment of visiting new countries, his status, and all other elements on the map, are dependent upon the salary his work provides or, like travel, are present in his life as a result of his work, which takes him to a number of international locations on a frequent basis.

Having mapped his current world, Ken may now choose to examine any of these satellite categories, such as 'travel', which will produce further offshoots of association as he explores what travel means to him and how it relates to his central theme of 'work'. This evolutionary exploration can go on for as long as you wish so that you fully examine all elements of the map as central concepts in their own right.

Creating a mind map is simple. Write down one main idea – such as 'work' or 'love' or 'family' or 'me' – summarized as a single word or picture, in the centre of your page and then work outwards to produce a web of words and images, which can be as complex and expansive as you wish. The central idea is a snapshot of your worldview at this point in time in relation to this particular theme. The ideas which grow from it are the associations and patterns within this reality.

To take the analogy of a journey, the central idea is the path you are now on; the associated ideas are the landmarks around you which create the environment you are in. The central idea will therefore change over time since we ourselves are changing as we continue on our journey. 'Work' is most important for Ken right now; tomorrow it may be 'health' or 'relationships' or 'religious belief'.

Or again, the central idea you choose is like the Sun at the heart of your personal universe; the associated ideas are the planets which revolve around it. And, of course, all of these planets are worlds in their own right and can form the centre of a further universe.

Ken might, for example, now take the concept of 'family'

and place this at the centre of a new map. He can then link associations to this to explore further what 'family' means to him and why, for example, his enjoyment of his family life appears to depend upon his satisfaction with his job and the income from it.

The advantages of the mind map are its very simplicity to create and to use and that the associations between key words and ideas are readily apparent and obvious.

Date and keep your mind maps together for reference so you can visit them in future to see how your world is changing as you continue with your journeys.

GATHERING INFORMATION

Once we have established where we are, the next step is to journey using the procedures we have already looked at, in order to learn more about the needs you have discovered using the mind map, the life wheel or the medicine wheel.

At the end of each journey, the techniques of Imagework can be used to explore especially significant and potent images from the material of the journey so you can more fully understand their particular impact on your life and the personal mythology you are subscribing to.

In a journey to examine a major life change she is planning, Clarissa finds herself riding over a fiery terrain on the back of a vast, black raven.

She is planning to give up her job, start a business of her own in a completely new field and, in the process of 'down-shifting' her life, to move to a new part of the country, which will have further implications for her social and emotional life. It is a big decision.

Her journey is a long and complex one. She is shown images and interactions from her past and current life and the unfolding of these into the future, all from the perspective of Raven, soaring high above the landscape of rock and flame. It is a disturbing journey but one which is also somehow exciting – she feels as if she is somewhere 'very real, a place where things really matter and are deeply connected'.

Her conclusion is that her future life may not always be easy, that she must sometimes travel through the flames and feel their heat, but that she will not 'get burned' if she makes the changes she has in mind.

On her return, she uses Imagework to learn more about Raven, her carrier and protector on this journey. What she finds is that Raven is a symbol for her of 'rising above', being more than a participant in the landscape; being a creator of it, one who has achieved a higher perspective and can travel over mundane, earthly difficulties. Raven, she knows, is also a powerful symbol of communion with spirit, a messenger of the otherworld.

Imagework adds useful information to the detail of her experience by explaining the role and intention of Raven, who is not just an ally in the journey, supporting and carrying her forward, but also stands as a principle for Clarissa of her active involvement in shaping her own destiny.

When you emerge from the journey, your insights will point a way forward for you. This in no way commits you to *having* to act in the way suggested, but often it will feel right to do so and you will want to make a commitment to change. At this point, ritual is a highly effective method for anchoring this positive energy.

'Anchoring' is the process whereby the internal change we wish to make is given energy through the use of a sign or symbol. This could be a gesture, a *mudra*, a word repeated silently to yourself as a mantra, an object such as a special stone, a representational image, a picture, or a spell or incantation. The symbol provides a focus to hold the energy of your intention. Like a hypnotic cue, every time your anchor word is repeated, or you hold the symbolic object, or call it to mind, you are reconnecting with the power of your intention. The ritual act is the first stage of anchoring. It is this which imbues the symbolic object or action with its transformational power.

MOVING TO RESOLUTION: THE
IMPORTANCE OF RITUAL

Rituals give a sacred quality to our actions by creating an energetic link between thought and action, spirit and matter, the inner world of mind and the outer world of personal expression and social interaction, unifying them to produce a powerful new form. They are at the heart of every shamanic work.

All rituals, as we have seen, are based on three elements – the severance of restrictive energy patterns from a previous life stage; the generation of new energy and its refocus on a definite goal or purpose; and then the emergence into our new selves, with clearly expressed intention to use our energies constructively to make practical, physical changes in our lives.

By using ritual, we are expressing this intention to ourselves and to the world. Instead of our resolution for change 'drifting' unspoken in our minds, we externalize it and 'speak it aloud' to name it and confirm our intentions, often before witnesses, giving ourselves the power and potential to move forward.

There are many techniques for creating rituals and ceremony, most of which are familiar in one form or another from their use in religious practice. They include prayer; the ceremonial use of food, such as fasting or feasting; chanting, singing, and other special use of sound; sacrifices and offerings; the creation of sacred space – the pilgrimage is a ritual, for example, where the entire path becomes sacred through the intention of the pilgrim and the significance of the journey itself. At the end, the pilgrim is a new person, one who has quested and been received by spirit.

The symbolic rebirthing of baptism; the taking of a new name; the use of the Earth in exercises such as the shamanic practice of the Burial of the Warrior, where we are literally buried for a time and physically reborn when our tomb is reopened; the use of fire to purify and burn away, or water to wash away the past, are also ritual expressions and there are, of course, many more. Even the stubbing out of the last cigarette on New Year's Eve is a ritual. It is a statement of intent, often before friends, of the decision to be free of something and to change.

Any ritual can be as simple or as elaborate as you choose since its potency does not come from the ritual event itself but from the faith and the power you invest it with.

Serge King even offers a simple ritual for blessing a new car, in order to ensure its long and problem-free life, remarking that 'In ancient times it was quite common to bless personal belongings like horses, chariots, carriages, boats.'[83] Now we live in the city and our carriages are cars, we do not have to subscribe to the industrial dream of 'built-in obsolescence', we can change the dream through our own intention.

King's ritual requires only a bowl of water. You start at the front of the car, sprinkling the water over it and saying aloud, 'May this car always provide useful and harmonious service to its owner' – or whatever words seem most appropriate to you – and work your way to the back, ensuring that all parts receive a sprinkling of water as a physical manifestation of the spiritual power of blessing. 'The main thing is not the prop you use, but how confident you are,' says King. 'It is your confidence that will change the pattern, and if there is also confidence in the symbol, so much the better.'

Radically different is the grieving ceremony described by Some, which followed the funeral of his shaman grandfather in Burkina Faso. The preparation of the dead is complex and takes many days, as does the singing and dancing which follows as the ritual expression of grief, the communication with neighbouring villages, and the honouring of and consultation with the dead person. Each stage is prescribed and precisely followed. 'Although there are certain ritual forms of mourning, it is no less sincere for all that,' says Some. 'Public grief is cleansing – of vital importance to the whole community – and people look forward to shedding tears the same way they look forward to their next meal.'[84]

One of my own workshops has the theme, 'The Journey beyond Fear to Empowerment'.[85] On the first day, we journey to meet Fear and consult with him as an ally and adviser in the same way as we have journeyed in this book to our inner child or our power animals. On day two, we journey to retrieve power by recovering our allies and power objects, again exactly as we have done in this book.

On the first day I ask people to bring with them an item which, for them, symbolizes their personal fears and whatever they feel is holding them back. This could be anything. For some it has been a stone, representing a past relationship which they still feel the weight of, an inhaler, to signify ill-health, a letter which summarizes unhappy events of the past, a credit card, a symbol of financial problems. We leave these items in the centre of the group during the workshop so we are all aware of them, sometimes intensely, sometimes peripherally, but aware nonetheless throughout the whole two days. During this time, they become so charged with energy that I have even felt shocks from some of these objects when handling them subsequently during their ceremonial disposal.

On the evening of the second day, I ask people to explain to the group what these objects mean to them. The telling of the story, giving voice to their fears at last, and the experience of *being heard* is itself an emotional and liberating experience for some.

I have previously arranged four bowls in the centre of the room, in the colours of the four elements – green for Earth, which contains soil; blue for Water, containing water; white for Air, which is empty; and red for Fire, where the symbolic object can be burned. There are also four candles – black or blue, yellow, white and red – in the colours of the Four Directions. After smudging the ritual space, I invite people to come forward and, to the steady beat of the drum, to allow these elements to take away the energies associated with their symbolic objects. Some choose to bury them in the earth, some to immerse them in water, some to allow the air simply to carry them away, many choose to burn the object and let the fire purify and carry it away.

Margaret, whose story we will hear shortly, elected to work with the energy of two stones, taking one (which she visualized as filled with the negative forces which were holding her back) and ritually disposing of it, while keeping the other (filled with love and positive energy for the future) as an 'amulet' or 'charm' which is always with her.

Simon chose to work with fire. In our life, we are all merely witnesses to events; there is no objective reality, only our perceptions and interpretations of significant episodes. Simon recognized that he had always interpreted one particular event in his life as extremely limiting and negative and had written this up during the course of the workshop as the 'diary notes of a Victim', which is how he had always seen himself in relation to this episode. He had really put a lot of effort and energy into the creation of this diary, using beautiful handmade paper to represent the intricate quality of the persecution story he had woven, and decorating the page with wonderful images. In a very moving ceremony at the close of the day, he burned the 'Victim story' of his life, with the group supporting him in this. He was no longer buying in to the Victim myth and he wanted us to see that he was free of it.

During the ritual itself, I sometimes lead the group in the singing of a beautiful Spirit Song which seems appropriate in the context of this ceremony. It was lent to me by an exceptionally brave man I once worked with, who had suffered much and still managed to retain his will and his sense of pride despite many hardships in his early years. It is a power song which was taught to him by the spirit of Water on a hillside in rural Wales, and has a wonderful tune, which I wish you could hear. Its words summarize the healing powers of the elements and the spirits who reside within them:

> *Spirit of the Water, I give you my soul to cleanse.*
> *Spirit of the Earth, I give you my soul to cleanse.*

Spirit of the Air, I give you my soul to cleanse.
Spirit of the Fire, I give you my soul to cleanse.

Later, I will remove the objects or the remains which are left of them, and dispose of them in the appropriate sacred manner.

While it is my belief that it is always preferable to create a personal ritual as a true expression of your *own* intentions, no matter how simple or complex it may be, it is also perfectly acceptable to use any 'standard' ritual technique, or an adaptation of the releasing ritual which I use, as a vehicle to express your own commitment to change. What is vital is that you *believe* wholeheartedly in what you are committing to and really visualize the energy of your resolution entering the ritual object or performance. And then see it vanish as you let it go.

EMERGING

Many people, when they emerge from the ritual experience, do feel a profound sense of release, often coupled with elation, excitement, and a strong commitment to move forwards. It is only natural, however, that we begin to waver once 'normality' hits us again – which is why it is so important to change our habits as well as our intentions so that we do not immediately fall back into our old ways again.

One way to do this is to keep a journal of your continuing journeys and experiences so that you record your progress and see a movement in the right direction. Another is to choose a ritual which enables ongoing visual expression of your commitment as a reminder of your intentions. One of my workshop participants created a 'collage of aspirations', including images of all the new things she wanted to introduce into her life. This now hangs by her front door so that she sees it each morning on her way out of the house, to give focus to the coming day.

Other people have taken simple steps to change their daily patterns so that things remain fresh and 'new' for them – even something as small as varying our route to work each morning can, literally, open up a new perspective on the world.

When don Juan was advising Castaneda on the technique for 'erasing personal history' (casting off our old self to give birth to the new), he recommended that Castaneda regularly change his perspective in just such a way. Castaneda was, at the time, a respected author and academic, which carries with it its own rules, expectations and limitations. Don Juan recommended that Castaneda 'vanish' from the circuit of lectures, 'appearances', and the fame of guru-dom in order to break the habits he was falling into and reconnect with his essential self. Castaneda did so, going from academic and new age hero to short order chef in a diner, a job he worked at for many months before resurfacing.

You do not have to go to these extremes to break the energetic bonds that habits can create, nor do you have to erase your personal history entirely, but it is good advice to vary your patterns periodically.

Reconnecting with your inner child through journeying and Imagework is also a useful way of remaining in touch with what is important to you. You are reborn through the ritual you have carried out, and as you emerge from it, you are young in the world even though you may look like an adult. The expert on this state of being is not the grown-up you, it is the child within you, so allow your inner child to become a consultant to the new you. Children are natural shamans who instinctively see the world in its purest, most natural form. Staying happy, free and purposeful is simple once this can be reduced to two simple questions: *What makes me happy?* and *What makes me sad?* There is no better authority on this than your inner child.

To recap, the format for energetic transformation is:

1.   **Locating the blockage:** Use the mind map, the life wheel or

the medicine wheel to describe yourself and identify areas of potential for change and empowerment. Use Imagework, if you wish, to explore the meaning behind the life shape you create.

2. **Gathering information:** Use journeying to better understand yourself and the issue, and to recover power. Imagework can then be used to explore particular elements of the journey, to uncover new symbolic meanings, and to embrace the power you return with.

3. **Moving to resolution:** Employ ritual techniques to anchor these changes or to let go of the things you no longer want or need.

4. **Emerging:** Affirmatory techniques, the breaking of old habits and customary approaches, and the setting up of 'reminders to the self' will all help you to stay in touch with the positive energy released when you broke through the blockage with ritual. Make it hard for yourself to forget and easy to see how your life is evolving for the better.

Not every issue you bring to the process has to be of dramatic importance, these techniques can be used in many different situations for clarity on the way forward. Nor does every journey have to be an epic: some have the flavour more of a 'quick check-in' with spirit for guidance and support.

The process of energetic transformation has been used by many people to change their lives, not always in a way suggestive of a Shakespearean drama, but in a way that had *absolute meaning* for them.

How *you* change is all that matters.

This is how three other people have used the process.

JASMINE'S STORY

Jasmine is dis-spirited. For two years she has felt restless, lacking in energy and direction, as if something is missing from her life. Something is. Her symptoms are classic indicators of power loss.

The life wheel she creates reflects this. She chooses to explore the categories of 'social life', 'health', 'career', 'interests' and 'spiritual belief', most of which end up in the 'low' section of the wheel, suggesting general dissatisfaction. Her 'social life', she says, 'feels tired and old. I'm ready for a change'. She enjoys reading historical romances and watching old movies, but they are also in the low category because 'they are solitary pursuits. I feel I would like to get out more and meet people'.

She is 'fed up with her job', which seems to be 'going nowhere'; her health is 'OK, but could be better. I could be a lot fitter, for example'; and her view of the world, consequently is that it is a 'boring place, with nothing really happening'.

These life qualities reflect a general lack of energy – 'nothing is moving'. Her whole picture is one of ennui, apathy and boredom with things as they are. She recognizes that she must 'give birth to a new me' and decides on a journey to explore what is holding her back in this.

Because of where she has chosen to place her life categories, the shape of Jasmine's life appears very sharp and triangular. She uses Imagework to become the shape.

I am a pyramid alone in a deep, vast desert. A wind blows past me, a wind which brings change, rearranging the sand around me, but I resist it.

Things were not always like this. Once I was living rock and organic materials. But I have been assembled in this way to serve a purpose and I must stay like this, in the design created by someone else. I am important to them in this form and represent something very special and sacred to them. But I feel as if I am neglecting myself. I cannot move, cannot experience or feel. I would like to be able to move.

What would happen if she did?

I see that I have life within me, buried kings and riches. I become the power that is held by these things and see that I can use it to give myself form. I walk out of the pyramid and into the desert. It is warm. There is life here and I am part of it.

Jasmine is clear that she must recover her energy and use it positively in order to experience life fully, and feels it appropriate to take a journey to recover her power animal.

Even before I leave the tunnel, I see an eagle waiting for me. To me, Eagle is a symbol of clear vision. I follow him to a hillside, on top of which is a man in a long black coat. He looks very severe. In that instant I recognize him as my father. He is handing me a bird in a beautiful cage. The bird has everything it needs – food, water, a mirror so it can see itself. But it is still locked in and the door is firmly bolted. The bird speaks to me. 'Remember the dream and the dark of the forest', it says.

At this point, I hear the call-back signal and ask Eagle if he will come back with me. He says yes. I hug him to me and start back along the tunnel.

Jasmine feels that she has reclaimed a lot of energy from this journey and feels 'lighter' as a result. But she is puzzled by some of the images she has seen.

She was surprised to have been told to 'remember the dream', although she does remember having a dream which she found very frightening as a child and which has stayed with her since. It was after hearing the story of Hansel and Gretel, who are held captive in the woods by an evil witch. She feels there is meaning there, but she cannot yet understand it.

She has some sense of the significance of the caged bird, but does not understand why her father was dressed in such a way when he handed it to her. 'He looked so severe,' she says. 'He was never like that in life.'

Jasmine uses Imagework to become her five-year-old self, the age she was when she had the dream which frightened her.

'I am scared by this story, which is perhaps not surprising, but what seems most to scare me now is that the children have given themselves away so easily. Why did they not try harder to escape?'

She becomes the caged bird:

This is a gilded cage, a fantasy land, totally perfect, just like the gingerbread house which attracted Hansel and Gretel. The bird can be happy here as long as it does not try to escape. But its nature is to be free, to be wild. As luxurious as this cage is, it does not want to be here. The bird does not perceive 'luxury' or 'beauty' in the same way as we do. To the bird, to be free is to have beauty in its life.

She becomes her father:

He loves me very much. He sees my perfection and my purity and wishes I could always stay this way and not have to go out into the world and all the darkness and corruption that is there.

With all of this information she has been given, Jasmine is able to reconsider her life and look objectively and clearly at the pieces.

Her father protected her when she was little, to the extent that she felt trapped in his world. She was always well-dressed, never allowed to get 'dirty', to really get involved with life. The caged bird is a reflection of that. The gingerbread house of Hansel and Gretel is another view of an unreal world which in some ways appears attractive but hides dangers, one of which is to make a captive of you within a fantasy.

Jasmine realizes that, even as a young girl, she has learned not to engage with the world to fully express herself, but to remain at arm's length from the 'darkness' which is out there, protecting herself with romantic novels and old films which embrace a fantasy of a different, harmless, world. But not a real one.

She has reclaimed her power in the clear-sightedness of Eagle, and sees that she must now emerge into the world to actively play her part in it.

Jasmine could have performed a 'letting go' ritual to exorcize the beliefs of the past and to free herself from their hold, or an 'accepting in' ritual in order to fully possess the new insights and energy she has recovered. In the event, she chose an acceptance ritual because this more fully reflected the new, positive approach she wanted to take to life. 'Letting go would mean a ritual to destroy old habits and I want to create now, not destroy,' she said.

Her ritual act was to begin making a collage of images torn from magazines, of all the new things she intended to bring into her life – exotic locations for travel, party scenes for a new, active social life, athletes to signify a greater focus on health and fitness. Once the collage was finished, she framed it and it now hangs on the wall by her front door so it is there as a constant reminder to her as she enters and leaves her house that she has made an energetic commitment to change.

One of the first things Jasmine did after taking this journey was to join a gym and to begin swimming regularly. She now looks and feels fitter. Through the gym, she has also met new friends and her social life has changed considerably. 'I am more prepared to take risks,' she says. 'Now, when someone asks me out, I don't think "well, I could stay at home with a good book and a cup of cocoa",' she laughs, 'I just go.'

She is also saving up for a holiday to Thailand – a big step since she has never before travelled further than Europe. Now she wants to see the world. And, while her job has not changed, she is actively looking for a new position else-where. 'To tell you the truth,' she says, 'I actually don't mind it so much any more. I have too many other things going on and plans for the future.'

Jasmine's stages of change reflect the process of energetic transformation. First, she created a map of her life which incorporated the qualities that best described her world as she experienced it.

She became the life shape her map represented to explore how it felt and what it meant to be this shape. Questions to ask at this stage might be *Is there another shape or form I would rather be? If so, how do I go about becoming this other shape? What would life be like if I did? What would this mean to me?*

She then journeyed to meet with her spirit allies to discuss what she had learned about herself and to recover a power animal which she brought back with her as a source of new strength and clarity of vision.

She used Imagework to explore any aspects of the journey that were not immediately clear to her, and this revealed that they contained more information.

Then, when she was sure about what it was she wanted to bring into her life (and let go of), she created a ritual which was appropriate to her and symbolic of her intention to change. It was a real, concrete, solid representation, which now acts as a permanent reminder and a focus for her commitment.

MARGARET'S STORY

Margaret separated from Keith, her husband of twelve years and the father of her two children, four years ago. She spent the first two years of the separation wanting Keith back and although she has had sporadic affairs since then, she has been constantly looking for someone 'just like Keith', someone who can fill his shoes. Her affairs have been short-lived, usually leading to disappointment and frustration.

Not surprisingly, she chooses to explore the categories of

'love', 'relationships', 'children' and 'social life'. She then adds 'health' (she has just taken up t'ai chi, which she loves) and 'career' which, for her, is uncertain at the moment.

'Love' and 'relationships' she places in the 'low' ring of her life wheel, reflecting her dissatisfaction with these. 'Children' and 'social life' both occupy the middle ring. She is relatively content with both areas, although she would like to spend more time with her children and to have 'someone special' to spend her leisure time with.

Using the medicine wheel, which she overlays onto the life wheel she has created, she places 'children' in the North to represent the physical demands they make on her. 'Social life' is also placed in the North because, she says, 'I'm quite happy with what I do but I would like somebody to share it with'. 'Health' is in the East and the 'high satisfaction' ring, for the new beginning of t'ai chi, and 'career' in the South and the 'high satisfaction' ring because, although her job is currently uncertain and she is emotionally concerned about what may come next, it is a position and a career she very much enjoys.

Margaret finds she has created a life shape much like an arrowhead which, in the context of the medicine wheel, points towards the East. Becoming the shape, she sees herself as a road sign 'pointing backwards'.

I look for the name of the place I am pointing towards. The road sign says 'Hope'. I walk down the road a short distance. It is lush and green and beautiful. There are flowers and wildlife everywhere.

How does she feel being here? 'Actually,' she laughs,

I feel quite bored. It is very beautiful, but I know wherever I go it will always be the same.

I return to the crossroads and look at the other signs. One says 'Destiny', the other 'Nowhere' and the third, for some reason, says 'Home'. I realize that I am drawn to 'Home', that 'Hope' is the road I have been walking on throughout my marriage, but the road I am now on is 'Destiny'. It seems more 'normal' than 'Hope', somehow, with downs as well as ups. It also seems to be the road that more people are walking. On the 'Hope' road, I was alone.

Margaret realizes that, although her past life was comfortable and predictable, very beautiful in many ways, it was ultimately unchallenging, too comfortable. The road of 'Destiny' is the one which most people are walking and she appreciates that she is not alone here. She would like to know where 'Destiny' is leading and decides on a journey to find out.

As soon as I enter the otherworld, my power animal is waiting for me. He seems very pleased to see me; it is a while since I have been here to see him.

He takes me to a waterfall, which flows into a lovely fresh pool of crystal clear water. I know that I am to bathe in it and climb into the pool, immersing myself in the fall of the water. 'This is to wash away the past,' I hear him say, 'and this is for your future.' He hands me a photograph of myself, just me, as I am now, and I am smiling. At first, I am a little sad, I know this is wishful thinking, but I was expecting to see myself with someone, perhaps a family. Then I realize this is the 'old me' talking and I need to find myself and be myself now instead of trying to fit into a new relationship where I am just part of someone else's life. Then I become angry – why can't I be myself? Why do I always have to be OK in somebody else's eyes?

When I come home, I still feel angry – like I've wasted part of my life wanting others to be with me, as if they were all that mattered and I had no value by myself.

The message was very clear for Margaret and she felt that she didn't need to do much more to understand its meaning. But she was curious to see where the image of herself came from that she was dependent on others for an 'OK' about herself.

Using imagework this is what she found.

I am a small piece of rock being held tightly in a clenched fist. I am the eldest of a big family and I always had responsibility for helping with the little ones. I realize that when I am 'good' and help out, I am rewarded with love and praise. I am a rock for the family, someone they can rely on. And I like it too, I like the feeling of being needed in this way.

When I do not want to help out, there is no punishment, just a feeling of the withdrawal of love, of letting the rock go and fall. When I have no-one to take care of, or to be taken care of by, I realize, I have been living as if I can be discarded, like I don't matter. But I do matter. I matter.

Now that Margaret can see this about herself, she can begin to move forward. She chooses a ritual which represents both a letting go of old ways and an embrace of the new. She finds two stones, important objects for her since they symbolically connect her with the way her family saw her – 'a small piece of rock'. One of these she names 'Hope', the other 'Destiny'.

She spends a few minutes reflecting on her past and the expectations that were held of her, that she had of herself, and concentrates on seeing these become part of the 'Hope' stone. The other stone, 'Destiny', she fills with blessings for her future and then places it in her purse so it is always with her. She then walks towards the container of earth and, digging a hole, buries 'Hope'. 'It was a false hope anyway,' she says.

A few months on from this experience, Margaret is still no closer to finding her ideal relationship – and she couldn't care less. She goes out, meets people, has affairs, but is not attached to any particular 'hope for the future': she is taking each day as it comes. She is living for herself. She still practises t'ai chi and has negotiated a new arrangement at work so she can workpart-time (which suits them as well as her) and so see more of her children.

MIKE'S STORY

Mike has a demanding job in the financial sector of the City. He works hard, but he plays hard too. He has taken part in the London Marathon twice, windsurfs, rollerblades, plays rugby, football, tennis, rides, and for many years practised judo. All that stopped three years ago, coinciding with what he calls 'a change in my life'. The change was meeting Elizabeth, 'the first woman I ever really loved', and settling down with her. Now he would like to get back into his previous active life but lacks the motivation to do so. He wants to know what is holding him back.

Mike places 'health and fitness', 'lifestyle' and 'energy' (he never seems to have enough) into the wheel as his key categories. He feels reasonably fit still, so the first category is placed in the middle ring. The two others are placed in the low ring, which surprises him. 'I'm less surprised about "energy", I know that's low, but I thought I had a good lifestyle. I was surprised when I decided to place it in the low category. But I suppose it's true.'

He adds the category of 'marriage', which he places in the middle ring, to represent his relationship with his wife, and 'children' in the high ring as he has a new son, Daimon, whom he is delighted with.

Mike's configuration gives him a diamond-shaped life map – which is interesting given his job in finance. He becomes the shape.

A diamond is permanent, for ever. Reliable, secure, solid. I see myself as a diamond with all of these qualities. I wasn't always like this. Once I was rough organic matter, but over time I have been compressed and changed my form. Now I'm hard, nothing can hurt me and I am here for ever. How very like my life! I used to take a lot more risks. Now I can't afford to. I have to be there for my family.

A diamond is clear. And I am clear about my job and my role. I'm here to provide for the people I love. I do miss the ability to be myself, though. Being a diamond feels so compressed and restricted.

Mike's journey takes him into his future so he is able to reflect back on the big picture of his life.

I was shown my own graveside as my funeral took place. 'He was a real diamond,' says my wife's mother. I almost laugh out loud. 'He always took care of you and the children' (Children – not child – there are two others, another young boy and an older girl). Daimon is about 12, standing at the graveside too. They will be without a father now. This saddens me.

My power animal is there with me. 'Being unavailable sometimes does not mean not caring,' he says. I took that to mean that I can have a life of my own too. I needn't feel held back by my desire to be with my family. I can do what I want to as well.

Mike realizes that he cannot just continue to work hard, he has to 'get a life' too, and although he does not believe he was witness to his actual death, he appreciates that without feeling able to be fully himself, the net effect will be the same. He will not 'be there' for his family, giving them his strength. He will have lost them, and they, him.

He wants to know where this feeling came from that he has to sacrifice himself totally for the good of his family, when he knows that by doing so, he is actually not giving them more, but less of himself. Only by being himself, can he be fully present for his family and truly giving of himself.

'This sounds dreadfully macabre but the image I wanted to work with was of me in the coffin. I became my dead self, at the end of my life, looking back. What was my most important memory? It was of my father. He was never home, always working. We came from a very working-class background and when my father had a chance to improve things,

314

he always did, which meant he worked long hours and was never home.

'Eight-year-old me remembers waiting to cut the cake at my birthday party till he got home. He never did. Ten-year-old me remembers my father taking me to a circus because Mom insisted. He didn't want to, he had other things, work things, to do. Fifteen-year-old me remembers taking evening classes at a college ten miles away from home and my father promising to pick me up. He never did. He said he'd had to work late so I had to walk home. I think it was at that point I vowed that my own family would always come first.

'Love, for me now, is very much about providing for my family and offering them security. Elizabeth and I rarely have time for our relationship; it really is a 'partnership', almost in a business sense, where security is the currency we use. Our expressions of love tend to be physical and with Daimon to think about as well now, it tends to be a bit mechanical.'

I ask what would help. 'Time away, maybe,' says Mike. I ask him to become the person he has in mind, spending some time away with his wife.

We're taking a weekend away at a hotel. There's a sauna and a gym and Elizabeth and I can swim together in the hotel pool. We're both feeling happy and free. We can talk together, make love, be with each other. I'd forgotten how nice that is.

Mike's insight was that he didn't need to be just a cash cow and provider for his family, that they got more from the unique person he is by his sharing more of himself and not just his wealth with them. Nor did he have to take a rational and mechanistic view of his relationship with Elizabeth. Expressing himself – revealing his essential, vulnerable, human self – was more important and gave his family a real person to connect with. He discovered also that by taking part in the things he naturally enjoyed, he became more himself, which he was able to share with his family. By sacrificing himself, he actually had less to give, but by taking time to be himself, he was able to give them more.

Mike decided that the transformation he was looking for was not about letting go of, or bringing new things into his life, it was about re-visioning the things he already had. He had come to see his life in a very linear, inflexible way – if he behaved in one way it meant that he loved and would take care of his family, which usually meant denying himself. If he behaved in a different way, where he felt free to be himself, it meant he did not love his family, and then he blamed himself and felt guilty.

He decided on a transforming ritual, working with art materials to 'redraw' himself. First, he pictured his life as he sees it now, with all his problems and unresolved issues. Then he redrew the image to show himself as someone who had changed their life.

Along with these images, he wrote himself two letters – the first describing his current life as he saw it; the second from the perspective of the person in the second picture who had made the changes he wanted to make. In this second letter, he included advice to his younger self on how he could make these changes.

The first letter he posted to himself. It would arrive two or three days later, to remind him of how he felt at that time and of his need for change. The second letter, I posted to him two weeks later. When he received this he would have had time to reflect on the changes he needed to make. The second letter would tell him how.

Mike decided to take decisive and committed action to change his life. He put his house up for sale and, with the money he has saved in his high-powered job, is in the fortunate position of being able to buy a new house outright, although smaller than their last. This is the first step in his move towards a simpler and more fulfilling life with his family.

He also decided to change his work status and has

negotiated a new position involving less frequent but highly paid consultancy work. With the simpler lifestyle he is planning, he will need less money; what he wants is more time for his family.

Almost as an aside, he has also started a programme of physical fitness again, which is interesting since this was his main concern at the start of this process. He and Elizabeth are also now planning a second child, which they both hope will be a girl.

MIND-MAPPING YOUR NEW REALITY

When you emerge from the energetic transformation process, you will have entered a new reality space, a new unfolding of the hologram. The world has changed because you have changed. Energy flows where your attention is directed, and a little energy can make a big difference, as Caroline Myss showed us.

The mind map can help here too, as a device for plotting your new position in inner space. For example, if you had recorded your pre-journey world using Buzan's technique your worldview would have created a particular map. Your new post-journey universe will have a different form and feel and different components. You can now compare one with the other to see where you have changed your world and to give yourself a progressive map which builds up the topography of your evolving reality.

What we call 'reality' is just one configuration of energy, one assemblage of the world, amid an infinite variety of potential forms. We always have control over what we see, feel and experience. Energetic transformation is a process where we use the power of our minds to reassemble this energy into a different form, one which answers our needs more effectively and serves us better by using the mind as a gateway to the world of spirit and to our own deeper resources.

EXPLORATIONS – USING ENERGETIC TECHNIQUES FOR CHANGE

1. USING THE LIFE WHEEL

The shamans of Tuva use stones to make divinations, which they often do before rituals of any kind. It is a very different approach to the rock divination method of the Sioux, which we looked at earlier.

The Tuvans use 41 stones of uniform size, which are often taken from the belly of a grouse. These are arranged into nine piles and divination begins from this.

What is interesting about the Tuvan approach is that if the arrangement of the stones suggests future misfortune for her client, the shaman may change and reconfigure them in order to create a more positive outcome, in addition to any further healing work which may be done to address the cause of the misfortune.

A similar phenomenon has been noted among the Yakut people of Siberia. Here, a shaman may have a premonitory dream prior to his healing consultations for the day. If conditions seem unfavourable, the patients who arrive will be sent away, in the certain knowledge that they are doomed. They may, however, return the next day so that the healing can proceed effectively to a positive outcome. By dismissing his patient, the shaman has, with this action alone, changed the future of the healing.

In our consideration of the holographic model we saw how this might be possible. Since we are parts of the giant hologram of the universe, even a small change in one area can have a large impact on the whole – again, similar to the invocation of a blessing or a prayer which releases the energy necessary to save a life by changing the outcome of a car accident.

The original configuration of divinatory stones represents *one possible future*, while the shaman's intervention at the micro-level changes the whole field of which his client is a part.

We can do a similar thing with the life wheel.

When you create the wheel which represents your life at the moment, you reveal the shape of the energies which are at play in your world. By *consciously altering* this shape on the page to produce what you see as a more attractive model, these energies become realigned.

In the West we are very taken with analytical and psychological explanations of effects such as these, so perhaps we can put it this way: by altering the shape that is created on the page, you bring focus to a particular area of your life. Your unconscious then begins to work on the changes necessary for you, presenting ideas and suggestions as to how they may be achieved. Awareness of what you would like to change is always the first, crucial step to be taken.

You do not even need to apply conscious thought to the process, but simply allow your unconscious to communicate with you, bearing in mind that it will do so through images and associations, dreams and synchronicities, rather than direct statements of purpose and fact. You need just to be open to these as they occur.

Changing the shape of the life wheel is also an expression of intention on your part to make changes, and we have already seen the power of intent.

This is a very simple exercise. Merely sketch out your life shape within the wheel and then reflect on the areas you would like to change – and then adapt your life shape to reflect these with *full intention* that positive changes *will* result for you. See what happens next.

2. USING THE MIND MAP

Working with the people concerned, use the mind map approach to plot the worldviews of the significant others in your life: your partner or children or parents. Try the exercise also for your 'enemies', the 'petty tyrants' who offer themselves as advisers to us each day in their behaviour towards us and their criticisms of our actions.

Place the map you create alongside your own and see where the two are similar and where they differ. People who have done so are sometimes surprised to see how closely they resemble the individuals they have come to regard as their enemies – but is actually not so surprising when we realize that we tend often to project our shadow selves onto others and to see in them the traits we would rather not have in ourselves. This revelation is often helpful as a first step in redefining the role of others in the world we are creating, allowing us to see them as our teachers instead of our adversaries.

The technique can also be used with those you love in order to make clear the differences between you, and to give yourself the option of bringing these things closer together by working with what is revealed. At the centre of your map may be 'family', for example, while 'career' may be the centre of your partner's. You now both have a choice of bringing the two into greater alignment for your mutual benefit.

Shamans say that we must have a 'strategy' for dealing with daily life, like a warrior who goes into battle with a clear plan of attack. Battlefield intelligence – information – is the first step in planning any strategy. This is one of the ways you can gather it.

3. WORKING WITH RITUAL

Begin thinking about meaningful rituals which you would like to create. These should ideally be personal to you, but two excellent ones to start with are:

• **Creation of an altar.** In the West, we are accustomed to seeing very grand altars in our churches, which is probably also the only place we do see them.

In Haiti, the situation is very different. Every home has

an altar to the ancestors and the gods, bringing their powers directly into the everyday world through the altar which is the energetic centre of the home. These are not grand affairs. You will see pictures of saints and spirits, as well as offerings of rum and food on these altars, the same food the family is now eating. The gods of Haiti like to eat and drink! There will also be family photographs, heirlooms and trinkets, symbolic of the fact that the gods and the people walk together.

Your personal altar does not need to be an elaborate affair. Rather, it represents the direct connection between you and your spirit. Your intention behind its construction and the faith that you invest in it are the most important ingredients for its success as an energetic tool.

Use items meaningful and precious to you, such as family photographs, candles, rocks and shells, souvenirs and trinkets, to create a full expression of *who you are* or *who you intend to become*. Use the altar space and colours, crystals and other power objects, to represent the Four Directions as well as the four elements of water, air (feathers, for example), earth (or rocks) and fire (a candle, perhaps).

Keep your altar clean and use it often as a meditation space, a doorway through which the spirits may enter to offer you advice and support in your life.

• **The collage of self.** Create a collage of images precious to you or which represent the life you intend to create, just as Jasmine did. Have this framed and hang it where you can see it each day. Every time you see this collage, use the opportunity to reaffirm your intention for positive change.

7

THE PSYCHOLOGY OF THE
SHAMAN'S OTHERWORLD

*In going down into the secrets of his own mind, he
has descended into the secrets of all minds.*
– Ralph Waldo Emerson

*I remember being amazed as a child when I learned that the
land we walk upon is a commodity which can be owned and
sold. How do you sell the oceans and the sky? What about
the waves and clouds: who owns them? Who does the Sun
belong to?*

*All of this is already ours. I simply could not understand
how anyone had the right to sell it. And how can it be bought
when we already own it?*

*Native peoples and all children feel this way. 'How can you
buy or sell the sky, the warmth of the land?' asked Chief
Seathl.*[86] *'Every part of this earth is sacred. All things are connected. The Earth does not belong to man; man belongs to
the Earth. Our God is the same God.' My children ask me
the same questions – and I have no answers for them – it is
not natural, not in our genes to want ownership of sacred
space. To partake in it is enough.*

*And yet, as we grow older, we get used to the logic of
ownership – so much so that we are prepared to squabble*

over feet and inches and kill each other over longitudes and latitudes, instead of embracing a planet which is rightfully ours, all of ours, in its totality. And while we squabble over inches, we forget what it is to be part of the whole.

'In the rainforest there are thousands of plants which are totally unknown to us – unless, of course, they are put to the torch in their first encounter with humanity,' says Dr Thomas David.[87]

During a trip to the Amazon, David was given a special tea used by the shamans of the rainforest to treat a variety of health problems. Back home in Europe, he tested the plants that compose this tea and discovered that they have a remarkable curative effect on patients with cancer, AIDS and other diseases of the immune system. Clinical trials by other medical laboratories have confirmed his findings.

'The rainforest does not just serve to regulate the world climate; it is above all a library with an irreplaceable collection ... If these plants or animals should become extinct, this information will be lost for ever,' he says.

And if they are?

Well ... pharmaceutical companies will have lost a major revenue stream and humankind a source of life-saving therapeutics since much of the drug technology we use today has been developed from naturally occurring rainforest species – from agrimony for asthma and typhus, to boldo for liver dysfunction – and maybe special and secret blends of these known only to shamans which might cure cancer and other crippling diseases.

But maybe we are prepared to live with cancer so the oil companies can profit and we can drive our cars.

The rainforest, the world's largest natural botanical garden, is also home to fruits and vegetables that we can only do our best to synthesize outside of her environment. If the rainforest goes, they go, and the species that depend on these fruits will also die. We will have lost them for ever. All it takes is one mistake by us as caretakers of these species and, once the rainforests are gone, there is no way back. They become just a memory.

Maybe we are prepared to take that risk too.

Oh yes, and there is something more. We will all be dead. Unable to protest or protect any more. From caretakers to corpses.

And so we go on wishing, for our own peace of mind, that things would change, that the oil companies would see sense, that someone would put a stop to all this . . . madness.

And all the time not really doing much to encourage it. But then, of course, we can still breathe. It will not be us choking, only our children.

Do we really have a right to buy and sell the Earth? And, if we do, is She not worth more than this?

'Man is what he believes,' wrote Chekhov. We have the power to stop this.

The techniques of shamanism allow us access to these new possibilities. Through them we can not only enter a new universe, but re-create it, shape it and focus its raw energy on personal and global transformation and a more fulfilling future.

John Perkins covers much of this ground in his books, *The World Is As You Dream It* and *Shapeshifting*,[88] which detail his life among the Shuar people of Ecuador and the teachings he has learned from them and now practises with individual students, groups and with major Western institutions and companies. It is possible, he says, to shapeshift, to recreate ourselves from a cellular level, using these physical, mental, emotional and spiritual powers to alter the very composition of our bodies in order to understand our illnesses and to fight off disease, right up to a corporate and cultural level to change the dream the world is living. All it takes is focus and the will to do so, so that we honour our lives and our world rather than abusing it and ourselves. We naturally have the ability to make it happen.

There is considerable scientific support for John's claims. Dr Edmund Jacobson has demonstrated a visible link between mental imagery and bodily changes which shows that we can change ourselves physically using the power of our minds alone.[89] Jacobson asked people to visualize themselves running and then measured the tiny muscle movement made by their bodies in response to their images. He found that they were essentially *the same* movements we would expect if the subjects had actually left the room and gone for a run.

Even more surprising is the work of John Basmajian, which shows that the control we have over ourselves through the use of imagery extends beyond the merely muscular right down to the cellular, at the level of the autonomic nervous system. The ANS takes care of the body's 'automatic' functions and because of this, had largely been written off by scientists as beyond conscious control. Nobody wants to have to remember to breathe, for example, as forgetting has some dramatic consequences.

What Basmajian found, however, is that people can actually control just about anything in their bodies, including the ANS – right down to the activity of *one specific cell*. Using biofeedback techniques, his subjects were able to locate and fire a single neuron in their bodies, a task which Michael Hutchinson, in *The Book of Floating, Exploring the Private Sea*, describes as 'more difficult than finding a single grain of sand in a desert'.[90]

This is shapeshifting – creating a new version of reality for ourselves – at its most fundamental, cellular level. And it is within the power of all of us if we use our bodies and our minds in a holistic way, instead of seeing them as separate, with the body (which includes the lump of grey material we call the brain) supreme in this, as our Western model dictates.

One of the ways we can use the body and mind creatively to evoke this new reality is by adopting specific trance postures. Trance postures give us access to shapeshifting, healing, and other dimensions of power. Shamans have known of the benefits of trance for thousands of years and of the power of *specific* trance postures for creating a range of effects, such as divining the future, calling to the tribe the animals which will sustain them as a source of food and clothing, and entering particular areas of the hologram to explore distinct territories of the otherworld.

We have used only one trance posture so far to enter both the lower and the upper world – the Jivaro posture taught to Michael Harner – which is a safe and effective posture for any and all trance journeys, whether to the lower, middle or upper world and for whatever purpose. It is a truly universal posture and the only one you will actually ever *need* to know. There are, however, at least eighty other postures now known, explored and their effects documented by the Cuyamungue Institute run by Felicitas Goodman and Belinda Gore, both of whom have written on the usage and purpose of ecstatic body postures for journeying.

TRANCE POSTURE JOURNEYS

I first learned of alternative posture forms from Howard Charing of the Eagle's Wing Centre for Contemporary Shamanism in London.[91] As he rattled in the healing posture called Bear Spirit (and more affectionately known as 'Grandfather Bear'), many of us in the group felt the presence of a vast shape behind us, some experienced running through forests with Bear, all of us felt a surge of energy in our bodies.

My own journey was one of brotherhood with Bear, of running through deep forests, the light and dark of the leaf canopy casting shadows and webs of light across my eyes. Eventually we came to the sheer face of a deep crevasse. 'It is this you will have to cross to take the next step in your healing,' said Bear: 'the first step into the abyss is always an act of faith.'

When the trance ended, Howard explained that this was, indeed, an ancient posture associated with healing and that Grandfather Bear is often experienced as standing behind the journeyer, using teeth and claws to rip away illness, to infuse the body with new energy, and to explain what is needed for personal healing.

My experience with Grandfather Bear had been so potent for me – I had, indeed, come to a point in my life where a leap of faith was exactly what I needed for my own sense of self-fulfilment – that I began to research these ecstatic postures. I began conducting experiments of my own and introducing the postures to participants in occasional workshops, using Belinda Gore's book, *Ecstatic Body Postures*,[92] as a reference source. My findings, although not always entirely consistent with Gore's, are that these postures do produce qualitatively different experiences for participants than those commonly found using the Jivaro posture.

I began to experiment further with the effects of different body postures, involving groups and other individuals in this work. More recently, this has developed into a more unusual form of experimentation, using the tools of urban shamanism – an online 'blind' test with volunteers from three 'cyber-shaman' communities, my own community at *AJourneyToYou-Shaman@egroups.com*[93] and two others. Members, who were given descriptions only of the body postures and not their meaning, characteristic effects or full names, were therefore separated not only by geographical distance but by the more ephemeral distance of cyberspace. All volunteers were essentially alone and had no method of comparison with each other.

Ten people took part in this experiment, which is probably not a sufficient number to set the statistical world on fire, but the results were, nonetheless, interesting. The aims of this experiment were:

1.   to see if the trance postures used produced a common effect and/or experience among participants;
2.   to see if these effects varied from those produced by the Jivaro posture; and
3.   to see whether the experiences recorded were congruent with those from the Cuyamungue Institute, where

experiments with trance postures are conducted in work-shop groups.

We will look at the results in a moment, but first let us explore where our knowledge of the shaman's trance comes from.

THE HISTORY OF TRANCE

'Great beings who inhabit the realm of spirit that we call the Alternate Reality have been around for thousands of years, helping humans through our journeys here on Earth, and hunter-gatherer and horticultural peoples around the world have both documented their presence and preserved the means of access to them through their artwork on cave walls, in totem poles, in delicate gold or silver work, or in simple pottery. Their images have been perpetually in front of our eyes,' says Gore.[94]

Even so, the true nature of these images was rediscovered just twenty-five years ago by anthropologist Felicitas Goodman, as an outcome of her research into glossolalia ('speaking in tongues'). Goodman's findings suggest that the figures represented in this artwork are, in fact, ritual body postures which enable ordinary people to enter non-ordinary consciousness and experience the spirit world in quite specific ways.[95]

The postures produce a common effect, according to Goodman, because they have in common the one thing we all share, the human body, which has remained unchanged in its basic structure and functions since the times of our earliest ancestors. Our nervous and endocrine systems are much the same as they were 30,000 years ago, says Gore, a fact which enables the urban shaman of the city to enter the same other-world as the plains or jungle medicine man, and just as effectively, through the same neural doorways used for thousands of years.

Dr Goodman identified several prerequisites for a successful trance experience:

- A sacred space must be created, with a special power and purpose for the individual.
- Participants must enter the trance state with the *intention* of having a sacred experience.
- A repetitive sound must be used to tell the nervous system to shift into non-ordinary reality. The rattle or drum is ideal for this and Dr Goodman's experiments confirm that a rhythm of about 200–220 beats per minute works best, which is consistent with other shamanic literature on the use of 'sonic driving' by tribal peoples.
- A method for silencing the inner dialogue of the mind is essential. Goodman's initial research was conducted in churches, where the minister's instructions to focus on the Holy Spirit served this purpose by enabling people to leave the material world outside the door and to focus deeply on the world of spirit. In her own experiments, Goodman used a simple breathing exercise instead to create a meditative space by focusing on the breath to quieten the mind.

The key factor, however, was that people needed a shared approach to the exercise, a belief system to be part of, which transformed the trance experience into a spiritual one. Ritual body postures provided this common reference by over-coming individual and cultural differences and creating a new sense of unity with the universe which all people could be part of. Trance postures worked for everyone, irrespective of their worldview or belief systems. In the words of Belinda Gore: 'Agnostic computer programmers could undergo a shamanic dismemberment during the fifteen minutes of an ecstatic trance session.'

Trance postures are designed for specific purposes. The 'Lady of Cholula' posture, for instance, connects us with what Gore calls 'a grandmotherly presence', who offers us loving advice and clarification, whereas the 'Tennessee Diviner' is the preferred posture for specific questions concerning ceremony, and 'Bear Spirit posture' – the one first demonstrated to me by Howard Charing and which is perhaps 8,000 years old – is widely known as a healing posture.

I offered three postures to my group, describing only the positions themselves, not their intentions. Should you wish to try these, the three I chose, with descriptions of the postures themselves (following Gore), were:

1   *Tattooed Jaguar* – Kneel with legs spread so knees form an open V and cross your right big toe over the left big toe. Rest your buttocks on your heels and bend forward slightly at the waist. Curl your hands the amount needed to hold an imaginary medium-sized candle. Place your curled left hand palm down on your left knee and your right hand on your right knee, tilted upwards slightly (so if you were actually holding a candle, it would point at 45 degrees towards your other leg). Keep your elbows relaxed and slightly bow your arms. Face forward with eyes closed.

2.   *Tennessee Diviner* – Begin by kneeling, then raise your right knee and place your right foot sole down on the floor beside your left knee. Continue to kneel on your left knee, with buttocks resting on your heel. Place your left hand palm down on the left knee and right hand palm down on your right knee, but slightly to the left of the kneecap. Cock your head very slightly to the right as if wanting to look over your right knee. Keep your eyes closed and protrude your tongue a little between slightly parted lips.

3.   *Realm of the Dead* – Stand with feet parallel about six inches apart and point your toes straight ahead. Keep your knees sightly bent. Place your right hand over your waist with the ball of the hand covering your navel and your middle finger extending along the waistline. Your left arm is against your chest, with your palm just above your right arm and parallel to it. Keep your upper arms relaxed and close to your body. Face forward with your eyes closed.

The Tattooed Jaguar may be 3,500 years old and is a shapeshifting posture which allows us to enter a new reality from the perspective of the animal kingdom. In Gore's words, 'many individuals become sensitised to the non-human world and grow in rapport with the animals'.

The Tennessee Diviner, dating from around 1,300 years ago, is a divinatory posture which enables us to contact a specific spirit whose expertise is advice on ritual. The spirit being contacted can be 'short tempered, brief and even cryptic' but 'generous with exacting details' concerning specific rituals for healing.

The Realm of the Dead posture, which has been traced back to Germany around 2,500 years ago, mediates experiences of dying and journeys to the land of the dead. 'The traveller wanders in desolate areas . . . but eventually something changes and the journeyer begins to rise into a new form and a new life'.

Some of the ten people who participated in my online experiment were workshop leaders themselves who introduced the techniques to their groups as an extension of this exercise. All reported markedly different effects to the ones normally experienced using the Jivaro posture. 'Each individual was successful in gaining a different perspective than normal [and in terms of] where they went spiritually, the journeys were intense,' said one workshop leader who introduced the postures to her group of six.

The Realm of the Dead (described to participants only as the 'RoD', so as not to disclose its purpose) produced the characteristic descent into the lower world and facilitated meetings with 'spirit guides that were unusual to the journeyer', she continued.

Another participant, who could only hold this posture for a short time due to a prior injury, commented: 'I got an impression of the incredible vastness of time and space rushing towards me as if I was travelling at a very fast rate of speed through space. I saw blackness and stars that were very far away from me . . . I didn't think I really got anything in that short time but since you asked specifically, I realize I did – and the impression is staying with me.'

The most intense of all postures was the Tattooed Jaguar, which is especially noted by Gore for facilitating the experience of reality through the eyes of a big cat. 'I journeyed in the posture of the jaguar and can report that I was unable until I left the journey to "get out" of the jaguar body,' said one informant. 'During the journey I met the "Mother Jaguar" – incredible. I was fully grown and compared to the size of the mother, I was a six week old kitten.'

'I truly knew what it felt like to be wild,' said another. 'I experienced myself running through the jungle, totally alert and aware, tracing my prey and then tearing it with my teeth, utterly primal, with no sense of the morals or taboos of our society. I was totally free of all that.'

Tennessee Diviner (described to participants as 'Tennessee D') – a divinatory posture, as the name suggests – on the other hand, had a more limited effect. In retrospect, this is not so surprising. The essence of divination is to hold a question in mind during the journey and without knowing the purpose of the posture, this was impossible. Participants mentioned only an 'intense' experience and a feeling of 'lightness'.

It seems clear from the experiences of those who took part that these postures produce quite different journeys to those normally taken using the Jivaro posture, that each trance posture was different in itself from others, and that broadly, the effects experienced are consistent with the findings of the Cuyamungue Institute.

Some postures by their very nature – such as the Realm of the Dead and the Tattooed Jaguar – do seem to open a specific doorway to a particular otherworld territory or state of being, while others like the Tennessee Diviner require a greater degree of intentionality in order to be effective in producing helpful journeying information as well as a specific state of altered consciousness. What this also does, of course, is underline very strongly the absolute necessity for a definitely expressed journeying *intention* prior to the journey itself.

OTHER ASPECTS OF MIND–BODY UNITY

Castaneda also tells us something about the unused potential of the mind–body partnership we use so little, when he talks of the power of the energy body, the natural energy which flows through us and which we can direct if we apply ourselves to it. He relates the story of don Genaro, a contemporary of his teacher, don Juan, who was able to scale the sheer face of a waterfall against the fall of the water, and without even using his hands or feet to help him do so.

Beyond the physical body we normally only think of as ourselves, we have a body which is made of fibres of pure energy, which can be focused, through our intention, into new types of limbs which are just as effective for climbing. Using this energy practically was the secret of don Genaro's climb.

I had a taste of this while climbing the steep hills of San Francisco last year. My colleague and I were both unused to the inclines which can be found in some of the streets there and were finding the going quite tough. I decided to use the fibres of my energy body to assist me and, projecting them forward from my solar plexus, was able to 'hook' streetlamps and other objects ahead of me in order to pull myself up quite effortlessly simply by 'seeing' these fibres as 'winching' me upwards, without any need for me to exert physical effort.

Having concentrated on doing so only for the few minutes it took to really get the hang of this, I turned to my colleague to suggest he tried it too – only to find that he wasn't there. When I looked back, I saw that James was, in fact, some 200 yards or so behind me and still struggling with the climb. I realized that I hadn't even felt the effort of it during the last few minutes. When I returned to the UK, I had the opportunity to use this technique again in the rather steeper hills of Wales and found that it worked just as well.

This body–mind partnership has other practical uses too. Serge King has explained that the body, not just the brain, contains our memories, so that any event has a physical as well as a mental and emotional component. When we try to remember something using the brain alone, we often find ourselves struggling, sometimes in vain, because this part of us has forgotten or even repressed the event. But if we allow ourselves to become aware of our physical selves at these times instead and to notice the position of our shoulders, neck, limbs, we will often find that we are using our body to replay the event in muscular or nervous tensions and movements, since our memories are also stored in particular areas of the body which reflect the effect that a specific incident had on us at the time. We may find that we automatically grimace or that there is stress in our shoulders or back as our bodies recall certain painful events which are still hidden within our brains. Then the trick is to fully experience the bodily sensation evoked and the memory of that event will return to us in full, just as the smell of coffee or a certain song will often remind us of a pleasant afternoon spent with friends, or a person we once loved.

These are some of the powers of our physical and mental selves, well known to shamans, which we in the West have forgotten we even have, yet alone know how to use.

Psychologists tell us that we only ever employ about 5 per cent of the capacity of our minds at any one time. While it may be true that over the course of the day, we use a greater amount of the range of our capabilities, it remains true that very little of our power is needed for any single activity or mental process; most of us can handle modern life on 'automatic pilot'. But if we can accomplish the miracles we achieve every day using just 5 per cent of our brains, imagine what we could do if we were able to use 100 per cent – or even just 50 per cent – of the powers we have available to us.

Some researchers have studied just this possibility.

Maxwell Cade carried out research with 4,000 people and found that, when they were shown how to use more of the whole brain at the same time, they were able to achieve feats which most of us would probably find miraculous.[96] This included the ability to consciously control pain, to heal themselves and others and to demonstrate highly developed intuitive – even telepathic – capabilities, simply as the result of achieving a more integrated use of the whole brain.

Anyone who has ever watched a shaman-healer performing her work with a client can have no doubt that this is exactly what is happening when the shaman enters the trance to communicate with her spirits.

Sharmanic healing may be very different from the journeying experience, far more active and aware. The shaman will drum, dance, perhaps sing or vocalize to narrate the journey she is taking, all the time communicating with her spirit helpers and with her client, flowing effortlessly between the primal, pre-verbal language of spirit and the rational explanation required by the person she is helping.

In one healing I observed recently, the shaman *physically* changed her appearance, *becoming* her bear spirit helper as she worked on her client, talking, smiling and consulting with her spirits, staring into what we around her saw as empty space, as she clawed and pulled the sickness from her client. Then, in the next second, she was entirely rational, directing her human helpers and talking quietly and analytically with her client. It was obvious to those who watched that the shaman was, indeed, using the whole of her psychic capabilities in an entirely holistic way, moving between the left brain and the right effortlessly in a completely unselfconscious way to harness her natural, intuitive powers for healing.

One interpretation of Eliade's description of the shaman as a 'walker between worlds' is exactly this practised ability of the shaman to walk across the corpus callosum, the rope bridge of nerves which separates the two hemispheres of the brain, her intention to heal providing the energetic link to integrate the two, which results in her 'magical' curative powers – powers we all may have.

THE INFINITE WITHIN US

Michael Hutchinson points out in his excellent book on the floatation tank experience, that none of our innate abilities, miraculous though they may be, should actually give us any real cause for astonishment as we have only to open our eyes and look about us to see the evidence of these powers in the world at large.

Yogis, monks and fakirs have been performing these 'miracles' of self-regulation for thousands of years, in blithe ignorance of our Western scientists who said such things could not be done. We need only think of Hindu firewalkers; of Tibetan monks who through meditative techniques, raise their body temperature so they can sit, in subzero snow, and dry scores of wet, icy blankets wrapped around them; of Yogis who are buried alive for days in airtight boxes; of healers and mystics who can puncture themselves with knitting needles yet experience no pain and whose bodies heal almost instantly.[97]

We might also mention the Ninja warriors who sometimes prepared themselves for missions by sitting for days beneath freezing waterfalls to acclimatize their bodies to the rigours ahead, the Shaolin monks who perform extraordinary feats of the body, and the yoga masters able to slow their heartbeats to practically unrecordable levels, all of it through the application of controlled thought and intention alone, a partnership of mind and body.

I have watched shamans from Siberia to Peru cure illnesses using only their will to do so and the sound of the drum. In Haiti, young boys drink bottles of rum laced with red hot peppers in possession trances and emerge sober and unharmed. In Turkey, I have seen people walk barefoot over crushed glass and beds of nails, all without injury.

In *Gifts of Unknown Things*, Lyall Watson tells of one of his own remarkable experiences, where he watched a shaman make a grove of trees vanish and reappear merely by dancing before them in order to express her intention that they should do so.[98]

Colin Wilson, in *The Occult*, tells of a blind Russian girl who was able to read aloud the words from a book by laying it flat against her stomach and 'sensing' the content of the pages.[99]

Taking this even further to demonstrate the power of intent as a focus for the energy of the mind, Wilson also reports a remarkable experiment which was conducted, successfully, to deliberately *create* a poltergeist, a sentient spirit.[100] In this experiment, a group of researchers simply invented the biography of a fictional dead boy they called Philip. Despite being entirely fabricated, Philip emerged as a real individual and autonomous entity with his own thoughts and will, who could move objects, answer questions, and interact with individuals and with the group, *even when he had not been 'called' by them to be present.*

The will of the group was so strong that its psychic expression manipulated the energies surrounding them to create a physical manifestation of their intention. Shamans have been quietly doing this for years. Some tells how the shaman in the Dagara culture can help the dead to walk. 'Why do the dead walk where I come from? They walk because they are still as important to the living as they were before,' he says simply.[101] Once we 'dismiss' our dead as beyond our world, they are gone, but if our intention is to honour them and to work with them, they remain – a fact which can create problems, of possession, soul loss, 'hauntings', as well as opportunities for greater communication between the worlds.

At what level does the frequency of such events mean that we must redefine them so that they become the norm of what is possible rather than extraordinary occurrences and miracles reserved for the gods? All of these things are recorded, although even now we are sceptical of them. In being so, we are really being sceptical of our own abilities since all of these things were achieved by ordinary people – flesh and blood – who were just more aware of their own, extraordinary potential. 'They can because they think they can,' as Virgil said.

There is a lovely song by the group Tindersticks, called 'My Sister', which illustrates beautifully the difference in perspective between two people, one of whom *should* feel disempowered but actually feels quite the opposite while the other, who has no physical disadvantage, just cannot see the world from the same position of personal power.[102]

The singer narrates the story of his sister who, he says, went blind at the age of five. Staring out of their bedroom window together, his sister would ask him to tell her what he saw. He would describe the houses opposite, their front gate with its rotten hinges, that was never fixed, and the grey drabness of the street. His sister would stand quietly for a moment, considering this, as if she was trying to picture the scene in her mind. Then she would reply with what she saw: the Christmas tree lights of beautiful, faraway stars; the bright orange planets which circled them; rainbow fishes dancing in crystal bowls.

Her brother, seeing only the cold, grey street and the grimy houses opposite, could only draw the curtains against the dismal scene and turn away.

Often, we would rather see the gate with its rotten hinges than Christmas tree lights in faraway windows, as long as the former offers us the hard 'linear evidence' our society craves, the ability to study, measure, record, and refer to peer group reports of similar results in the libraries of pre-analysed experience. But clearly, there is something going on; there is too much evidence to believe otherwise.

To the shaman, our reliance on the brain, so preciously regarded in the West, is often seen as holding us back from achieving our true potential. Instead, they say, when we still the chatter of the brain and achieve inner silence, we are able to strengthen the intuitive abilities which come from an integration of the whole body, mind, emotions and spirit within us and achieve far more in this world. Otherwise we are using only one quarter of our total potential, our physical abilities alone.

For shamans, the brain means little, it is just another part of the body, with all of its potentials and limitations. The *mind*, however, is a gateway to the otherworld and a different matter entirely. The mind flows through us, across the whole holographic plate of the body, and is the energy which unlocks the door to spirit by allowing us to connect with the wider potentials of the universe.

THE HUMAN CORE OF POTENTIAL

Michael Hutchinson's *The Book of Floating*, is a record of this direct experience of connection with the otherworld through his use of the sensory deprivation technique of the floatation tank.[103]

Hutchinson originally set out as a journalist to discredit the new fad of floating, which he saw as 'so California' but he rapidly became converted to the practice once he began to try it for himself. In the floatation tank, you are suspended in a warm saline solution at body temperature, unable to distinguish the point at which your physical self ends and the environment takes over. You are 'at one' with the world you now experience, a feeling which is enhanced by the darkness of the interior and silent isolation from the world outside.

People in this situation slip easily into a trance state with the descent from normal awareness to the Theta brain patterns described by Bearwalker Wilson in Chapter 4 of this book, as characteristic of the shamanic state of consciousness during journeying. People find themselves suddenly and intensely involved with the visions and experiences well known to the shamans. For many, the experience is one of enlightenment, with new insights and the development of new powers and abilities, and a different way of seeing and engaging with the world when they emerge.

Certainly this was so for Hutchinson. So much so, in fact, that his article turned into a detailed and exhaustive study of the trance state of floatation and of the research literature and experimental results on changes in consciousness and human potential arising from this state. Hutchinson's evidence is so impressive and, indeed, the floatation experience so similar to the shamanic state – the darkness, the silence, the sense of relaxation and focus on the self, as well as the visions and sensations which arise from these two specific uses of the mind and body – that I would like to share some of his findings here.

TRANCE STATES PRODUCE NEW POSSIBILITIES FOR SELF-DEVELOPMENT

Research shows that the influence we have over our bodies and our minds is significantly increased when we enter a trance-like state of controlled relaxation. Rats temporarily paralysed with injections of the toxin curare, for example, are able to develop much greater control over those parts of their bodies they still do have power over – their 'internal' states – and are able to manipulate these as well as any advanced Tibetan master, including raising and lowering their bodily temperatures in highly specific areas of their body – at will.[104]

One of the implications of this is that when we are taken out of our normal ways and means of interaction with the world, it is quite easy for us to rechannel our energies into new directions and to use the power of the mind to address the new challenges of the situation we find ourselves in. Instead of focusing outwardly on the stuff of the material world, we can use our infinite powers as explorers of the inner self to truly know ourselves in this world.

I have no doubt that we can choose consciously to do so. Indeed, when I was writing this book, I would sometimes ask my mind, in the relaxed state before sleep, to continue working on the text as I slept. I then found that whole pages of writing would be delivered to me as I dreamt. These were not normal dreams, where information appears in symbols and metaphors, these were dreams in which I could play an active part. I could clearly read the words I was being shown and amend them and work on them as the pages were presented to me as whole typewritten sheets. In fact, everything in this chapter so far was written in exactly this way. Last night I asked my spirits or, if you wish, my unconscious self which has access to this world, to work with me to write this section and to produce some tangible work for me. They not only did so, but woke me at 4 a.m. to get the information down on paper so I did not forget what I had seen, before allowing me to sleep again.

Around 40 per cent of our life is spent asleep. If we can use this time constructively, how much more productive we could be. The shamans recognized this and developed techniques for 'lucid dreaming', where the real, alternative world of dreaming was given intention and focus so that this time asleep could continue to be used in an effective manner for problem-solving, healing work and explorations of the other-worlds. Castaneda, in books like *The Art of Dreaming*, describes these techniques in some detail.

The key, for Castaneda, was the act of will – to give the mind firm instructions prior to sleep about the problem it was required to work on. Next, it was important to be aware, while sleeping, that an answer to the problem was emerging in the dreamscape and to begin to interact with the solution in a conscious way, to direct the flow of the action of the dream.

Castaneda's advice for learning *dreaming* is to concentrate first on becoming aware of your own hands in your dream. This connection with your body in a first-person sense begins to put you in charge of the dream space, and you can then build up to full body awareness and 'physical' control of your whole dream environment.

Unfortunately, this is a practice which can take years and which some of us never achieve. I have never managed it fully. But thankfully, it may not be totally necessary since I have found, once again, that intention is far more important. You must firmly intend the dreaming self to continue to work on the assignment you set for it and then relax and allow another side of yourself to take over. It won't work every time, but when it does, it certainly gets the job done.

Trance states give us information from *new* sources

When we enter the Theta state of trance, we enter new realms of possibility much deeper than our everyday consciousness, a place of 'sudden insight, creative inspiration . . . a mysterious, elusive state,' as Hutchinson calls it.

This is a place which is particularly conducive for the resurfacing of unconscious material and childhood memories, accompanied by new insights into their meanings and our own origins.

Biofeedback researchers, Elmer and Alyce Green used laboratory techniques to teach people how to consciously enter these Theta states, although the success of tribal shamans, as well as Buddhists and others who meditate regularly without the benefits of such technology, suggests that the technology itself matters less than the self-knowledge that we are successful in achieving a deepening level of trance. This is enough for us to validate our own experiences and assess our improvements over time.

When people are deep in trance, said the Greens, usually unheard or unseen things come to consciousness . . . rather like an experience, a 'reliving', and people often report 'integrative experiences leading to psychological well-being' as a result of this reconnection with their deep selves.

Whatever happens in Theta, it is not just a simple memory, it is *real* – a 'reliving' – and one which produces powerful effects in the present and the future, as if the outcome of the event itself is changed by the experience of reliving it.[105]

One of their conclusions was that we produce 'new and valid ideas or syntheses of ideas, not primarily by deduction, but springing by intuition from unconscious sources' while in this altered consciousness state. In other words, the reality we find in trance can be just as real, and the information we receive there at least as valuable, as when we approach the world from the viewpoint of ordinary consciousness: 'Valid ideas' from 'unconscious sources'.

Theta patterns tend to be more prevalent in children, certainly till the age of 10 or so, by which time we have been taught to use more 'socially acceptable' areas of our brain, to focus on the material body rather than the inner self or the spiritual dimension, and to concentrate on rational thought. It is at this point that the adult beta pattern begins to emerge. It is perhaps not so surprising, therefore, that entering the theta state again, the world of the child, gives us this ability to relive childhood memories and to reconnect with the power of our inner children.

OUR POWERS OF INTUITION REMAIN, DESPITE THE BEST EFFORTS OF SOCIETY

By studying people like 'PS', who have had the two hemi-spheres of their brains separated by surgery, researchers have found that each side of the brain is essentially responsible for its own interpretation of reality. The work of Karl Pribram and others suggests that there is no reason why this *should* be, if all thought crosses the mind – or, indeed, the whole body – in a giant latticework of holographic potential. So perhaps it is just physiological convenience that encourages us to deposit certain types of information in these different sectors initially, while we all have the capability for more holistic thought ultimately. Or perhaps these separate functions of the brain have simply been found there because that is where the researchers have looked.

The Western world is certainly preoccupied with the qualities it has ascribed to the left brain, which was thought to handle the 'linear' aspects of reality, all the logic and rationalization of 'doing' rather than 'being'. We may be more inclined to question the assumptions of society when we remember that we all enter this world with a highly developed sense of connection to our imaginative selves, that this is our primary way of engaging reality, and that it is the urban dream we are born into which then channels us away from this. Away from what, we cannot know. We will never know what we *could* have become or how we *might* have shaped the world unless we can reconnect with this early experience and allow our children to develop in a different way. I imagine that it would be a more peaceful, accepting and loving world.

But we do not. By the time they get to 10 or so, our children have been encouraged to turn their backs almost fully on the intuitive landscape they entered at their birth. I still remember from my own childhood being able, physically, to walk on water and I know how that sounds!

There was a particular bodily movement and a certain feeling associated with the action of doing so. The movement was something like a skip, like skimming a stone across water, of treading lightly so as to connect only with the surface tension of the pool. It was accompanied by a feeling of being lifted, of being light, and of focus on the other side of the watery divide. I doubt whether I could have travelled great distances this way, but I certainly could skip across expanses of water 20 or 30 feet across and, as I did so more often, I was getting better at it. Nobody had told me it was impossible.

Then one day someone did.

I was at the seaside on holiday with my parents and began walking out to sea. As I continued, still only ankle deep in the water, I looked back to shore, now several hundred yards away, and noticed my parents on the beach in a state of excitement and agitation, and my father begin wading out after me.

Not knowing quite what all the fuss was about, I continued. Beneath me, what I was walking on felt soft and mossy, slightly slippery but also somewhat adhesive, so that I was 'caught' and held by my next step. Still the water only lapped at my ankles.

I looked around, and there was my father next to me, shoulder deep. I was looking down at him.

He shouted at me to come down, that I must be standing on some underwater object that had allowed me to walk dangerously far into the sea and that I was at risk of drowning.

His panic startled me and, without my taking a further single step, merely standing where I was and sensing his fear, my world collapsed around me. Whatever was beneath me vanished and I was plunged into icy water, suddenly five feet below the waves, coughing and spluttering and, just as he had predicted, almost drowning. Then his strong arms had caught me up and, holding me, he took me back to the safety of the shore.

He was my father, he knew best. And his worldview had nearly killed me.

I put all thoughts of walking on water well behind me and from that day forward never tried the trick again. Except for once, when I had to.

I was, perhaps, eight years old and they were building houses near where I lived. I liked playing on the building site, full of adventure and new experiences and, one day, was overjoyed to find that a deep hole had been newly dug, presumably for the foundations of a house. The sides were very steep and, as it had been raining recently, very slippery, and at the bottom was a deep pool of water and mud.

My friend Kevin and I were ecstatic – an adventure for heroes! How to cross it? As I stood at the edge pondering, I slipped in the mud and fell, ending up neck deep in water right in the middle of the pool below. Which wouldn't have been so bad except, I realized, beneath the water was a deep body of liquid mud and I was sinking.

There was no way Kevin could reach me and, even if he could, nothing that he could have done without endangering himself.

They say your life passes before you as you prepare to die and this was true for me. Being eight, it wasn't incredibly profound – going to school for the first time, my favourite TV programmes, my first stabs at independence and finding my own way in the world. That was what did it – the realization of my own experiments with life, of finding out what was possible, and my memory of being able to walk on water, even though my father – who, as an adult, *must* be right – had said it wasn't possible. In that moment, which lasted for ever, I struggled with what I knew was possible, what I had been told was possible, and came to one of my first important decisions about life: anything *is* possible but what we *believe* is possible can empower us or kill us.

The next thing I knew, I was standing on the other side of the muddy, water-filled hole that had almost killed me. I had absolutely no idea how I had got there: by all rights I should have been dead. Kevin was no help. As the only witness to all that had just taken place, he took one look at my wet and bedraggled body, screamed and ran home, leaving me wondering what on earth had got into him. If I had just done what I suspected I had done – walked to the shore on the surface of the water – it was perfectly natural as far as I was concerned. We were all capable of it, I was nothing special, so what was my friend so concerned about? His reaction, however, was the final straw which convinced me that I should not go about doing this sort of thing any more and it was not until years later that I developed some understanding of what had gone on then and how it was possible that I could do these things.

I was in my twenties and studying martial arts, ninjutsu and aikido, when our instructor showed us one day the power of our minds over our bodily states. He asked a volunteer to sit on a chair in the middle of the room and four people to stand around him. The person in the centre was instructed to 'think himself heavy' by projecting his weight deep into the Earth and imagining himself anchored, immovable.

I imagine the person in the middle must have weighed maybe 11 stones, with chair, but four men, each at least of equal weight, could not lift him.

He was then told to 'think himself light' by projecting himself upwards and seeing his body mass as a column of light stretching to the stars which were pulling him up to meet them. The four people around him began to lift again and, expecting another struggle, they exerted at least a similar effort, but this time, it was visibly clear that there was no resistance at all and the volunteer on the chair was lifted to shoulder height effortlessly.

This was exactly what I had done when I had been skipping water pools. I had felt the sensation of being lifted, thought myself light and unable to sink beneath the surface, and the water had conspired to work with me.

After the class, with some trepidation, I told the sensei (the martial arts Master and teacher) of my early experiences of walking on the water. Instead of the ridicule and disbelief I still expected, he had an even more fantastic story for me.

'When I was about the same age as you,' he said, 'I was taken to a lido, an open air swimming pool, by my parents. I couldn't swim but I was so excited by the water that I just dived in – and promptly sank.

'I was there some time at the bottom, I'd say maybe 20 minutes before anyone noticed. I should, of course, have been dead by then, I realize now.

'When my parents noticed I was missing and then saw me at the bottom of the pool, there was blind panic, people scrabbling about and diving in to get me out. I couldn't understand what all the fuss was about, I could quite happily have sat there and amused myself for a while longer and, I guess, if I really wanted, walked to the shallow end and climbed out.

'They were scared because what I was doing was not possible. I wasn't scared because, possible or not, I was doing it.'

Breathing underwater is perhaps even more fantastic than walking on it, but it's do-able. We all did it for the first nine months of our lives, and our bodies remember. It is the worldview of others which convinces us that it can't be done.

Despite all the encouragement from society for us to abandon these natural intuitive abilities early in our lives, however, perhaps we never actually lose them. Instead, they remain dormant within us, and quite separate from the intellectual and analytical powers we refine in response to the social world.

Hutchinson quotes a piece of research from as long ago as 1963, just a little earlier than my own experiences, which compared academic performance with the intuitive abilities of students in an American college and found 'almost no correlation' between their work grades and their powers of intuition. We keep our natural abilities quite separate from the rational abilities we learn to work with to get by in a linear world.

The research also suggests that we may well be capable of developing this intuitive side of ourselves – perhaps infinitely so – as long as we start to use it. After all, if we can learn as children to develop one part of our minds in response to social demands and the self-sustaining rewards that our compliance brings to society, we can certainly do the same with our intuitive, spiritual selves for the rewards that it gives to *us*. Including, perhaps, the ability to survive when we really should have drowned, simply by doing the 'impossible'.

WE ARE EMOTIONAL AND INTUITIVE
BEFORE WE ARE EVER RATIONAL

Just to underline the potential we have to develop the more emotional and instinctive side of ourselves which society asks us to repress, there is now considerable evidence to suggest that our interpretations of the world around us continue to be, first and foremost, instinct-driven before our rational mind is even used.

Scientist Paul MacLean describes human beings as having a 'triune brain' which is arranged in layers, as if one part had grown on top of the other during our evolution to enable us to function effectively in the new world we were creating around us.[106]

The first of these levels, what MacLean calls 'the reptile brain', came first and enabled us to control our 'automatic' body functions such as breathing, without conscious thought, which freed up our thinking power for other evolutionary tasks. This was followed by the limbic system and, finally, by the neocortex – the top part. This is usually seen as the most important of the three in the Western world because of its developmental recency and its role as the brain's centre for analysis and interpretation of the outside world.

Messages received from the outside world, however, must first pass through the limbic system *en route* to the neocortex – and some very interesting things happen there before the neocortex even gets a look in. Hutchinson tells us, for example, that an electrical current applied to the exposed brain at this point will produce very strong emotional re-actions, including rage, terror, bliss, and panic, which has led to the scientific belief that, even though the neocortex may be our *rational* centre, the limbic system controls emotions and our intuitions about the world.

And since all the information we take in from the external world passes *first* through the limbic system before it gets near the neocortex, our first experience of the world, every day of our lives, may actually be more emotional, intuitive, and spiritual, than we currently believe.

The consensus scientific view is of *rational* human beings, acting on our emotions and intuitions – if at all – only after our analytical brain, the neocortex, has dealt with them. Our society is structured to support such an approach, with many rewards for using our analytical and interpretative abilities and sometimes severe penalties, even legal repercussions, for acting on our emotions.

According to MacLean, however, our brains may really work the other way round. This is a conclusion supported by the findings of Simon Baron-Cohen, lecturer in Psycho-pathology in the Department of Experimental Psychology & Psychiatry at the University of Cambridge, who works with synaesthesia.

Baron-Cohen points out that there are more limbic fibres in the body, both in size and number, than all other fibre systems:

> *In other words, we had the primary direction of flow backwards all these years. While we think that the cortex contains our representations (or models) of reality – what exists outside ourselves – it is the limbic brain that determines the salience of that information ... it is an emotional evaluation, not a reasoned one, that ultimately informs our behavior.*[107]

Limbic structures, he says, are inclined towards experiences of reality which he calls 'seizures', producing physical and mental effects, one of which is *qualitative alteration of consciousness*, including episodes where there is no distinction between our dreaming and waking realities. This sounds similar to the journeying and lucid dreams of the shaman, and suggests a natural human affinity with the limbic world – a place of ancient wisdom and old truths – and a place we touch in the trance state.

Baron-Cohen gives another example of the power and primacy of the limbic system – the emergence of a patient from coma, where consciousness returns first with involuntary, then voluntary movements, then rudimentary speech. Behaviour begins to become more rational only if recovery continues. 'In other words, intellect [*neocortex*] cannot be reclaimed unless emotion [*limbic system*] recovers first.'

If we compare Baron-Cohen's description of coma with what Bearwalker Wilson has said of the deep trance state and the emergence from both into rational thought on the one hand, and ordinary reality on the other, we again see parallels which suggest that the shaman's intense trance is connected with the deep architecture of the intuitive, emotional self.

'The limbic brain alerts us to what is meaningful,' says Baron-Cohen.

> *We know more than we think we know. And yet are we not always surprised at our insights, inspirations, and creativity? And do we not just as often reject our direct experience in favor of 'objective facts' instead?*
>
> *Emotion – irrational, a-rational, and non-verbal knowledge – is what actually directs our thoughts and actions . . . What we feel about something is more valid than what we think or say about that something.*
>
> *Reason is just the endless paperwork of the mind. The heart of our creativity is our direct experience and the salience that our limbic brain gives it.*

The rational, interpretative overlay of data and 'facts' is the way of society – one possible society of our own creation – while the way of the shaman, and the natural predisposition of all human beings, is intuitive, ancient and holistic.

In other words, the non-ordinary reality of the shaman is the same ordinary reality we all use every day: the interpretation of the raw information of the universe. The shaman merely *chooses* to enter the information flow deliberately and selectively, to *trust* his interpretations of what he finds there and to use it with *intention* as a doorway to the spirit world.

BELIEF IS WHAT IS REAL

During trance, says Hutchinson, the limbic system blocks the secretion of hormones such as cortisol, which have an arousing effect on the body, while increasing those, such as endorphins, that have more beneficial effects.

Research (for example, by psychologist Candace Pert) shows that reductions in cortisol create a feeling of greater confidence and the certainty that we are in control of ourselves and our environment.

In using the shamanic journey for self-healing, we may sometimes choose to revisit old wounds or explore future challenges to recreate the past or to find a solution to a current problem by understanding the future. When the cortisol of trance flows through our bodies, we are naturally able to go into these situations from a position of enhanced power and greater control. A childhood event which may have disempowered us at that time is now disempowered itself *by the very act* of challenging it.

Endorphins, the body's natural 'highs', are also released during trance, creating a sense of deep well-being as well as reinforcing the potency of the images that emerge for us.

Placebo studies have shown that we can stimulate the release of endorphins and the positive physical and mental effects which arise from them, using the power of our minds alone. Hutchinson quotes an experiment in pain relief, where people were given injections of either morphine or a placebo.[108] Those given the placebo were able to resist pain just as effectively as those who received morphine. They believed they were pain-free, and so they were.

The placebo group was then given a shot of naloxone – a substance which blocks the painkilling effect of morphine – and they then began to experience pain, even though they did not receive morphine in their first injection.

Their *belief* in the effectiveness of the placebo had generated a real bodily effect, releasing endorphins to block their pain. The naloxone had cancelled this painkilling effect. In other words, we can *choose* to experience pain or not. It all depends on our beliefs.

In a second experiment by Harris Hill, people exposed to exactly the same level of pain as others actually experienced the pain quite differently if they thought they were in control of it. Control – belief in themselves – was the key. Those who thought they controlled their experience actually *felt* the same level of pain but *experienced* it as less painful than those who thought they were powerless.

In both experiments, people accepted the worldview of another, the experimenter, and with his encouragement, were able to create real physical effects within themselves. Our power of belief is an incredible force – how much more so if we were able to accept *our own power* instead of that of another.

THE JOURNEY IS ENTIRELY NATURAL

Journeying takes us back to the pre-verbal world of the child where direct experience is possible without the intermediary of social conditioning. In a further link to childhood, Hutchinson remarks that in pregnancy, women release up to eight times more endorphins into the bloodstream they share with their unborn child. The foetus experiences the effect of endorphins as one of its first tastes of the world. Through the trance state, we are not only reconnecting with our earliest selves, we are entering and re-experiencing the world we were naturally programmed for.

All of the foregoing, looking at the more instinctual powers of the brain and their role in shaping our present world, becomes even more interesting if we look at where in the mind the shamanic experiences takes place.

If we divide the brain, conceptually, into four areas according to the evolutionary age of the brain matter concerned, and the function of this part of the brain (the rational left side, or intuitive right side), we end up with a map on which we can pretty much plot the twists and turns of our consciousness during the shamanic journey.

The rational mind is where we as journeyers will use our analytical skills to phrase the question which is the intention for our journey. This is the rational space of the neocortex, the new brain, the left hand, verbal, side of ourselves, which is in full, Tonal, awareness.

Rational thought stops when the imaginative part of the mind is entered and the journey begins. This is the seat of conceptual and metaphoric thought where we begin to get in touch with a deeper, more ancient part of ourselves. At this point, we take our first steps into the Nagual world of the personal-universal. It is the gateway to the transpersonal, where we will come to know ourselves as aspects of the whole.

As the trance state deepens, we also become more in touch with the older, emotional brain and memories and qualitatively new insights will begin to emerge. If we are journeying to understand an emotional experience in our lives, we will 'live' the experience again and reconnect with the emotions we had at that time. We are now at one with the Nagual, in so far as this nameless energy can be understood by human beings, and as we draw this information within us, we find our own repertoire of experiences and understanding, expanding and growing.

When we emerge from the journey, we again use the practical, left brain to analyse the information we have received, and to decide on the changes we will implement in our lives as a consequence. We are now re-emerging back into the Tonal world, but with the deeper understanding of the Nagual as part of our new power-base of skills and the new reality we are a part of.

In this sense, the shamanic journey is a completely holistic experience, allowing all of our mind to play its part.

We know from the work of Maxwell Cade and others, that the powerful effects of such integration can result in increased healing abilities as well as transpersonal experiences such as telepathy. The latter happens frequently in journeying groups, so that occurrences and images are shared by entire groups of people through the externalization of personal experiences and what should be individual images.

In one of my recent workshops of ten people, working in pairs, each person was asked to journey for the other and to bring back a gift of empowerment for their partner. One person journeyed first as the 'shaman', while their partner simply relaxed as 'client'; they then swapped roles without discussion. In the subsequent feedback circle *every single client–shaman partnership* shared key elements of the same vision during their individual journeys.

The use of the mind in this more intuitive and holistic way, where we truly use its vast capabilities, can have a dramatic effect on our physical and mental abilities, as the works of Jacobson and Basmajian show. Hutchinson writes about a further study, by Alan Richardson,[109] which also proves the point.

Richardson asked one group of schoolchildren to practise basketball throws every day, a second group to visualize making perfect shots, but not to actually practise, while a third group did nothing. Twenty days later, the first group showed a 24 per cent improvement in performance while the last group showed no change at all, neither of which is surprising. The second, non-practising, visualizing group, however, had improved by 23 per cent, not much below those who had actually used the ball. In other words, when the mind *perceives* something as real, it generates bodily responses *as if* it was real. The result, to all intents and purposes, is that it *becomes* real.

THE IMAGE IS AN ALLY OF THE SHAMAN

We often receive information in images when we shamanize. Some shamans do hear verbal instructions from their spirit helpers, it is true, particularly during active healing. But it is also common during journeying to experience images and visions.

Images, it appears, are such a natural way for the human mind to handle information we may even have almost photographic memories of them.

Ralph Haber showed 2,560 photographs to his subjects, followed by 2,560 *pairs* of photographs – the original photo-set and a further 2,560 – and then asked them to pick out only those from the first group shown to them.[110] They were able to do so, with an accuracy level of up to 95 per cent.

In Lionel Standing's experiment, thousands of slides were flashed in front of subjects, and sometimes even shown backwards as a mirror image.[111] Despite this, accuracy levels were again so high that Standing commented, we have an 'essentially perfect' ability to absorb information in image form.

We saw the power of images and our natural affinity with them when we looked at Imagework earlier. Images can also be used in a less deeply involving and therapeutic way, as a fast solution to the more immediate problems facing us, without the need for a detailed journey. One of the ways that shamans do so is to enter the dreaming of another person or thing to investigate the cause of a problem or to find a solution to it, much as we did in the exercise where we tuned in to another person using Imagework.

Because in shamanic terms all things are alive and have information for us, and in the world of the scientist, all things are connected as part of one giant hologram, all parts of us are encoded in all things. We can therefore enter the reality of the thing we need to deal with, see how the world looks through its eyes, and change it if we need to.

Helen lost her car keys one day right when she needed them as she was already late for a doctor's appointment. I had taught her this technique of dreaming another reality but, in her panic, she had completely forgotten to use it. After 10 minutes of charging round the house, however, she suddenly remembered and sat down to take a breath and calm herself. Then she allowed herself to enter the reality that her car keys were now dreaming.

The technique is simple. You merely allow the body to quieten down and to still itself so the mind is no longer racing, and then close your eyes and imagine the object you are looking for in its new space. If you were the lost keys, how would your world look and feel and seem right now and what would you like to change?

What Helen saw was darkness, combined with a sense of claustrophobia, and a feeling of extreme warmth. The dream of the keys was one of freedom and escape.

In that instant she remembered: she had left her keys in the pocket of the coat she had worn the day before, which she had hung in the wardrobe without removing them. When she checked the pocket, they were wrapped up in the tissues she always carries with her and warm to the touch, in the dark enclosed space of her wardrobe. The reality of the keys was one of darkness, claustrophobia and warmth, exactly as her dreaming of them had told her.

The 'key' to the lost keys was an image, not the panic and loss which accompanies the failure of rational thought.

There is a similar technique from Imagework which you can use as a problem-solving exercise for any issue that currently faces you. This one is simplicity itself – you simply relax and in Dina Glouberman's words, 'allow an image to emerge of your tension and then transform the tension'. If the image you have of your current situation is of bait being gnawed at from all sides by predators, see the bait becoming whole and alive again and simply walking away. It may not fix the problem – but at least you are now aware of it – and 'the tension goes right along with it'.[112]

THE SHAMANIC EXPERIENCE OF FLOW

'Flow', a term invented by Mihaly Csikszentmihalyi of the University of Chicago, describes a state where action 'just takes place' without any need to force it: we simply move effortlessly from one action to another, in control of every movement, a holistic experience with no distinction between the environment and the self, or between past, present, and future.[113] No space and no time. Perhaps we have all been there at least once in our lives. The experience of flow enables us to ditch 'the self *construct*, the intermediary which one learns to impose between the stimulus and response', and gain direct access to our full potential without the rational mind stepping in to tell us that something can't be done or isn't possible.

'Flow' is also the experience of the shamanic journey, where we are in direct contact with aspects of ourselves that normal reality tends to edit out. In the trance state, we are aware of, but may *choose* not to acknowledge, the socialized self with all of its rules of perception and personal mythologies. Instead, we stand back from it or *consciously include it* in our journey, rather than blindly responding to its whims. Sometimes we might deliberately study the self and explore its responses, but we do not engage it. We are in touch with a deeper level of personal awareness and are able to 'let our *selves* go'. The result is similar to Csikszentmihalyi's description of flow. We have 'no active awareness of control but [are] simply not worried about the possibility of lack of control. Later, in thinking back on the experience, he [we] will usually conclude that, for the duration of the experience, his skills were adequate for meeting environmental demands; and this reflection might become an important component of a private self-concept.'

This last observation is interesting. What it means is that by successfully exploring the landscape of the shaman to discover new truths about ourselves, we automatically integrate this knowledge *and the experience of our success* into a new view of ourselves. The process of positive change and re-empowerment begins with *the experience of trance itself.*

RELECTIONS ON THE INNER JOURNEY

What have we learned during this quick voyage through the inner landscape and how does it relate to the world of the shaman?

The overriding conclusion, once again, is that our perception of reality is no simple matter. Reality and its possible outcomes depend greatly on our approach to it.

If we *believe* we can do something, that something is possible, then we can, and it is. In fact, our whole organism will mobilize its resources and reassemble reality to ensure that it happens – as Miller and DiCapra's Zen-like rats demonstrated, as well as Maxwell Cade's pain control experiments.

Our brains are a blend of ancient and modern technology, so perhaps it is not surprising that the timeless techniques of shamanism can work so well for us in the twenty-first century of the holographic universe. We enter and engage with the older brain when we shamanize, and it has remarkable properties, allowing 'unheard and unseen things' to become known to us, as Elmer and Alyce Green concluded, old memories to become conscious and a greater range of symbolism to enrich our perceptions. The trance postures identified by Goodman and Gore perhaps enable us to make this connection more strongly.

The older brain is the reception point for emotion and the filter for all information. Before we react rationally to anything we see, hear, smell, sense, we react *intuitively* to it and this colours our response. We are more empathetic than we think. The neocortex, in fact, with its rationally wired technology, does not just fail to supply us with the fullest basis for understanding our world, it may actually *exclude* us from much of its meaning. By prohibiting its emotional and intuitive content, we do not see the whole picture and the full potential of the reality we are exposed to, part of, and inherently capable of being. But we can change that.

As we enter the trance state, we access these new worlds of the senses and meet our full potential – and the sheer act of moving our consciousness to these sites of enhanced wisdom can itself create positive bodily effects. We *are* as we think.

We can create – by thought alone – the ability to stop pain, to perceive reality in a new way, even to benefit from exercise we haven't actually taken, except in our minds. And to learn new skills, as well as controlling our reactions right down to a cellular level, as Basmajian's research proves. These are just a few of the natural, magical capabilities of ordinary human beings.

During the shamanic journey, ordinary human beings are able, perhaps for the first time, to use the whole brain in an integrated way, which will itself produce beneficial effects, while using images – a mode of processing information for which we are perfectly designed – to explore these wider realities.

And the best news of all is that we get better with practice.

Our brains create reality. We already know this from the evidence of the holographic model and the experience of trance postures as old as recorded time itself. What we now know, from our study of the mind – and what the shamans who created the trance postures discovered by Goodman have, perhaps, always known – is that we have the innate ability to create any reality we want. I had a deeper insight into this potential recently while reflecting once again on the journey I made earlier into the destiny of human souls.

There was a part of that journey where I realized that we are multiple beings, able to exist everywhere at once and at all times, exactly as the holographic theory suggests. It is the conscious exercise of our will, our intention, which enables us to become our full experience at any one of these infinite points of light. And so, perhaps, this is what the mystics have been alluding to when they talk of reincarnation. We simply fix our attention on a single point of interest to us and so, in a sense, become that new life while the rest of us, consciousness withdrawn, cease to be. We are as we intend; we live the life we will.

When my daughter, Jodie, was a baby, we would often listen to her through the intercom which connected her room with ours, as she stirred, then awoke, then cried.

Sometimes, however, before I could even get up from bed to go to her, I would hear a second voice soothing her, as any mother would. When I went into her room to see her, Jodie would be peacefully asleep again.

I have journeyed to this second voice since those days and met its owner, Jodie's spirit mother.

We are all born from one world to another. Our children come to us from spirit and leave us to return there. Just as we grieve for our lost ones and are still 'there' for them, so it is with our spirit parents; they do not leave us abandoned while we come to terms with this alien material world.

Jodie's spirit mother remained with her for at least the first year of her life, by which time Jodie had decided to remain in our world. Her tiny mind would now begin to learn *our* rules, *our* ways of being, instead of the spirit realm of pure potential she had left behind.

The challenge for us all as parents is not to make our children choose *absolutely*, or to sacrifice one world of potential for the limitations of another. Our children should continue to have access to the pure, natural, intense capabilities they – and we, too – are born to in this life.

EXPLORATIONS: EMPOWERMENT AND INTEGRATION

1. The scientist and the shaman

There is real power in the integration of our right and left brains which can be used not only for a more expansive and harmonious world vision but in matters of real physical healing.

Robert Assagioli, the founder of psychosynthesis, offers good advice when he asks us to 'obey the urge aroused by the great need for healing the serious ills which at present are affecting humanity; let us realize the contribution we can make to the creation of a new civilization characterized by an harmonious integration and cooperation, pervaded by the spirit of synthesis'.[114]

Close your eyes now and imagine two people standing before you, one a scientist at the leading edge of quantum discovery, the other a powerful shaman from the jungles of the Amazon or the heartlands of Siberia, representing your logical, analytical left brain and your intuitive, insightful right brain.

Take a few moments to ask these two, in turn, for their respective answers to the questions that now concern you. Notice where their viewpoints differ and where they are the same.

Become the scientist and the shaman independently and see how the world looks through their eyes. *What do they know about the world that you do not? How would you approach the problems that face you from the world-view that is theirs?*

Step back from this interaction now and see the scientist and the shaman as two separate people once again. Introduce them to one another and let them debate the question you have presented to them both. Ask them to come back to you when they are able to agree on a single answer to your question which is respectful of both viewpoints and synthesizes their worldviews in a solution that is *practically* helpful to you.

What is the answer they give you and how does it differ from the answers they were able to give you independently?

Continue to ask questions if you wish, taking advantage of the combined wisdom of these two great thinkers and transformers of energy, or addressing specific questions to each in turn.

Finally, see these two people as merging into one being before you, with all the power and understanding that comes from this synthesis of spiritual and analytical wisdom, the union of the condor and the quantum.

Ask any further questions you wish of this powerful being, and ask also that she remain with you as an ally and adviser that you can return to in the future.

2. The empowerment posture

Belinda Gore describes a trance posture, known as the empowerment posture, which brings with it the wholesome feeling associated with the integration of all aspects of the self. In Belinda's words, it helps to 'get the life force flowing again'.[115]

Trance postures may work by aligning the body in particular ways so that new neurological and chemical pathways are opened along the body's meridians in order to stimulate the experience of specific states of non-ordinary consciousness.

When I use the empowerment posture with groups, it typically produces feelings of 'wholeness'. As one participant put it, 'I felt as if all of me was experiencing this, not just my mind or my body or my emotions, but all that I am, all parts of me.'

According to Gore, 'it is typical for people in this posture to experience flows of energy and to emerge from the trance feeling able to do anything'. One of her participants reported that by using this posture 'the floodgates opened and all channels were filled'. Those who enter this posture in stressful situations, says Gore, 'return from it with radiant, peaceful energy'.

Try it.

Kneel on the floor with your heels together and knees apart, your buttocks resting on your heels. Keep your spine straight and your back 'long', and raise your arms to shoulder level, bent at the elbows with hands together at your chest.

Your hands are curled with your knuckles interlaced and the back of your hands facing upwards. Your mouth remains slightly open throughout.

Try to maintain this position for about 15 minutes and, if you have one, play your drumming tape as you do so.

You may feel as if some energy or force enters you at the crown of your head, or find yourself swaying backwards and forwards. This is natural.

The empowerment posture is one you can also use for physical and psychological healing since, in the words of Belinda Gore, 'the abundance of energy obtained can be extremely helpful if you have been unwell and are beginning to recuperate'.

Try the posture by itself first to see how it feels to you. You can then take if further by using this posture as the position for a journey taken with *intent*, to explore 'what it means to me to feel whole and complete'. How would the world look and how would you feel to be living harmoniously from a position of power as a more integrated person? I have also found this posture rewarding during journeys for guidance on *specific* issues of healing or empowerment.

3. The way of the blind
Victor Sanchez, in *The Teachings of don Carlos*, includes an exercise he calls 'Temporary Blindness'.[116] The technique is simplicity itself, although it demands a fair degree of dedication and self-discipline: you simply remain blindfolded for extended periods of time. In a more advanced form of this exercise, you do so while going about your normal daily business in the home and, in a more advanced form still, in the outside world. Although Sanchez recommends keeping the blindfold on for periods of 'several hours to several days', I confess that the longest I have done so is for only three hours at a time.

Even so, in this new and unusual universe of darkness you are suddenly plunged into, that may be enough, since the impact of being forced back on your own natural resources is an immediate and powerful one, where even something as simple as making coffee becomes a major act of will.

You are forced to remember and to draw upon all that you *know* and all that you *are*, a true merging of the body and the spirit, the intellect and the intuition, the left side and the right, until, eventually, you are operating from instinct alone, as one integrated and holistic system, as you were at your birth.

I suggest that you practise this exercise for short periods of time at first and build up to more extended periods. There is a 'frustration barrier' to get through after about 30 minutes and a desire to end the experiment quickly, so it is important to begin it with full commitment and, obviously, to have the uninterrupted time to do so.

After that, once your mind realizes that you intend to stick with this, there may be a momentary feeling of panic as it begins to relinquish control and a deeper, more intuitive, bodily wisdom takes over. From this point onwards you will act more fully as an integrated being, from a position of left and right brain unification.

But what is really interesting is how you feel when the blindfold is finally removed and you see the world for the first time from this new sense of being.

8

INFINITE JOURNEYS:
THE FOUR ENEMIES TO FREEDOM

Knowledge has been, is now, and will ever be POWER. He who knows does not die like he who does not know.
– Santeria priest

They have been making art here in this silent landscape of Greece. Behind me someone has drawn a lizard on rock, Aboriginal style, as an ancient symbol of change. In front of me is the image of a snake eating its own tail, a symbol for infinity, a perfect circle, mandala for the self, image of change and becoming.

Between these images, I am myself part of the art form, a flesh-sculpture of evolving man between two symbols of change. I am caught in, and part of the flow of change between them. Life experiencing itself.

The double helix is the snake-like building block of life. The circle, an archetypal symbol of unity, and the basic form of organic life, as the scientist, Kerkule, realized, after a dream . . . of a snake eating its own tail.

We are born, live, grow, die. Our remains become food for other life forms who are born, and live, and grow, and die. And whose remains become food for others. Infinite circles.

In the Peter Carey novel, Bliss, *Harry Joy dies for the third time and his soul leaves his body to merge with the universe. Part of Harry Joy becomes the forest and his new lifetimes are mapped by the circular age rings of the trees.*[117]

This connection to the infinite is echoed in the words of Lisa Alther, who reflects that: 'The enzymes in grasses closely resemble those in an elephant. The sap flowing through the forsythia bush, in composition almost identical to blood which, in turn, was identical to dilute sea water – from which all life came, to which it would return. We had origins far greater than the cinder we inhabited would indicate.'[118]

We give our very selves to others, feeding them mentally, emotionally, spiritually with what we are in life, physically with what we become in death – all of it energetic transformation, a cosmic exchange of energy – so that they may grow and experience too.

'If you give life, you must necessarily give death . . . life always ends in death and must be renewed through death,' said Aldous Huxley. As you read this line of text, at least 100,000 of the atoms within you will have disintegrated.

It's a one-way trip, and what we have en route *is experience. That is all we know. Life is all experience, all movement towards the release of our energy back into the void and our inevitable decision to experience more. Meanwhile, the journey is one of understanding and the creation of purpose; the invention, and experience of personal reality; a giving of meaning to a universe of our own creation.*

Whatever we can do to enhance our ability to feel, to experience, also strengthens our life force and our ability to Be. Knowing ourselves better is the first essential step.

I stand up, gather crystal and bone, and begin the journey home.

We spend our entire lives trying to remember and recover what we already knew when we were first born.

We are creatures of experience, we live for experience. Life is a powerful, magical energy which is immensely attractive to us.

It is also an extremely complicated affair. We must constantly reorder the information we take in about it in order to make sense of our personal worlds.

When we were babies, our exposure to life's complexity was minimal and we were able to experience its energy in a pure and formless way. It was delicious and we wanted more, so we learned to talk, to move, to structure, to think, in order to discover more and to experience more life. We became experience junkies, constantly seeking new experiential highs, unable to function effectively when deprived of sensory stimuli.

The isolation wing at Alcatraz prison, 'The Rock', houses a row of cells, each room a rectangle of about two metres by three, each one totally black and almost soundproof, where prisoners were held in solitary confinement, in a space beyond space, a time outside of time. Prisoners entered this formless blackness and were buried alive in a living death while years passed by on the outside. Total sensory deprivation. It was the most feared punishment on Alcatraz.

Yet even here, in the black soundless solitude, the mind will not abandon the search for experience. Prisoners reported hallucinations, visions in the void, the projection of inner worlds onto outer darkness. They created a new sensory universe for themselves, a *holographic* universe of one, where meaning is found in the shapeless mass of swirling dark and light.

John Lilly, in his pioneering experiments with sensory deprivation and floatation tanks reports a similar phenomenon – the emergence of visions and images as the brain accesses its own library of resources, creating a new world of experience to feed itself in the absence of nourishment from the outside.

Human consciousness *is* the third beam of laser light which connects with and makes sense of the interference patterns on the holographic plate and creates an image of ordered reality. Our sole purpose is to be part of this creative experience. Progress and evolution is no more than our generation of new experience to be part of.

As babies, we had simple needs. But as adults we must play a more active role in the creation of our worlds. This demands the development of personal power and the conquest of the enemies which stand between us and our goal. Once we get beyond these enemies, we realize that we are ultimately powerful and naturally able to control our worlds. Shamanic powers for personal development, for community healing, for global evolution, become entirely possible for us – and natural *to* us.

We must first become aware of our enemies, and then greet them, before we can understand that our enemies are in fact the greatest allies and teachers we have on our journey to self-awareness and self-empowerment. Without our enemies to confront us, to challenge us, we would lose ourselves in a world of sensory stagnation. Our enemies are there to awaken us and to set us free. There is nothing in this world that we have not ourselves created. Our enemies are no different – we have created them for the purpose of liberation.

And the first of these enemies is Fear.

FEAR

Our first fear is the realization, as children, that the world is 'not-us', that we are physically separate and there is a void of mystery beyond us. 'Mother', 'food', 'toy', 'drink', all of these things exist outside of us and we do not control them. They have substance, will and existence apart from us.

We do not understand the deeper, energetic connection between things and, in an effort to make sense of this new world so seemingly out of reach and beyond our control, we accept what we are taught about it in order to illuminate its darkness. What we 'know' to be fact about this world, however, is actually agreement, a symbolic compromise, a linear model. It is a communication tool, a social necessity which lets us meet our fellow travellers in a marriage of perceptual convenience. But it is not fact.

The stark reality is that we are completely alone, as separate in our private universes as the prisoners of Alcatraz. No-one else lives in our world, and if it were not for us, the rest of the world would not exist at all.

This is a terrifying discovery for many people, and it throws us back into the existential darkness of childhood and brings godlike responsibilities with it, adding to the weight of our fear. The immense responsibility for generating our own reality and for recreating the world each day is first among these. It brings the responsibility for living each moment as if it truly mattered, as if it were our last, of dealing with our lives impeccably. It is a responsibility too heavy to bear and yet we must. For, once we have met Fear, there can be no return.

'Our deepest fear is uncertainty,' reflects Tim Lott.[119]

The world is, by its very nature, a deeply uncertain place that we can only fleetingly grasp through a continuous series of isolated moments of sense-impressions. To counteract this essentially chaotic, ungraspable world, we start from the moment we are born to create our own inner world.

One of the most popular myths is, and always has been, that we live in a just, ordered universe. This gives us the certainty that we are in control of our lives. That if we do the right thing, sooner or later – even if we have to wait for an afterlife, or reincarnation – we will receive our reward.

Which is where we came in: a linear model which we now know to have limited value. For there is no order to the universe, only that which we give it. There is only the Infinite Now and the connections we make with the energy around us.

Some people will look up briefly and see Fear waiting on

the path for them, and will turn back and walk away, contenting themselves with more limited experience, a life more ordinary, if only they do not have to face Fear.

But they will always know that Fear, like Death, is waiting. And one day, inexorably, their world will become so claustrophobic, so tiny and exhausted of experience that they know they have no more choice. They must look up again, with intention, and they must speak with Fear or die.

It will be hard, it always is, but only by speaking with Fear and by understanding its nature can the first enemy be overcome. In this sense, Fear is merely a teacher, one with our best interests at heart. If we allow him to, he will liberate us from the constriction of self-imposed limitations and perceptual agreements and bring us insight and clarity. Fear will teach us that the world is of our own making – and then we will face the second manifestation of Fear. Ourselves.

Knowing that we are gods in our own right, that the world is as we dream it, will naturally create all sorts of self-doubts – that we are not worthy, that we cannot create a perfect world all by ourselves (you are right – but you *can* create a perfect world for *you*) – resentment (why me?) and anxieties (what if?).

Susan Jeffers has given us a comprehensive list of self-limiting fears, which is eminently worth considering in depth, but 'at the bottom of every one of your fears is simply the fear that you can't handle whatever life may bring you,' she says.[120] But if not you, then who?

You have managed to create a world for yourself up until now – perhaps without even realizing that you were doing so. The next step is a small one, a baby step: it is simply *acknowledging* this fact, remaining aware of it and choosing to act *consciously* in respect of it. The words of Marianne Williamson, used by Nelson Mandela in his 1994 inauguration address, offer us wise counsel in regard to this:

Our deepest fear is not that we are inadequate.
Our deepest fear is that we are powerful beyond measure.

It is our light, not our darkness that most frightens us.

We ask ourselves, who am I to be brilliant, gorgeous, talented and fabulous?
Actually, who are you not to be?

You are a child of God.
Your playing small doesn't serve the world.
There's nothing enlightened about shrinking so that other people won't feel insecure around you.

We were born to manifest the glory of God that is within us.
It's not just in some of us – it's in everyone.

And as we let our own light shine, we unconsciously give other people permission to do the same.
As we are liberated from our own fear, our presence automatically liberates others.[121]

We have a *right* to be fearless. In fact, as these words suggest, it is as if we have a *duty* to be fearless so we can act for the best possible good. We are all connected. If we act personally to create a better world, the world responds in kind. Like the pieces of the hologram, each fragment is the image of the whole. God, however you define Her, is manifesting through us and we through Her. Our duty is to make ourselves great, not humble, so the whole universe is empowered.

When we recognize this and act beyond Fear – or *in spite of our fears* – when we feel the fear and do it anyway, we have recognized this truth and we are beginning to move into our power.

It is paradoxical, therefore, that the next enemy we face is . . . Awareness.

Once we are aware that it is we and we alone who create our world, then our view of the world must change. We can no longer see the world as a dreadful place, full of war and hate and challenge, which we are powerless to change, or a playground of earthly delights like the Eden of the Bible. We can only see ourselves reflected. It is the working of our mind that we see in the world 'out there'.

It is a world without meaning, full of meaning. We can truly see the universe in a grain of sand. It is our sand. It is our universe. And, at the same time, the world just is.

Awareness means that we have entered our power and taken mastery of reality. We know that to change our world, we need only change ourselves.

More responsibility. More potential.

'I often think that our job as human beings is not to find God, but to create him,' said Asimov.

For some, the experience is liberating: 'I could no longer go back to the old ways. Everything was alive, everything was new, and I was at the centre of it,' said Lucinda after taking the journey into the destiny of human souls that I described earlier.

For others, it is confusing and they must learn to come to terms with their new vision: 'Nothing made sense. The only thing that was real was how I felt about the world that day,' said Scott. The feeling is different but the words are the same.

Some become evangelists, preaching the new reality; others become recluses, embracing their world in physical as well as existential isolation.

Once we are aware, the old patterns must go. We may no longer have much in common with the people we knew before, those who have not yet spoken with Fear and accepted the fruit that was offered, because now we know a great secret. *The* greatest secret of all. All the old spiritual platitudes and truisms turn out to have essential meaning and wisdom. The truth *is* within. Now try telling that to your friends.

And so, we have moved beyond Fear, we have embraced Awareness, and we have our reward: the potential for greater, more intense and more personally meaningful experience. And so we meet the third enemy. Power.

POWER

Unless handled properly – impeccably – power can lead, on the one hand, to arrogance, on the other to complacency. If we give in to either of these options, we give away our *genuine* power and accept a pale imitation in its place.

Arrogance is a shield for ourselves from true power, allowing us to hide behind a façade of self-control when actually we do not engage with the responsibility of using our power at all, we merely exercise it in words and actions without depth. In a sense, we are *afraid* of power and may even come to use it in an exploitative way so that we do not have to accept full responsibility for our decisions and our actions. Instead we rely on an habitual approach to the problem of power, using the Western definition of 'control' to guide our actions. In doing so, we make ourselves the slaves of another's dream.

Complacency, meanwhile, is the denial of power, the switching off of responsibility and self-control so that others may step in to control us.

We must occupy the dynamic space of tension between these apparent opposites, walking a tightrope between extremes. This is an act of courage which requires intense self-questioning, self-knowledge and, at times, self-doubt, which we must find a way to come to terms with. Every act must be examined so that we are entirely clear about our intention and certain that we are not acting from unconscious motives or hidden agendas. Only then can we act authentically and *in* our power.

To know the true nature of reality is power beyond the experience of most people, which may lead us to believe we have some supernatural calling or cosmic importance. This is arrogance. The truth is that *maybe we do* have supernatural powers and cosmic significance – and it is still totally irrelevant, because only by acting with authenticity, moment by moment, can we retain our power and our focus. Purposeful intention is the key – otherwise we become just one more madman talking to the trees.

Kowing the true nature of ourselves as powerful creative beings can also lead to fatalism and a feeling that nothing matters. If you are the only person in your world, then what is the point of reaching out to others? Why must you struggle alone beneath the immense weight of recreating the world anew each day?

Giving in to this feeling is an act of complacency. The truth is that there *is* no point in reaching out to others, and yet we have no option. A decision to take no action is an action in itself. Your existence – and even your non-existence – has an effect on others and both are parts of the whole.

By abandoning Fear and gaining Awareness and Power, we have at once achieved free will – and given ourselves no choice. The only option we have if we are to remain anchored to our world is to explore our power and learn to use it sensibly and meaningfully, to make it truly ours. The alternative is to float adrift in the worldview of others, allowing them to decide our fate according to their whims and their personal interpretation of the reality we share.

We have seen the historical effect of such abdications of power. Wars are an obvious example. Millions are killed in confrontations orchestrated by power-hungry politicians who never enter battle themselves, and fought by soldiers who have given away their absolute right to retain power over their own lives.

To retain our power, we must seek balance in order to live authentically, but without any attachment to outcomes – without even, in fact, an attachment to non-attachment itself. We must live our truth at all times, as if every day is our last on Earth and every decision our final one.

And then behave as if none of this matters.

To act otherwise and attach importance to an outcome is to give it meaning, to name it, and to give away power.

Our poets and musicians have wise words for us about how to remain true to ourselves, deciding always to act *in our power* no matter what confronts us, by seeing each of our experiences as an opportunity to express ourselves and to discover new strengths rather than insurmountable problems to escape or hide from. The solution is in our own definitions and vision for ourselves.

The James song, 'Ring the Bells', is a call to arms for the exercise of our personal power.[122] The words tell us that when we are let down and fall as a result of the actions of another towards us, we can use this as an opportunity to grow our own wings, instead of crashing to the Earth defeated; when we are abandoned and left to drown, we have the power to grow our own fins and gills so we can explore the depths of our personal sea. We can always adapt and overcome – if we truly want to.

Sometimes it is easier to just drown in our own tears and face the world defeated. That is our personal choice. But there is always the option to see the world and the setbacks it throws at us as another opportunity to learn from the universe, and to use our power in the best way for ourselves as agents of change in the world.

FATIGUE

Acting authentically is hard work and many succumb on occasion to the easy comfort of acting from habit, repeating the actions and thought patterns they have been taught from birth, instead of the one that has true meaning in the moment. A lovely song, 'The Weeping Song', by Nick Cave, illustrates this well.[123]

The singer describes a strange and melancholy, eternally separate world, where men and women must always be apart, both crying for one another across the abyss which divides them without once questioning the habitual basis of this pattern. It is an odd and alien world Nick Cave describes – and yet it is the world we all inhabit, where we are kept apart by patterns and expectations rather than being willing to explore what may be possible.

Children follow the patterns we set for them – if we create a world of sadness and distance, this is the world they will grow up to believe in. And yet this song also suggests a seed of hope for us all. The singer tells us that our children are *merely crying*, rehearsing their sorrow; there is still a chance for them – and for us all – to avoid *true weeping* by changing the pattern of our lives.

Tiredness, ennui, fatigue with the whole process is an ever-present danger, for we can slip once again so easily into the habitual expectation of *true weeping* which is why, after all the hard work we have done, Fatigue is not only the final enemy we must face, but also the hardest of the four to overcome. But we must try, because it makes a difference to us and to our children, and it shapes our world.

To behave inauthentically is to give up on life and on truth; to strive for truth is to be truly alive, to embrace life and to play an active role in the creation of the world.

Where we are in life will always be some way along the continuum of Fear–Awareness–Power–Fatigue. Life is a process, a journey, a cycle. There is no beginning and there is no end. Just when you feel you have overcome Fear and are comfortable with your new awareness of yourself as creator of your world, a new situation will arise to confound you, and you will see yourself back at square one.

You won't be, you will have moved on and you will be stronger and more resourceful than before, but in the jaws of each new challenge it may seem as if once again you are adrift in a cold and meaningless universe. Trust and Faith are your allies. The universe is a reflection of yourself. Perhaps you cannot change it directly – to do so would be like trying to grasp a phantom, a hologram – but you can change it indirectly, by changing *yourself*.

When you feel most alone, tired, cold, defeated, you are actually being handed a gift, if you choose to see it this way – the gift of your shadow-self revealed, and, once you see it, you can change it. There is nothing you can do before that point.

So these moments of Fatigue are opportunities to work gently on yourself without blame, or recriminations, or guilt. And the universe *does* respond. Just when you feel you are too tired of accepting your Power and striving to live impeccably, you will find a new definition, new meanings, new people, who bring new energy to your life.

And you *will* go on.

This is a path not without hardship. There are no easy solutions, no quick fixes. That is why it is a Hero's Quest. But you do not walk it alone. There have been many others before you and there are many more to come.

It is also a road full of joy, truth, insight, and beauty, a 'path with heart', Castaneda calls it. Not many get the chance to create a new world every day, to be truly free and to know that all things are possible and within their power.

Ultimately, it is a journey which we all must take. For the good of ourselves and every one of us. For the children, and for all our relations. To make a better dream.

ALLIES FOR OVERCOMING THE FOUR ENEMIES TO FREEDOM

We have looked at many of the shaman's techniques to help you accept the power that was always yours, to reclaim your birthright. The Four Enemies stand before you on the path to reclamation and, in that sense are also your guides and your allies. The techniques we have looked at – journeying and Imagework, and those contained in the Explorations sections – are all at your disposal as you tackle each of these enemies and allies.

I also offer the following, not as a formula, but as a

framework for dealing with each of these enemies as they appear to you.

Fear

By re-educating the mind, you can accept fear as simply a fact of life rather than a barrier to success. – Susan Jeffers.

Throughout our lives, we are taught that fear is somehow unnatural, something to be – well, afraid of.

In fact, fear is entirely natural. What we call fear is simply a physiological reaction which helps us to better focus our energies in the direction which most needs our immediate attention. The metallic taste in the mouth, the shaking, the 'tunnel vision' that accompany our fears are all useful insights into ourselves and will shift energy to the parts of our body where it can do most good in protecting us. Self-protection is perfectly natural; the feeling of fear is in no way strange or alien.

All of these reactions are driven by the release into our systems of adrenalin, a very useful biochemical which boosts our levels of energy. Energy, pure and simple. What we do with this energy – the name we give it, the meaning we attach to it – is up to us.

We saw in the first chapter of this book that the release of adrenalin always causes a bodily effect. But tell one group that effect is fear and they feel fear; tell another group it's joy and they feel joy.

The next time you are afraid, for whatever reason, do not dismiss the feeling, try to be rid of it or deny it in any way. Instead, explore it fully, stripping away the emotional content stage by stage, asking always 'What is behind this sensation?', then what is behind the next sensation or emotion which appears, until eventually you are left with a pure nameless energy. This energy is not 'fear', it is simply what is. So now decide to relabel this sensation. Call it 'excitement', 'readiness for action', 'purpose' or 'personal power'.

Kathy, an actress, has stage fright every night when she walks out into the darkness of the theatre to confront the unknown. She tells herself she is just anxious to get onto the stage to perform, to demonstrate her creative genius to an audience that is there to appreciate her, and she acts *as if* this were true. And so it is true.

This technique is used by many performers and those who address large audiences – who then find that the motivating and energetic effects of the adrenalin reaction become extremely helpful for them. It is only the self-limiting belief that we attach to fear, the label we apply to our bodily sensations, which makes us feel that our experience necessarily means that there must be something wrong, that we should feel apprehensive and to find this sensation unpleasant.

Instead, use the energy your body is giving you in a constructive way – that is why it is there.

'Mind is the creator of everything,' said Paramahansa Yogananda. 'You should therefore guide it to create only good. If you cling to a certain thought with dynamic willpower, it finally assumes a tangible outward form. When you are able to employ your will always for constructive purposes, you become the controller of your destiny.'[124]

An ally for dealing with Fear:
Knowledge. In any situation of Fear, finding out more about the nature of your *specific* fear will empower you. Fear works with the unknown but is disempowered in the face of knowledge. Fear is just an energy like any other and is there to serve us.

Awareness
Your beliefs are your reality. Beliefs are assumptions about the nature of reality and you will have many 'proofs' that reality operates the way you think it does. – Sanaya Roman

It is very easy to slip into the belief that one is 'enlightened' – and the world will respond by giving you opportunities to prove it. Which is not so surprising, since you are the one creating your reality and the opportunities it brings you. We all create the reality we want to see.

By living according to a pattern of belief – any pattern of belief: 'nine to five man' or 'enlightened being' – we are still in prison, all still locked in the Alcatraz of our own world-view. Subscribing to one belief system over another does not make us incrementally more or less 'aware', more or less free; it is just a different jail.

The challenge now is to remain open, not to believe we have the answers, that we are somehow better. We are just different – which is what we have always been. 'Before enlightenment, chop wood, fetch water. After enlightenment, chop wood, fetch water', are ancient wise words and they are valid still.

A helpful way to keep our feet firmly planted is to use Descartes' technique of doubt to see whether the information we use to guide us can truly stand up to tough and in-dependent scrutiny. Ask yourself always 'Can this be doubted? Could it be opinion rather than hard fact?' If your information passes the test, congratulations, you have just discovered a new universal Truth. If it doesn't, it is simply a personal belief like any other. And while that belief may be the absolute foundation stone of your approach to life, or mine, neither of us has the right to inflate our own world-views over those of others.

Sometimes it is better to work quietly on changing the world from within.

> **An ally for dealing with Awareness:**
> **Compassion.** The mission of the shaman is not to become enlightened. That, if anything, is a by-product. The mission of the shaman is to understand his power and to use it effectively for a purpose and with *strategy*. The job of the shaman is not to preach but to make a better world

through effective action. Sometimes this may mean allowing people their own beliefs and working within their belief system rather than confronting it. Our job is to change *ourselves* and, through that, to serve our community which, in today's society of instant and global communications, means the entire world.

The journey is always firstly an inward one, for control of our own power. Refusing to accept this power or using it to manipulate rather than *influence* the future are both the acts of a dictator.

Power

> *It doesn't interest me where you live or how much money you have. I want to know if you can get up after a night of grief and despair, weary and bruised to the bone, and do what needs to be done for the children.* – Oriah Mountain dreamer

The best advice I was ever given to ensure that I do not get drawn into the battle with Power, and remain true to my vision for myself, is to pay frequent visits to the child I hold within me.

Children have a very developed relationship with Power. They will fight absolutely for their right to be and do exactly as they wish, as any two-year-old will show you. But they will also let that go completely when appropriate: the war cries and screams of rage will recede and the child will move on with no resentment or attachment to the moment or to their past act of will.

When my daughter Millie was two she would often demand something from me as a perfectly natural expression of her own inner power. If I refused, she would use her incredible energy to rage and scream, sometimes for hours. Then she would sleep and when she awoke the matter would be completely forgotten.

I remember her lying down in a pool of mud in the park one day because I would not carry her the remaining 100 yards to the car. She was soaked through, covered in mud, and quietly refusing to move until she got her own way. What Millie did not know at that age is that she inherited her stubborn gene from me and so I, also refusing to compromise and unwilling to just leave her there, simply got down in the mud with her and also refused to move until I got *my* way. A real battle of wills on a battlefield of mud.

And so there we lay, the two of us, both caked in mud and dirty water, attracting quite a crowd of concerned mothers and nannies who could not understand quite what was going on here and saw only an abused child (or father, depending on their perspective) lying in a pool of water, watching in silence as the sky revolved above them.

Looking up at the anxious and querulous faces above us, Millie and I both began to laugh. Neither of us could understand how these people, who had presumably never touched mud or experienced the Earth, could take all this so seriously. We looked at each other, Millie and I, and smiled. The spell of the moment was broken and we walked back to the car, soaked through, amidst much murmuring and 'tutting'. Millie had completely let go of the feeling that had driven her so passionately just a few minutes before. She had found something else which amused her and engaged her energy with more involvement and so decided to find the whole thing funny instead. I tried to do the same.

Our inner child is like that too. He is the small, quiet, soul within us who knows that everything is within his power – no-one has yet convinced him that it is not, could not be, otherwise. At the same time, he has never been exposed to the concept of Power. He acts with authenticity because he does not know there is an issue to address. The child can focus intensely, passionately, on his own needs but is not so attached to outcomes that he cannot let go when necessary. There is a universe out there to explore; why get locked in the moment of one time and one space when we have the whole of alternity?

If power should become an issue for you, in my experience it is always helpful to visit your own inner child and to ask his advice. And then act upon it, with faith.

> **An ally for dealing with Power:**
> **Innocence.** The effective use of power is not attachment to a single event or outcome. Nor is attachment an effective use of power. The two are not the same.

Fatigue

Man's main task in life is to give birth to himself. – Erich Fromm

The journey we are on is not a race to a finish line, and there is no winner or loser. We all finish together and without each other, we do not finish at all.

There will naturally be times when we are tired, downtrodden, fatigued. Who can hold a universe together and not feel tired sometimes? There are times when we must rest – but we must always remain vigilant, like a hunter who stays awake and alert to the movements of his prey even as he makes temporary camp.

We have a choice about our lives only if we are active in our world. If not, then someone will be active for us. They may do this with the best of intentions, carrying us when we are weary, or they may do so from a perspective of control. Either way, effectively they take away the power we have over ourselves by the actions they take on our behalf. We only have a choice for as long as we exercise that choice.

Nick Williams quotes Stamford University research in his book, *The Work We Were Born To Do*, which shows that the achievement of success is regulated entirely by a formula, where skills, abilities and qualifications contribute just 14 per cent, while attitude, intention and purpose account for 86 per cent. What we do and who we decide to be is always more important.

Success in life is no different: maintaining our own sense of destiny and purpose remains paramount. When we can all do that, the world we occupy will be a better, more honest, and more powerful place. 'I started to see myself as someone who had purpose and I experienced the meaning of love for the first time in my life,' says Susan Jeffers.[125]

Rest when you need to. But always return to Self, your true self, and never the prescriptions and expectations of others.

An ally for dealing with Fatigue:
Intention. Always come back to intention, your purpose in being. This is your world, no-one else's – but if you do not make choices in your world, then someone will surely make them for you. You have a choice in this too.

The final journey: Keeping Death as your adviser

Shamans say that we must keep Death as our adviser, that Death always stands at our left shoulder and offers insights into our words and actions. By this they mean that ultimately we will all cross one final bridge between the worlds and it will be a journey from which we will not return in this life-time. This is the final truth by which we may measure all other events of our lives.

Recognizing this, some things which bother us now tend to become less significant – so what if our bodies are not an 'ideal' shape, that we have wrinkles, that we are not as young as we once were: soon it will not matter at all, so let us embrace what we *do* have and ensure we live as fully as we can in each of the moments we have chosen in our lives.

At the same time, some things take on new meaning and become truly important when we recognize the imminence of Death. Perhaps these are the same things – in which case, the time to act upon them is *now* – or perhaps other things turn out to be more important when this moment is our last on Earth. Awareness of our own mortality can make a mockery of our current priorities.

The simple fact of life is that we all came here to die, there is no escape from this fact. This is the true secret behind the initiation crisis of the shaman, the life-changing event that takes him to the brink of death: his realization in that moment of the vast importance of life. We must live each moment *as if* it were our last, to give it meaning and richness and to act responsibly, for there may be no time later to apologize or explain, recant or forgive. We must make a difference to the world we are a part of right now. It is crucial that we face our fears, achieve awareness, deal with our power, overcome our fatigue and go on to make a difference in the world and with our lives. At the same time, ultimately, it matters little, for we all return to the universe in equal measure. But it will be a very different and better world that we create and come back to if we choose to make it so in this lifetime.

Where we stand in this, the difference we choose to make, is a personal choice for us all. Here is an exercise to help you clarify your thoughts on this.

Allowing yourself to die to become your own adviser
Imagine this: you have just one week to live. The best medical authorities in the world have told you this. There is absolutely nothing to be done.

Really feel this. And fully accept how you feel, embracing all of the sensations and emotions which come to you.

What is your first reaction?

What illness do you have and how does this tie into your lifestyle? Does it make obvious sense, or is there anything here that your unconscious is speaking to you about?

Explore honestly all feelings that arise. What is important to you during this last week and what do you really need to know; what last things do you truly want to do? Is there any unfinished business that needs to be taken care of, things left unsaid, people to connect or reconnect with, last-minute goodbyes and explanations or statements to make? Who are these people that you need to connect with; who matters most to you at this time?

Many people may visit you during your last few days.

Some will be among the living and some, perhaps, long dead. Who are they – who has made the most significant contribution to your life, either 'positive' or 'negative'? They will all be here – how do you feel about them now? Notice the flow of energy between you, too – are you giving this to them or receiving it from them?

This is a time for goodbyes. So who do you really want to ensure that you say goodbye to, and what do you want to say to them? Since you now walk between the worlds and can sense the world of spirit very clearly, do you have a message of truth for these people, to help and guide them in their own lives?

As you also reflect on your own life, allowing the events and pictures of significant moments to pass before you, what do you notice in particular that was, or has become important? How did it change you and help to make you who you are? Is there anything which leaves you unhappy or unfulfilled, or do you feel that there are things left unresolved in any way? What do you most regret or wish you had done? What needs to be said and made 'right'?

You are visited by your spirit helpers this week as you prepare for death and, since you ask, you are given one last sentence to sum up all that is important to you in life, which will now be broadcast to the nation – what is it? – and one question to ask of Life itself – what is that?

Time's up. How does it feel to die?

Your spirit floats above you now and you can look back at the shell of your body, the Earthly carrier of your spirit, in a totally impartial way. How do you look from this perspective outside of yourself? The same as you imagined you did when you occupied that body, or quite different? What sense do you have of how you have reacted to, and presented, yourself in life?

You do not die alone, there are others present to support you. How do they react to your death? What do they say about you now you are gone?

Since you are curious, you decide to stay around for a

while to watch your funeral take place. Who is there and what do they have to say – about you and to each other? How do they feel about your death – and what do *you* feel about it now? And about them?

What are the words on your tombstone? Who wrote them? And what does your obituary have to say about you? Would you have written it that way. Does it accurately portray you and your contribution to the world? Whose words are these and what do they mean to you?

Look back over your whole life and reflect upon it. What patterns do you see? What are the key events – and how do they tie into your other lifetimes? What do you feel happy, sad, good, bad, about, and what would you change if you could do it all again?

Sit down and reflect on all of these sensations and now make a long distance call to your younger, human self, reflecting on your experiences this last week and on your death. What will you say to the human being you used to be? In what way could they have made better choices, and what information would they have needed to do that? Do you have any advice for them or suggestions about how they could live more happily, healthily, powerfully, purposefully and well?

The alarm clock rings. This has all been a dream. But strangely, you notice a 'message waiting' sign on your answering machine and, playing it, you are surprised to hear your own voice and the words you just spoke to your younger self: you now. Are you sure this was a dream? It is a very thin tissue indeed between the worlds. Reflect on these words and be grateful for them: they give you the absolute possibility of changing your life right now.

What will you change?

Make a commitment to do so right now – because actually this is not a dream; it is merely a reflection on something that *will* happen and *is* inevitable in every life. The only difference between you and every other person on this planet is that you have seen it and were privileged to be there as the inevitable unfolded. Because of this, you also have the strength, the wisdom, the insights and words of knowledge from your spirit self to guide your actions in this world and to encourage you to do what is right, while so many others do not.

Write down the thoughts or resolutions that come to you now and, if you can, create a ritual for yourself to anchor this experience and keep it with you. We are all depending on you to make a difference.

And so we come to the end of this journey and to a new beginning. If there is one key message from this book, it is this: *You are a powerful being and an essential part of a vast, complex and beautiful universe which welcomes you and values your contribution.*

This has been a book about the shared vision of the scientist and the shaman, and so it seems only fitting that I leave you with two quotations – one of them from the greatest scientist of the twentieth century, the other from a timeless poet and mystic, both of which confirm the boundless energy and potential that is within you. You have only to set it free.

A human is part of the whole, called by us, Universe . . . He experiences himself, his thoughts and feelings, as something separated from the rest – a kind of optical delusion of his consciousness. This delusion is a kind of prison, restricting us to our personal desires and to affection for a few persons nearest to us. Our task must be to free ourselves from this prison by widening our circle of compassion to embrace all living creatures and the whole of Nature in its beauty. – Albert Einstein

Everything you see has its roots in the unseen world, the forms change yet the essence remains the same. The source is within you and this whole cosmos is springing up from it. – Rumi

Embrace your power; you were born to it.

EXPLORATIONS: BEFRIENDING YOUR 'ENEMIES'

1. Dealing with Fear by flaying the ego

We are all connected through the energetic web, of that there is no doubt. The Ego's desire for self-importance, however, will often lead us to believe that we are the 'only ones'. The 'only ones' to feel so alone, the 'only ones' to feel this pain, the 'only ones' to have ever truly felt like this.

The Ego is only one part of us – but it is an important part. I am not one of those people who advocate trying to rid ourselves completely of the Ego – and even if we ever did, if this were truly possible, how would we know we had achieved it since the Ego is what gives us self-reflection and allows us to pass judgement on such matters?

But I certainly do recognize the overbearing nature of the Ego, is penchant for self-importance and blinkered views, and the need we have to control it so that all parts of ourselves are given equal voice.

To deal with Fear, we must at least temporarily silence the Ego in order to reconnect with all that is, for the agenda of the Ego is to focus on our selves entirely as separate and crucial parts of the universe, according to its own limited worldview.

Fear, at its most basic level, relies on the illusion of separation. We are afraid because there is a world out there, a darkness, a not-knowing that we have no part of. *We are intimately a part of it* and the illusion of separation is exactly that, *illusion*, but it is hard to hear the song of harmony sung by the universe behind the self-important chatter of the Ego.

Reconnect now with a time in your life when you were fearful and note down on a piece of paper how you felt at the time. Now summarize what you have written in a paragraph, a sentence, and finally, in one word –

'helpless', 'alone', 'abandoned', whatever makes sense to you.

Ask yourself what was behind that feeling and, again, distil your answer into one word. Continue stripping away the layers until the Ego is naked and has nowhere else to go. The word you will finally arrive at, in one form or another, is *separate*. It is at this point that you can reconnect with all that is by focusing on the web which links us all.

At every stage of this exercise, you are returning more and more energy to yourself which was previously taken up by maintaining the illusion of separation. Eventually you will come to a quiet space where no more layers remain between you and the energy of the cosmos. Use this quiet time to reinvent yourself in the moment. *Just for now . . . just for now . . . act as if you are a warrior without fear.*

From this perspective, look back on the first event in this chain, the one that caused you to fear. How does it look now from this new space you occupy?

No-one is ever truly alone. It is said that there are only six degrees of separation between all the peoples of the world. We are all connected. We need only to see this.

2. Awareness through the eyes of the child

Have you ever noticed how children paint – before we 'teach' them the 'right' way to represent what they see? They are able to capture the very essence of their world and there is spirit in the paintings of small children which teaches us about the direct connection they see between themselves and the universe. There is no distinction between things, no fundamental separation in the paintings of the child – their splashes of colour, blendings of tone and blurring and merging of shapes are indicative of the unity they see between everything that is. This is how our children see the world, in a way which is similar to that of traditional shamanic communities.

The Navajo still produce sand paintings – creations of form in coloured sand, which they give to the land itself, with no intention of keeping the painting as a material thing. A sand painting is a sacred thing, a blessing, which is given away to nature as soon as it is made and the wind begins to disperse it once again to the elements.

Navajo sand paintings are made for two purposes. One is for use in a healing or blessing ceremony performed by the *hataalii*, the medicine man, who crafts the painting from natural objects – flowers, crushed stone, charcoal, pollen, cornmeal, earth and coloured sand. It is completed within a day and destroyed on the same day.

The second type of sand painting is created as a sacred art form in celebration of the unseen. These paintings are religious objects with symbolic content, designed to restore *hozho*, balance, health and blessings. Because they are transitory, we do not know what they looked like for certain, even 100 years ago; we have only the words of the medicine man and the paintings of today.

Shamans and children have a similar approach to the world.

A scientist, Professor Semir Zeki, has recently made a study of art and the effects on the brain of creating such works. He finds that different parts of the brain are responsible for different aspects of a painting.[126]

The area he calls V1 (For 'Visual 1') is the collection point for the information we take in with our eyes. It is then parcelled out to many other areas, which deal with the specifics of this information – V1, V2 and V4 have specialized cells for dealing with colour; V1, V2 and V5 deal with the interpretation of motion; V3 is responsible for line and form. Each has its own tiny visual system and processes its information in parallel with the others. It is the coming together of the whole operation that produces the total image as all of this information and all of these elements are reassembled by the brain.

It may be possible to work on each of these areas

independently and develop our abilities to truly *see* the world in all its aspects, by concentrating on colour only, or on movement or on shape, and then representing this element alone in a painting only of this. In doing so, we repattern our normal response to 'reality' and see it in a totally new way.

Try it, by sharing the pleasure taken by the child in playing with and painting his world. Find an object or a scene to paint and spend a little time really *seeing* this thing in its pure essential form. And then set to work to capture this *essence* – as a splash of colour or a combination of shapes rather than a literal representation. Work with each part of the brain, so you produce a work of colour or of shape or of movement, or turn away and paint the scene from memory alone.

You will be strengthening your brain so that no particular part has dominance and lazily acts from rote to reconstruct the world according to the Western dream and the areas of our minds we have been socialized to rely upon as prominent and most (self)-important. You will be seeing the world in an uncommon way – and reconnecting once again with the reality of the child.

3. Death as an adviser on Power

For dealing with issues of power and control, when you need to see beyond the mundane into the essence of the problem and what lies behind it, you can use the power of one of your most important allies – Death.

Death is a real energetic entity, not just a 'condition' or a negative to be avoided, but a true ally with whom you can meet and interact for guidance and support. Journey to Death and ask him to show you your true purpose, your reason for being in the world and the real essence of yourself. It is a journey you need take only once because the answer will be very clear.

Ask to see the nature and pattern of your life revealed, the challenges which have been placed before you (which are often very different from the challenges we think we have faced) in order to strengthen and to help you, as well as the energy blockages which are not serving you in your soul's mission.

This journey can be taken like any other to the lower world and, again, your intention is the key. Find the form of words that is most comfortable to you and that reflects your resolve. The following is my own suggestion for this journey: '*I am taking a journey to the shamanic lower world to meet and consult with Death as my adviser so that my soul's purpose will be revealed to me, as well as the issues in my life which present challenges to this.*'

Meet with your power animal if you wish and ask to be guided to where Death waits for you (a hint: look for trees – many who take this journey find that Death waits for them among woods or forest).

When you find him, look closely at him and note his features. See who he looks like and, indeed, what *his* purpose is, since we all of us have an intention in being here and a role to play. Then ask your question of Death.

He will answer you from the sure perspective that we are all of us mortal and each moment may be our last, and so his answer will be exquisitely honest. Our most fundamental challenge always is to act impeccably in accordance with our purpose so that we leave no un-finished business behind us, energetic or otherwise, should our last moment be now.

4. Feeding the hunger of Fatigue
Energy will always tell you what it wants, although it appears sometimes to talk in riddles.

When we are physically tired, our body's manifest energy is often telling us not to rest but to exert ourselves physically, to blend with the sensation and then reverse it upon itself. When we do so, by taking exercise for example, we often feel energized instead of more tired.

It is the same with the mental and the spiritual process.

Our tiredness results when we are not actually *thinking* but worrying over or dwelling on a particular issue. We are not connected to the problem, but make ourselves entirely separate from it.

When we activate the mind by thinking, with clear focus and attention, we create a proper expression of mental energy. Then we can let go so that our unconscious can use its natural problem-solving capacity, the infinite power of the mind, by entering through the energetic gateway we have created into the greatest encyclopaedia of empowerment we have access to as human beings: the world of spirit. This is the productive use of energy and results in less fatigue.

The next time you feel mentally drained, going round in circles, try this approach. Really *focus* on the issue and think about it with solid concentration. Mind map it, make notes, write it down, really hold it in your mind – then let it go by deliberately distracting yourself from further thought. Allow your unconscious to do the work for you during this time, and then come back to it later. The issue will seem clearer, of less concern and emotional impact, and you may even find that the problem has been solved for you.

What we are doing is feeding fatigue by giving it the focus it requires and then releasing it in not-doing – distraction being a not-doing of fatigue.

THE FINAL CHALLENGE:
A GIVE-AWAY TO UNDERSTANDING

To put the conclusion crudely – the stuff of the world is mind-stuff.

– Sir Arthur Eddington

We have completed many exercises and explorations during this journey, but what follows may be the hardest of all for some. I would like you to burn this book.

By retaining it, it becomes a possession, a material thing, and by referring to it you are referencing your life against my words, my beliefs and those of others I have quoted. These words and thoughts are not your own and are dis-empowering. By referring back to them you give away your natural power and your right to create reality as you see it and determine it to be.

By freeing yourself from these words, you free yourself to be the perfect being you truly are and you liberate yourself from the guidance, teachings, expectations and assumptions of others. The final outcome of this journey, then, is to ultimately Be Yourself.

If you can accept this challenge, do so in a sober, reflective and sacred manner. If you cannot, that may be, in itself, an idea to ponder.

Let us assume you do. A fire ritual seems appropriate to me – you may think differently – to release the energy invested in these pages and those parts of yourself which you have given to these words.

Build the fire that you will use in a totally focused way, fully in touch with your intention in doing so. You may wish to journey first to see how and where this should be and, perhaps, to use the walk of attention to locate exactly the right materials for this. Then construct the fire as if you were building an altar in sacred space.

Intend to fully reclaim your power from these pages as you watch them burn. Give thanks to the words and to those who have contributed to them, to the paper and to the tree which has given generously of itself for you, to the ink, and to the energy of thought which has been invested here – from Plato right through to the experiments of modern physics and to the ageless wisdom of the shaman which underlies it all. And see it all as yours, always yours.

In reading through this book, you have created a space which now exists for ever, outside of time and space. The knowledge you have accumulated will always be yours and will always exist for you. You can journey to this knowledge at any time you wish, using your own natural power to do so. You do not need the words of others to be part of and embrace our wonderful world of change and to know your own power within it.

It always was this way.

In three words, I can sum up everything I've learned about life: It goes on. – Leo Buscaglia

THE COMMUNITY OF SHAMANS

Readers with internet access are invited to join an online discussion group which exists to support this book and its subject matter. As well as discussion of shamanism and its relationship to other forms of healing, empowerment and Earth medicine, one of the intentions of this group is to undertake journeys together, members entering the otherworld from locations in ordinary reality as geographically distant as America, Russia, Europe and the UK. We then share experiences, validate 'coincidences' and examine the details of these journeys with the intention of mapping the otherworld to produce a representation of the landscape of non-ordinary reality and to understand and work with the Spirit People who live there.

Joining this community is entirely free of charge. First, go to *www.egroups.com* and register as a member, then search for the list, AJourneyToYou-Shaman (full address: *AJourneyToYou-Shaman@egroups.com*). We look forward to your contribution.

NOTES

1. Malidoma Patrice Some, *Of Water and the Spirit. Ritual, Magic and Initiation in the Life of an African Shaman*, Arkana, 1995.
2. Dick Olney, in *Walking in Beauty*, ed. Roslyn Moore, DO Publishing, 1996. Copies available from PO Box 103, Mendocino, CA 95460, USA.
3. Robert Assagioli, in *The Elements of Psychosynthesis*, Will Parfitt, Element, 1997.
4. Fritjof Capra, *The Tao of Physics*, Flamingo, 1992.
5. Carlos Castaneda, *Tales of Power*, Pocket Books, 1992. I have Castaneda to thank for giving a name to my early experiences and to setting me on the path of shamanism. And even today, as I re-read his books, I find more and deeper wisdom within them than in the majority of the other books on my shelves.

Castaneda is not without his critics. Indeed, Richard De Mille, in his excellent book, *The Don Juan Papers, Further Castaneda Controversies* (Ross-Erikson, 1980) devotes more than 500 pages to 'unmasking' Castaneda as 'the bogus fieldworker' behind 'the most intriguing episode in anthropology since the Piltdown forgery' and as 'one of the greatest intellectual hoaxers of all time'.

Did Castaneda make it up? I have four answers to this question: *No*, *Maybe*, *Yes*, and *Who Cares?* The *No* answer is simple enough. I have studied with teachers who worked with Castaneda during his early years and who shared some of the experiences he relates. I have no reason to doubt my teachers or to question the authenticity of Castaneda's work during this time. And, more importantly, it *feels* real.

Maybe. Some of what Castaneda has to say, however, does not ring quite so true. But then, I have experienced some remarkable things myself in shamanism and some of them are related in this book. So who knows? Whether Castaneda's personal experiences are wholly true or not, what he has to say is, for the most part, entirely valid and contains a deep wisdom which is worth exploring in its own right.

Yes. There are clearly passages and episodes in Castaneda's work where fiction plays a greater role than fact, and De Mille has catalogued these extensively. This is the way of the storyteller, to create dramatic devices to hold the interest of the reader and to help him understand the message which is being taught. It is also the way of the trickster-shaman who may use deceit in a purposeful way, to get across important information which is of real benefit to readers.

To me, these fictionalized episodes never interfere with the deeper message of Castaneda's work. And this is the essence of my *Who Cares?* response. We know when something is real. Because it feels real – whether it comes to us as a work of fiction or fact.

Despite what we may think of Castaneda, we do have much to thank him for. Without his books, many of us would never have discovered the world of the shaman at all.

6. Stephen Hawking, *A Brief History of Time*, Bantam Doubleday Dell, 1998.

7. Dina Glouberman, *Life Choices, Life Changes. The Art of Developing Personal Vision through Imagework*, Thorsons, 1995.

8. Philippe Ariès, *Centuries of Childhood. A Social History of Family Life*, Random House, 1965.

9. Michael Harner, *The Way of the Shaman*, Harper & Row, 1990.

10. R. D. Laing, *The Ghost of the Weed Garden*, in *The Politics of the Family*, Vintage Books, 1972. For biography and discussion of Laing's work, see John Clay, *R. D. Laing: A Divided Self*, Hodder & Stoughton, 1997.

11. Liz Tomboline, personal communication, January 1999.

12. *Daily Express*, 27 November 1999.

13. Carlos Castaneda, *A Separate Reality*, Pocket Books, 1991.

14. Colin Wilson, *The Outsider*, J. P. Tarcher, 1987.

15. Carlos Castaneda, *Tales of Power*, Arkana, 1990.

16. T. S. Eliot, *Little Gidding*, from *Four Quartets*, Harcourt Brace, 1974. First published 1943.

17. Carol Pearson, *The Hero Within*, Harper & Row, 1986

18. V. D. Auvergne, in *Bihar and Orissa Research Journal*, 26(2), quoted by Starseed © 1996 – web site at http://ms-services.com/starseed/crys.potporri. htm

19. Simon Baron-Cohen, 'Is There a Normal Phase of Synaesthesia in Development?' in *PSYCHE*, 2(27), June 1996.

20. Edward Hall and Mildred Hall, *Understanding Cultural Differences*, Intercultural Press Inc., 1990.

21. Michael Talbot, *The Holographic Universe*, HarperCollins, 1996.

22. John G. Neihardt, *Black Elk Speaks*, Bison, 1989.

23. Judith Hooper and Dick Teresi, *The Three-Pound Universe*, J. P. Tarcher, 1991.

24. For Castaneda's explanation of the tonal and the nagual, see Carlos Castaneda, *The Eagle's Gift*, Pocket Books, 1991.

25. Leo Rutherford, *The Principles of Shamanism*, Thorsons, 1996.

26. J. S. Mill, *On Liberty*, Cambridge University Press, 1989. (First published 1909).

27. Olney, *Walking in Beauty*.

28. Karl Pribram, interviewed by Jeffrey Mishlove on *Thinking Allowed*, Thinking Allowed Productions, 2560 Ninth Street, Suite 123 Berkley, CA 94710. www.thinkallowed.com/about.html. Transcript at www.intuition.org

29. Baron-Cohen, 'Is There a Normal Phase . . .'

30. John Lilly, *The Centre of the Cyclone: An Autobiography of Inner Space*, Granada Publishing, 1997.

31. Paul Pearsall, with Linda G. S. Russek and Gary Schwartz, *The Heart's Code. Tapping the Wisdom and Power of Our Heart Energy*, Broadway Books, 1998.

32. Nick Williams, *The Work We Were Born To Do*, Element, 1999.

33. Olney, *Walking in Beauty*.

34. Pribram, on *Thinking Aloud*.

35. Cerridwen Connelly, 'The Cosmic Computer. The TechnoPagan's Guide to the Universe', unpublished manuscript, 1999, personal communication.

36. Carlos Castaneda, *The Art of Dreaming*, HarperPerennial Library, 1994.

37. Talbot, *The Holographic Universe*.

38. Amit Goswami, *The Self-Aware Universe*, J. P. Tarcher, 1995.

39. Talbot, *The Holographic Universe*.

40. Alan Tickhill, Raven Lodge of Shamanic and Personal Development. Web site at www.shamana.co.uk

41. Olney, *Walking in Beauty*.

42. Some, *Of Water and the Spirit*.

43. *Ibid.*

44. Jim Schnabel, *Remote Viewers: The Secret History of America's Psychic Spies*, Dell, 1997

45. Mircea Eliade, *Shamanism. Archaic Techniques of Ecstasy*, Princeton/Bollingen, 1974.

46. Some, *Of Water and the Spirit*.

47. Eliade, *Shamanism*, Princeton University Press, 1972.

48. Quoted *Ibid.*

49. Harner, *The Way of the Shaman*.

50. Carlos Castaneda, *The Teachings of Don Juan, A Yaqui Way of Knowledge*, Ballantine, 1972.

51. John G. Neihardt, *Black Elk Speaks*, University of Nebraska Press, 1988.

52. Jaya Bear, 'Dancing with the Wolves: an Interview with Don Agustin Rivas Vasquez,' in *Sacred Hoop*, 24, Spring 1999.

53. Eliade, *Shamanism*.

54. Joseph Bearwalker Wilson. Web site at *www.metista.com/bearwalker/resume.html*

55. Maya Deren, *Divine Horsemen. The Living Gods of Haiti*, McPherson, 1953.

56. Stephan A. Schwartz, 'E.S.P.D. Blue,' *Kindred Spirit*, 47, Summer 1999.

57. Castaneda, *Tales of Power*.

58. Castaneda, *A Separate Reality*, Pocket Books, 1991.

59. Serge Kahili King, *Urban Shaman*, Fireside, Simon & Schuster, 1990.

60. Jonathan Horwitz, *The Absence of 'Performance' in the Shamanic Right: Shamanic Rites Seen from a Shamanic Perspective: II*, Scandinavian Centre for Shamanic Studies, Artillerivej 63, Lejl. 140, DK–2300 Copenhagen S., Denmark.

61. Villoldo's comments come from an interview given to Jeffrey Mishlove on *Thinking Allowed*. The web site of the Four Winds Society is at *www.thefourwinds.com*

62. Victor Sanchez, *The Teachings of Don Carlos. Practical Applications of the Works of Carlos Castaneda*, Bear & Co., 1995.

63. Eliade, *Shamanism*.

64. James Watson, *The Double Helix*, Penguin, 1999.

65. Maxwell Cade and Nona Coxhead, *The Awakened Mind: Biofeedback and the Development of Higher States of Awareness*, Delacorte Press, 1979.

66. Carl Jung, *Memories, Dreams, Reflections*, Vintage, 1989.

67. Glouberman, *Life Choices*.

68. *Ibid*.

69. Castaneda, *Tales of Power*.

70. Olney, *Walking in Beauty*.

71. *Ibid*.

72. Glouberman, *Life Choices*.

73. *Ibid*.

74. *Ibid*.

75. Carl Sagan, *Cosmos*, Abacus, 1995.

76. Castaneda, *The Eagle's Gift*.

77. Caroline Myss, *Why People Don't Heal and How They Can. A Practical Programme for Healing Body, Mind and Spirit*, Bantam Books, 1998. Caroline Myss has a web site, including details of her books, audio and video tapes and events at *www.myss.com/index.html*

78. Tony Buzan, *The Mind Map Book: How to Use Radiant Thinking to Maximize Your Brain's Untapped Potential*, Plume, 1996.

79. Neihardt, *Black Elk Speaks*.

80. Rutherford, *Principles of Shamanism*.

81. Kenneth Meadows, *Earth Medicine. A Shamanic Way to Self-Discovery*, Element Books, 1989.

82. Jack Black, MindStore. Contact MindStore House, 36 Speirs Wharf, Port Dundas, Glasgow G4 9TB, UK. Web site at *www.mindstore.com*

83. King, *Urban Shaman*.

84. Some, *Of Water and the Spirit*.

85. For more details on the author's workshops and other publications, write to the address at the back of this book.

86. *The Great Chief Sends Word. Chief Seathl's Testament*. Saint Bernard Press, 1977.

87. Thomas David, *Miracle Medicines of the Rainforest*, Healing Arts Press, 1997.

88. John Perkins, *The World Is As You Dream It*, Inner Traditions, 1994; *Shapeshifting*, Inner Traditions, 1997.

89. Edmund Jacobson, 'Imagination of Movement Involving Skeletal Muscle', *American Journal of Physiology*, 91, 1930; and 'Evidence of Contraction of Specific Muscles during Imagination', *American Journal of Physiology*, 95, 1930.

90. Michael Hutchinson, *The Book of Floating. Exploring the Private Sea*, Quill, 1984. In his book, Hutchinson quotes from John Basmajian's, *Control and Training of Individual Motor Units*, *Science*, Vol. 141 (1963).

91. Howard Charing is a director of the Eagle's Wing Centre for Contemporary Shamanism, and offers shamanic training, books and products. Write to 58 Westbere Road, London NW2 3RU, UK. Telephone 0207 435 8174 or e-mail: eaglewng@dircon.co.uk. *www.shamanism.co.uk*.

92. Belinda Gore, *Ecstatic Body Postures. An Alternative Reality Workbook*, Bear & Co., 1995.

93. To join this shamanic community, see details in 'The Community of Shamans' section, p. 398.

94. Gore, *Ecstatic Body Postures*.

95. Felicitas D. Goodman, *Where the Spirits Ride the Wind. Trance Journeys and Other Ecstatic Experiences*, Indiana University Press, 1990; Lisa Alther, *Kinflicks*, Plume, 1996.

96. Cade and Coxhead, *The Awakened Mind*.

97. Hutchinson, *The Book of Floating*.

98. Lyall Watson, *Gifts of Unknown Things*, Coronet, 1977.

99. Colin Wilson, *The Occult*, Llewellyn Publications, 1971.

100. Colin Wilson, *After Life*, Llewellyn Publications, 1987. Reissued in 2000 as *After Life: Survival of the Soul*.

101. Some, *Of Water and the Spirit*.

102. Tindersticks, 'My Sister,' © 1995, Quicksilver Recording Co.

103. Hutchinson, *The Book of Floating*.

104. N. Miller and L. DiCara, 'Instrumental Learning of Urine Formation by Rats: Changes in Renal Blood Flow', *American Journal of Physiology*, 215, 1968.

105. Elmer and Alyce Green, *Beyond Biofeedback*, Delacorte Press, 1977.

106. Paul MacLean, *A Triune Concept of the Brain and Behaviour*, University of Toronto Press, 1973.

107. Baron-Cohen, interviewed on *Thinking Allowed*.

108. J. Adam, 'Naloxone Reversal of Analgesia Produced by Brain Stimulation in the Human', *Pain*, 2, 1976. See also, research by Candace Pert reported in *Omni* magazine, February 1982.

109. Alan Richardson, *Mental Imagery*, Springer-Verlag, 1969.

110. Ralph Haber, 'How We Remember What We See', *Scientific American*, May, 1970.

111. Lionel Standing, 'Learning 10,000 Pictures', *Quarterly Journal of Experimental Psychology*, 25.

112. Glouberman, *Life Choices*.

113. Mihaly Csikszentmihalyi, *Beyond Boredom and Anxiety: The Experience of Play in Work and Games*, Jossey-Bass, 1975.

114. Assagioli, *Elements of Psychosynthesis*.

115. Gore, *Ecstatic Body Postures*.

116. Victor Sanchez, *Teachings of Don Carlos*, Bear Publishing, 1995.

117. Peter Carey, *Bliss*, Vintage Books, 1996.

118. Alther, *Kinflicks*.

119. Tim Lott, *The Scent of Dried Roses*, Penguin, 1997.

120. Susan Jeffers, *Feel the Fear and Do It Anyway*, Arrow Books, 1991.

121. Marianne Williamson, *A Return to Love*, HarperCollins, 1996.

122. James, 'Ring the Bells', on *James: The Best Of*, © 1992 Mercury Records Ltd.

123. Nick Cave and the Bad Seeds, 'The Weeping Song', on *Live Seeds*, © 1993 Mute Records Ltd.

124. Paramahansa Yogananda, translated by Christopher Isherwood, *How To Know God*, Vedanta, 1996.

125. Jeffers, *Feel the Fear and Do It Anyway*.

126. Semir Zeki, *Inner Vision – An Exploration of Art and the Brain*, Oxford University Press, 1999. Also see experimental results at web site, *The Painter's Eye www.physiol.ox.ac.uk*

SELECTED RESOURCES

The following are all experienced practitioners that I have either worked with directly or whose work I know, respect and trust.

SHAMANIC TRAINING

- **Aloha International** – Serge Kahili King's organization for Huna shamanism. PO Box 665, Kilauea, Hawaii 96754, USA.
- **Cornerstone Healings** – Workshops and healing. 1010 Ridgeway, Rose Hill, Kansas 67133, USA. Web site at *http://cornerstonehealings.com*
- **Dream Change Coalition** – John Perkins's organization, offering shamanic workshops, courses and trips to work with indigenous shamans. PO Box 31357, Palm Beach Gardens, Florida 33420, USA. *www.dreamchange.org*
- **Eagle's Wing Centre for Contemporary Shamanism** – Run by Leo Rutherford and Howard Charing, and offering shamanic courses, training and very good drumming tapes. 58 Westbere Road, London NW2 3RU, UK. Telephone 0207 435 8174 or email: eaglewng@dircon.co.uk *www.shamanism.co.uk*
- **Foundation for Shamanic Studies** – Michael Harner's organization for shamanic teachings. Box 670, Belden Station, Norwalk, CT 06852, USA.
- **Four Winds Society** – Run by Alberto Villoldo and offering classes and programmes in the medicine wheel, soul retrieval, energy medicine, and expeditions to sacred sites. Telephone (561) 832 9702 email: avilloldo@thefourwinds.com *www.thefourwinds.com*

- **Imagework** – Training courses, designed by Dina Glouberman, offered by the Skyros Institute, 92 Prince of Wales Road, London NW5 3NE, UK
- **Inner Voice** – Shamanic workshops, offered by Liz Tomboline, 48 Priors Hill, Wroughton, Wiltshire SN4 0RW, UK. Telephone 01793 814313 email: *liz@netcomuk.co.uk*. Web site at *www.members.tripod.co.uk/InnerVoice/index.html*
- **The Sacred Trust** – A shamanic organisation run by Simon Buxton which offers UK workshops and shamanic training courses, plus a huge library of shamanic books and materials for sale. PO Box 603, Bath BA1 2ZU. Web site at *www.sacredtrust.co.uk*
- **Scandinavian Centre for Shamanic Studies** – Jonathan Horwitz's centre for shamanic training. Artillerivej 63/140, DH–2300 Copenhagen, Denmark.
- **Skyros** – Therapeutic and holistic holidays in Greece and the Caribbean, 92 Prince of Wales Road, London NW5 3NE, UK. Telephone 0207 267 4424 email *skyros@easynet.co.uk*. Web site at *www.skyros.com*
- **Soluna Tours** – Trips to work with traditional shamans in their own communities. *www.solunatours.com*
- **TechoPagans Unlimited** – An international pagan organization run by Cerridwen Connelly, offering rituals at sacred sites in Britain and North America, and online discussion and teachings on Tuatha healing techniques. PO Box 937, Lone Pine,CA 93545, USA. Telephone (760) 876 5018 email *technopagans@qnet.com*. Web site at *www.qnet.com/~technopagans*

SHAMANIC CRAFTS AND PRODUCTS

- **Magonia** – Native American crafts and shamanic healing. *WhiteBearWoman@aol.com*. Web site at *http://magonia.cjb.net*
- **Pathways Heartlodge** – A variety of crafts available and made to order, including drums, rattles and power objects. Run by Nick Wood who also publishes *Sacred Hoop* magazine. PO Box 16, Narberth, Pembrokeshire, West Wales, SA67 8YG, UK. Telephone 01834 860320. Web site at *www.sacredhoop.demon.co.uk*
- **Raven Lodge** – Shamanic craftwork and teachings. 35 Wilson Avenue, Deal, Kent CT14 9NL, UK. Telephone 01304 381614. Web site at *www.shamana.co.uk*

- **World Tree** – Shamanic drumming CDs. For each one purchased Lee Russell will contribute £2.50 to the Dream Change Coalition for rainforest preservation. Department B, 33 Atherton Road, Sawbridgeworth, Hertfordshire CM21 0BS, UK. Web site at *www.wakan.freeserve.co.uk*

FLOATATION PRODUCTS

To purchase floatation tanks and for a list of UK float centres, go to web site: *www.cyberfloat.clara.net/5.htm*

For floatation tank purchases, also see Floatworks, Winchester Wharf, Clink Street, London SE1 9DG. Telephone 0207 357 0111. Web site: *www.floatworks.com*

CYBER-COMMUNITIES AND ONLINE SUPPORT

AJourneyToYou-Shaman@egroups.com – A cyber-community run by the author to promote the potential of shamanism for personal and global change, which readers are free to join.

CoreShamanism@egroups.com – An online community for people who have completed basic training in Core Shamanism.

sacredhoop@egroups.com – Join Nick Wood's Sacred Hoop cyber-community at this address.

Shaman-L@egroups.com – General shamanic discussion.

Shamana@egroups.com – A support group for students of Alan Tickhill's home study course in shamanic techniques.

Carrefour@egroups.com – For students and practitioners of Vodou.

Santeria@egroups.com – For students and practitioners of Santeria.

VoodooEnergy@egroups.com – Run by the author for discussion of the practical applications of voodoo and shamanism as energetic forms.

Infinite Journeys:
Trance Drumming for the Shamanic Journey

Shamans use many methods to achieve the altered state of consciousness necessary for the shamanic journey, but their principal technique remains the use of sacred sound, whether it is the singing bowls of Tibet, the click sticks and didgeridoo of Australia, or the drums of Haiti and Africa.

This high-quality tape has been specially recorded by the author as a companion to the books, *The Journey To You* and *Spirit in the City*, and offers a combination of shorter and longer trance sound accompaniments for the journeys described – and for any others you may wish to take.

The cassette features drums (the shaman's 'horse'), rattles and other traditional instruments played at the specific tempo required to induce the shift in consciousness which facilitates entry into the otherworlds – just as they have been played for thousands of years by shamans and priests to support and guide their own journeys of the soul.

Each track includes an orientation beat to allow you to express your intention, and phrase your question for the spirits, a journeying beat, and a call-back signal to assist your return to normal consciousness.

Featured instruments: Growler drum, bodhrán, Vodou gourd asson (priest's sacred rattle), African pod-rattles, hand-crafted English rattles, and African rain stick fetish.

Price: £10. Please send payment (cash preferably by registered post, or cheques made payable to Ross Heaven) plus a stamped addressed *padded* envelope to:

**PO Box 2747
LEWES
BN7 1HF**

Workshops and Courses

For information on workshops by the author, presentations, training material and other activities, please send an A4 sized stamped addressed envelope to the address above.

NOTES

NOTES

NOTES

NOTES

NOTES

NOTES